Nottingham

Adrian Henstock, Principal Archivist, Nottinghamshire County Council, 1971-2003.

Nottinghamshire Past

Essays in honour of Adrian Henstock

Edited by

John Beckett

Merton Priory Press
for
Nottinghamshire County Council
2003

First published 2003

Published for Nottinghamshire County Council

By

Merton Priory Press Ltd
67 Merthyr Road, Whitchurch
Cardiff CF14 1DD

Cover photography and design by Trevor Clayton

ISBN 1 898937 59 1

Printed by Technical Print Services Limited, Nottingham, England.

Contents

List of Illustrations vi
List of Contributors vii
List of Abbreviations viii

Foreword — *David Lathrope* ix

Introduction — *John Beckett* 1

1 The earliest history of Wollaton Park and its Lords, 1283-1345 *David Crook* 7
2 Enclosure and the Depopulation of Stanton-on-the-Wolds, *Alan Cameron* 21
3 The Wages of Sin: sex, shame and retribution in Nottinghamshire, 1560-1640, *David Marcombe* 38
4 Emma Child, née Barnard, formerly Willughby (1644-1725): records of the life of a gentlewoman', *Dorothy Johnston* 59
5 'The pleasant and glorious condition of this noble forest': mapping Sherwood Forest before 1800, *Steph Mastoris* 77
6 'The Warmest I have': Henry second Duke of Newcastle and Nottingham Castle, *Trevor Foulds* 99
7 'An Officer and an Antiquary: Major Hayman Rooke and the beginnings of archaeology in eighteenth-century Nottinghamshire, *Sarah Speight* 116
8 Edward Trollope, the Archbishop's Palace, and the Founding of the Diocese of Southwell in 1884, *John Beckett* 137
9 Unhealthy Areas in Victorian Nottingham: the Rookeries, *Ken Brand* 155
10 The Royal Visit to Nottinghamshire, 1903, *Philip E. Jones* 172

Adrian Henstock: An Appreciation — *Barbara Sharp* 186
Adrian Henstock: a Bibliography — *Corinne Phillips* 190

Index 195

List of Illustrations

Adrian Henstock	Frontispiece
Stanton-on-the-Wolds Village	25
David Allan, The Stool of Repentance	46
Accounts of Lady Child, 1717	73
Thomas Langdon's map of part of Kighill and Ravenshead, Newstead, 1613	89
A sketch map showing brecks in Allamore Side, Blidworth, late 17th century	91
Elizabeth Cavendish	105
Plan of a large Roman Camp on Sherwood Forest	125
A South-west view of Rowtor Rocks	126
Pen and ink drawing … Villas Urbana and Rustica	130
The Archbishop's Palace, Southwell	143
The Proposed Nottingham Central Station, 1881	162
Goad's Insurance Map, 1886	167
King Edward VII at Rufford Abbey	182

List of Contributors

John Beckett is Professor of English Regional History at the University of Nottingham, and Chairman of the Thoroton Society.

Ken Brand is Vice Chairman of the Nottingham Civic Society.

Alan Cameron was formerly Keeper of Manuscripts at the University of Nottingham and editor of *Transactions of the Thoroton Society*. He recently retired as Company Archivist to the Bank of Scotland.

David Crook is an Assistant Keeper at the Public Record Office and a former editor of the Thoroton Society's Record Series.

Trevor Foulds is Documentary Historian for Nottingham City Council.

Dorothy Johnston is Keeper of Manuscripts at the University of Nottingham.

Philip Jones is a Member of the Council of the Thoroton Society.

David Lathrope is Assistant Director, Leisure and Community Services, Nottinghamshire County Council.

David Marcombe is Director of the Centre for Local History, University of Nottingham.

Steph Mastoris is Curator, Snibston Discovery Park, Leicestershire Heritage Services.

Corinne Phillips is Special Collections Librarian, University of Nottingham.

Barbara Sharp is Senior Assistant Archivist at Nottinghamshire Archives.

Sarah Speight is a lecturer in the School of Continuing Education at the University of Nottingham, and archaeology editor of *Transactions of the Thoroton Society*.

List of Abbreviations

BL	British Library
CCR	*Calendars of Close Rolls*
CFR	*Calendars of Fine Rolls*
CSPD	*Calendars of State Papers Domestic*
HMC	Historical Manuscripts Commission
NAO	Nottinghamshire Archive Office
NJ	*Nottingham Journal*
NUMD	Nottingham University Manuscripts Department
PRO	Public Record Office
RBN	W. Stevenson, *et. al.*, eds., *Records of the Borough of Nottingham*, I-IX (1882-1956)
Thoroton	Robert Thoroton, *The Antiquities of Nottinghamshire* (1677)
TSRS	Thoroton Society Record Series
TTS	*Transactions of the Thoroton Society of Nottinghamshire*
VCH	Victoria County History

Acknowledgements

In addition to individual acknowledgements mentioned in the footnotes of the essays below, the editor would like to thank the following for their assistance in the preparation of this book: Janice Avery, Trevor Clayton, Claire Geeson, Valerie Henstock, David Lathrope, Philip Riden, Paul Roper, Barbara Sharp and Christopher Weir.

Foreword

David Lathrope

On 31st January 2003 Adrian Henstock retired as Principal Archivist to Nottinghamshire County Council, after thirty-two years in the post. He was a superb archivist and a remarkable colleague. Somehow amidst all the calls on his time, he was also able to research and write history, as well as to edit jointly the county journal, *Transactions of the Thoroton Society,* for most of the past three decades. It was in recognition of this achievement that the County Council wanted to commemorate his career, and I am delighted to be able to introduce this volume of essays prepared in his honour by colleagues and friends from across the county. Adrian's eclectic interests covered a whole range of subjects, many of which are discussed in this volume. Each essay is based securely in the archival resources of Nottinghamshire, and they open up topics previously neglected or not fully understood. They cover county and city, as well as (in John Beckett's essay) the Diocese of Southwell, which had been part of Adrian's remit since 1978.

It is my great pleasure to see Adrian Henstock celebrated in this volume as a historian, for which he has not always been fully appreciated amidst the everyday tasks associated with being Principal Archivist. Having left the employment of the County Council he will have more time to practise as a historian away from the demands of a modern county archives service. It is also my pleasure to thank the contributors, many of them with long connections to the Thoroton Society, of which Adrian has been such a key player for so many years, for their contributions to our understanding and appreciation of the history of Nottinghamshire, expressed in this volume.

Introduction

John Beckett

The history of Nottinghamshire was first written in the seventeenth century by the great antiquarian, Dr Robert Thoroton. At the end of the eighteenth century Thoroton's work was updated by John Throsby, who reprinted the original text with additional comments of his own relating to the churches, country houses and personalities of the county.[1] Other projected county histories did not materialise, and the nearest successors to Throsby were to be found in the county directories, notably those compiled by William White of Sheffield in 1832 and subsequently.[2] No further county history was attempted until the early twentieth century, this time in the form of the Victoria County History, for which two Nottinghamshire volumes appeared before the project faltered and died.[3] Subsequently only Professor A.C. Wood has had the courage to attempt a 'county history', and his single volume work, published by the Thoroton Society in 1947, began with the Romans and ended with the 1832 Parliamentary Reform Act.[4] Since then historians have lacked either the ambition or the wherewithal to write about the county as a whole. In part this has reflected the sheer weight of knowledge which has accumulated,[5] and in part it is also because the nature of 'county history' has developed since the days of Thoroton, Throsby and even Wood, to embrace the whole range of

---

1 Thoroton; J. Throsby, *Thoroton's Antiquities of Nottinghamshire* (1790-6, reprinted 1972).

2 White's *Directory of Nottinghamshire* (1832, 1844, 1853 etc.).

3 VCH, *Nottinghamshire*, 2 vols (1907, 1910).

4 A.C. Wood, *History of Nottinghamshire* (1947; reprinted 1971).

5 Michael Brook, ed., *A Nottinghamshire Bibliography: Publications on Nottinghamshire History before 1998* (Nottingham, 2002).

social, economic and cultural history, in addition to politics, religion and similar matters. The task now is such that in those counties where the VCH remains active it can take ten or more volumes to write the county history successfully.[6]

A county archivist has, somehow, to keep abreast of current research, and to maintain a broad knowledge of the history of their county across all time periods and all subjects. The result, predictably, is that they often feel jack of all trades and master of none, but they have little option but to seek such a range of knowledge and understanding even while local historians shy away from following Thoroton and Throsby to write the history of the county. Adrian Henstock, to whom this volume of essays is dedicated to honour his thirty-two years as Nottinghamshire county archivist, has had to appreciate and understand the developments in our knowledge, and the published record of Nottinghamshire's history. This has been achieved not least through the annual volume of *Transactions* published by the Thoroton Society, the county's leading archaeological and historical society, of which Adrian has been the history editor for most of the time he has been Principal Archivist to Nottinghamshire County Council. Such a long period at the coal face of the county's history puts Adrian Henstock at the forefront of knowledge about Nottinghamshire. He is also the first to admit that there are still numerous gaps in our understanding, and plenty of scope for reinterpretation and rethinking, particularly as we learn more about the county's past through historical research and archaeological enquiry. The essays in this book add to the corpus of knowledge about Nottinghamshire, and help to illuminate many of the remaining dark corners. At the same time they celebrate the career of someone who has overseen and promoted many of the advances made in our understanding, and helped us to appreciate the depth and breadth of the county's history.

The first two essays remind us of just how much we still have to learn about Nottinghamshire prior to c.1500. David Crook uses documentary sources in the Public Record Office, now part of the National Archives, and in Nottingham University Manuscripts Department to unravel the early history of Wollaton Park, as it was

6 Thus Hampshire was completed in 5 volumes, but Cambridgeshire in 10, and Oxfordshire has now published 13.

developed by the Morteyn family from about 1312. He shows how the family ran into financial difficulties, and as a result their land passed to the Willoughbys, whose possession of Wollaton was confirmed in 1355. Alan Cameron shows how the process of enclosure in the later medieval period led to the reduction of Stanton-on-the-Wolds to little more than an area of pasture, although it never quite became a deserted medieval village. Dr Thoroton found it much decayed. The village did not really recover until it became a favoured haunt of Nottingham commuters in the second half of the twentieth century.

Post-1500 the subjects discussed in this book range from individual buildings such as Nottingham Castle and Southwell's Archbishop's Palace, to broad swathes of the county such as Sherwood Forest, through the lives and work of individuals such as Emma Barnard, the second Duke of Newcastle, Major Hayman Rooke, Bishop Edward Trollope, and Dr Edward Seaton, and to the personal habits of numerous people in the early modern era, as witnessed in the church courts. David Marcombe's discussion of the role of the church courts in the administration of justice for moral offences, demonstrates how this role changed during the sixteenth and seventeenth centuries. The courts retained a moral role beyond the Reformation and into the seventeenth century, but their influence was hit and miss in terms of who was caught and who actually did penance. Many of those convicted simply bought themselves out of penance, while others just disappeared. Despite these inadequacies, substantial numbers of people were brought before the church courts in this period, although tailing off by the eighteenth century.

Sherwood Forest occupies a large swathe of Nottinghamshire, and although much reduced in size and scale today it remains a major tourist attraction because of the links with Robin Hood. Steph Mastoris discusses the development of the Forest prior to about 1800, and he does so through the unusual angle of the maps produced and the reasons for their production. For the most part maps were made because the Crown and, later, private owners, wanted to know the extent of their holdings, but by interpreting the evidence of the maps we can learn a great deal about how the Forest changed and developed across time. We also learn, in Sarah Speight's essay, about Major Hayman Rooke, whose military title of Major was given to the largest oak in the Forest, which is still maintained by Nottinghamshire County Council as a result of its supposed link with Robin Hood.

The role of buildings in history has long been a favourite theme of Adrian Henstock, and three essays in this book address the fate, or otherwise of buildings. Trevor Foulds writes about the furnishing of Nottingham Castle by the second Duke of Newcastle and his wife, and their subsequent occupation of the building. The Ducal Palace, as it should more correctly be called to distinguish the present building from its medieval predecessor, was the brainchild of the first duke, but its completion and furnishing fell to his son. Yet it was never a satisfactory building, and the impression gained is that the family preferred Welbeck, while visiting Nottingham twice a year primarily to establish a political presence in the town. After Newcastle died in 1691 the Palace was gradually abandoned. The great building debate in Southwell at the time of the founding of the Diocese of Southwell in 1884 was the future role of the Archbishop's Palace, the largely ruined medieval building which had once been the home of Cardinal Wolsey. John Beckett shows how the funding of the new diocese required capital to be raised for the bishop's income. Bishop Edward Trollope, suffragan Bishop of Nottingham, agreed to fund the restoration of part of the old Palace as a home for the diocesan bishop, by way of completing the endowment fund. Unfortunately the Ecclesiastical Commissioners judged his restoration work inadequate, the new diocesan bishop, Dr George Ridding, refused to live in Southwell, and good intentions turned into a sorry mess. The present Bishop's Manor, which sits amidst the ruins of the old Palace, was built only after the deaths of Trollope and Ridding.

Housing on a different scale altogether is discussed in Ken Brand's essay on the redevelopment of the Rookeries area of Nottingham during the 1870s and 1880s. Under legislation of 1875, and the guiding hand of Nottingham's first Medical Officer of Health, Dr Edward Seaton, one of the town's worst slum areas was cleared during the 1870s and 1880s. The problem was what to do with it? Lying between the market place and Parliament Street, it was prime commercial land, but the corporation had to tackle problems relating to the re-housing of the local population, and the construction of business premises in the area. In the end it made a substantial loss on the scheme, and fought shy of similar future projects, although the architectural legacy of the King and Queen Street area of central Nottingham remains with us today.

Finally, three essays pick up interesting issues which have sometimes been thought to lie outside the main stream of historical research. Dorothy Johnston unravels the life of Emma Barnard, successively married to Francis Willughby of Wollaton Hall, and the London financier Sir Josiah Child. From documents in the Willoughby family collection she recreates Emma Barnard's life as daughter, wife, mother, employer and householder, to provide an intimate portrait of the lifestyle of this otherwise almost forgotten woman, whose son became the first Lord Middleton. Sarah Speight writes about Major Hayman Rooke, who, after a modest military career retired to Mansfield Woodhouse and turned himself into an antiquary. He is particularly associated with Roman finds around Mansfield Woodhouse, but he was a pioneer archaeologist within the county. Despite having no formal training, he was well versed in a range of archaeological fields, and a significant contributor to the journal *Archaeologia*. Philip Jones writes about King Edward VII, and his annual visits to Rufford Abbey where he stayed during Doncaster race week each September between 1903 and 1909. The formality of the king's visits, despite the fact that they were only semi-official, contrasts with the relative anonymity he enjoyed which allowed him to travel round the county almost incognito. Although the chief constable was told of his movements, no special arrangements were made for his protection. Despite the fact that he travelled by car and train, it all seems a world away from the security conscious monarchical arrangements which are the norm today.

These essays contribute to our understanding of Nottinghamshire; indeed, we now know so much about the county that it would be daunting for any individual to take on the business of writing a single volume history. A county archivist may need to know about everything, but archaeologists and historians can safely hide behind their own specialisms. Over the years Adrian Henstock saw and used many of the county's archives, simply because they were in the office(s) where he worked, and he solicited, edited and even rejected, work on different aspects of the county through his editorial work for the Thoroton Society. The essays in this book offer additional insights into the history of the county, and in so doing they add to the corpus of knowledge that Adrian Henstock has been instrumental in developing over the past three decades. But at the end of his active archival career, and despite the array of learning which these essays contain, Adrian Henstock would probably not wish to change his own conclusion, written six years ago, that:

the wealth of material now available, both in archive and published form, makes the task enormously complex: perhaps one might be forgiven for echoing Thoroton's pleas about his county history: 'I allow no man for a judge who hath not done something of this nature himself'.[7]

7 Quoted in John Beckett, ed., *The Thoroton Society* (1997), 12.

1

The Early History of Wollaton Park and its Lords, 1283-1345

David Crook

Wollaton Park, which has at its centre the Hall which was formerly the seat of the illustrious Willoughby family, is the most famous public open space in the environs of Nottingham, constantly in the public eye. In 1976 Alan Cameron, then a keeper of manuscripts at the University of Nottingham, wrote an article on the deserted medieval village of Sutton Passeys, based largely on the documents then in his care, in which he demonstrated that the original Wollaton Park was not on the same site as the one which is now so familiar. It was in the area later known as Old Park, north of Wollaton village and the Nottingham to Ilkeston road, and up to the boundaries of Strelley and Bilborough in the north. This was the land which, until the house-building of the mid twentieth century consumed it, contained Old Park Farm. Cameron also suggested that the modern park which replaced it may have originated in an enclosure made by Sir Henry Willoughby in 1493.[1] Much has been written about the house and park both before and since 1976, but no attempt has been made to ascertain when the original Wollaton Park was created, and by whom. Recently some new information bearing on these matters has come to light.

The Morteyn family were lords of Wollaton for about two centuries, from the reign of Henry I to that of Edward II.[2] On the death of William

---

1 A. Cameron, 'The deserted medieval village of Sutton Passeys', *TTS* 80 (1976), especially 48-50, 57, 59. The area can be clearly seen on the 6-inch Ordnance Survey map, Nottinghamshire sheet XLI (1913, with additions in 1938).

2 Thoroton, 220, 222.

de Morteyn on 6th November 1283, without direct male heir, he was succeeded by Roger son of Roger de Morteyn, his nephew.[3] Roger was then said to be 21 years old and to have been born in late September or October 1262. The inquisition post mortem taken after William's death, on 7th December 1283, includes a great deal of information about his estate.[4] He had lands in several counties, but of particular importance was his Lincolnshire manor of Dunsby, near Bourne, where his widow Joan de Morteyn was in 1290 preparing to create a chantry for masses for his soul and for those of their predecessors and successors.[5] The property Roger inherited from William in Nottinghamshire consisted of the manors of Wollaton and Cossall, held of the honour of Peverel for the service of a knight's fee, of which a detailed extent is given in the inquisition. In Wollaton it included wood with heath, the herbage of which was worth 20s. a year, and the underwood worth 6s. 8d. a year, elements of the estate which probably formed the basis of the future park.[6] There is no reference to a park at Wollaton in 1283, whereas the separate inquisition post mortem on William's Staffordshire estate shows that there was one in his manor of Walsall in that county, the pannage and herbage of which was worth 13s. 4d. a year.[7] It was already by then well established, having been founded by William le Rous in the reign of King John.[8] It therefore seems clear that the park at Wollaton was created by Roger de Morteyn some time between 1283 and 1312, when the first explicit reference to it is found.

---

3 *CFR 1272-1307*, 197.

4 *Calendar of Inquisitions Post Mortem*, II, no. 508; J. Standish, ed, *Abstracts of Nottinghamshire Inquisitions Post Mortem [Notts IPM]*, II, TSRS 4 (1914), 20-2.

5 *Calendar of Patent Rolls 1281-92*, 385. Joan was given Dunsby in January 1284 because she and William held the manor jointly by grant of Master Thomas de Lichfield and Oliver de Sutton, bishop of Lincoln: *CCR 1279-88*, 250. Earlier William had had a wife called Emecine: *VCH Staffs*, 17, (1976), 184. Joan was the daughter of Philip Marmion: *CCR 1288-96*, 269-70. She died some time before 1298: *CCR 1296-1302*, 174.

6 *Notts IPM*, 21; PRO, C 133/37, no. 7: Et herbagio bosci cum bruerio valet per annum 20s. Et subboscus ibidem valet per annum vj s. viij d. All original documents cited are in the PRO unless otherwise stated.

7 C 133/37, no. 7. The park is mentioned in 1276: *CCR 1272-79*, 339.

8 *VCH Staffs*, 17, 184.

The young heir was not slow to try to develop and consolidate his new estate by extending his hunting rights over it. Roger received the Morteyn lands only in mid January 1284, and as early as 12th February that year at Lincoln he obtained a royal charter of free warren for his demesne lands in his manors of Wollaton and Cossall, Dunsby, Walsall, Braunston in Leicestershire, and Eyam and Risley in Derbyshire.[9] This might have been a conscious preliminary step towards establishing a further park or parks on his lands, but there is no evidence that one was constructed or even planned at Wollaton at that date. The charter gave him the same control of hunting of beasts of the warren over his own land that was first coveted and then enjoyed by the many lords who had received such charters in England, especially from 1251 onwards.[10] If his rights were breached he could deal with the offenders in his own manorial court, or use royal justice by obtaining a commission of oyer and terminer to deal with the interlopers, as he did when his park at Walsall was broken into and deer hunted there in 1292.[11]

Roger de Morteyn's family were not themselves strangers to illicit hunting outside their own property. Robert de Morteyn, William de Morteyn's brother and therefore another of Roger's uncles, was the most important of a group of nine men, including at least four from Wollaton and two from Cossall, including its reeve, who on 12th June 1264, during the period of the regime of Simon de Montfort immediately following the defeat of Henry III and his son Edward at the battle of Lewes, hunted red deer in Ravenshead wood in the king's forest of Sherwood. They took a stag which they carried to a house at Nuthall. They had also twice hunted on Bulwell moor, on 7th and 8th June 1264, taking two hinds and a fawn. By the time these offences came at last before William de Vescy's Nottinghamshire forest eyre in 1287, three of the hunters were dead and five were outlawed, but Robert de Morteyn and the reeve of Cossall, Robert son of Roger, clearly the ringleaders, were imprisoned and had to be ransomed at a

---

9 *CFR 1272-1307*, 197; *Calendar of Charter Rolls*, II, 272.

10 D. Crook, 'The "Petition of the Barons" and charters of free warren, 1227-1258', in M. Prestwich, R. Britnell and R. Frame, eds, *Thirteenth Century England*, 8 (2001), 33-48.

11 *Calendar of Patent Rolls 1281-92*, 514.

cost of 100 shillings and half a mark (6s. 8d.) respectively, and find pledges both for their ransoms and for their future good behaviour in the king's forest.[12] William de Morteyn himself, however, was a royalist during the war years, holding the forfeited lands of suspected rebels like Robert de Strelley, and being appointed keeper of the peace in Nottinghamshire and Derbyshire in 1267, with responsibility for pursuing the king's enemies and the right to take refuge in Nottingham castle when he needed to.[13] He was careful to obtain royal permission for his own hunting activities. In 1263 he obtained from the crown a licence to hunt foxes, hares and wild cats with his own dogs in all the royal forests in Staffordshire.[14]

The creation of a park at Wollaton by Sir Roger de Morteyn[15] in the last years of the thirteenth century or the earliest years of the fourteenth was not an unusual event, but part of a long-term development throughout England. About thirty-five parks are mentioned in Domesday Book,[16] and many royal and private parks were enclosed in the twelfth century, but the creation of private parks in really significant numbers did not begin until after 1225. Oliver Rackham calculated, on the basis of a sample of eight counties, that there were about 3,200 parks in England by around 1300, covering about 2 per cent of the country, with approximately one park to every four parishes in the lowlands.[17] In Nottinghamshire many of the new parks were in areas, particularly in the east of the county, which had formerly been part of the royal forest but were disafforested in 1225

---

12 H.E. Boulton, ed, *The Sherwood Forest Book*, TSRS 23 (1965 for 1964), 110. It seems unlikely that he was the same Robert de Morteyn as the one who was lord of Grove in north Nottinghamshire and who died in 1299: J. Standish, ed, *Notts IPM*, II, TSRS 4 (1914), 83, 89, 168-9.

13 *Calendar of Patent Rolls 1258-66*, 558; *1266-72*, 133-4; *Calendar of Inquisitions Miscellaneous*, I, nos. 644, 645, 849.

14 *Calendar of Patent Rolls 1258-66*, 247.

15 The date at which he had assumed knighthood is uncertain, but not earlier than 1286, when he was named in a charter witness list behind three men who were already knights, and not later than 1298: *CCR 1279-88*, 428; *VCH Staffs*, 17, 169.

16 H.C. Darby, *Domesday England* (1977), 201-3.

17 O. Rackham, *Ancient Woodland* (1980), 191; O. Rackham, *Trees and Woodland in the British Landscape* (2nd edition, 1990), 152.

and 1227 under the terms of the Charter of the Forest. Wollaton was one of the smaller number in the disafforested lands in the west beyond the River Leen.[18]

Within fifteen years of entering his inheritance, during which period it is highly likely that Wollaton Park was first established, things began to go wrong for Sir Roger de Morteyn, as he got into debt. The reasons are as yet unascertained, but the fact that he was summoned for military service against the Scots in 1297, 1298, 1300 and 1301 may have some relevance.[19] By the late 1290s he was defaulting on debts owed to townsmen and registered under statute merchant legislation.[20] In the spring of 1296 he borrowed fourteen marks from Peter de Thornhaugh, citizen and merchant of Lincoln, and, together with Adam de Cossall and Robert de Wingfield, twenty-six and a half marks from William de Normanton of Nottingham, the loans being registered before the mayors of the two towns in accordance with well-established practice. By early 1297 Normanton was suing for recovery of his debt, and Thornhaugh took action about his own in the early summer of 1300.[21] Sir Roger also contracted debts recorded on the close rolls of Chancery in those years, secured against his Lincolnshire lands: £19 13s. 4d. from William de Bernewell, tailor of London, in 1298, and £40 from Gilbert Pecche in 1300.[22] In 1302 even Roger's tailor, Thomas de Stamford, owed £11 to Pain de Sevenak, a debt registered before the mayor of London.[23] These sums were relatively modest in size, and that to Bernewell is known to have been paid off by 1303,[24] and since no loans are recorded for some years thereafter matters may not have been unmanageable. Then, however, in the early years of the reign of Edward II after 1307, matters seem to have got much worse.

---

18 D. Crook, 'The development of private parks in medieval Nottinghamshire', *TTS* 106 (2002), 73-80.

19 *Parliamentary Writs*, I, 287, 309, 310, 334, 355, 357.

20 I am deeply indebted to Dr Pamela Nightingale for generously supplying me with many references to the Morteyns from her database of statute merchant and statute staple proceedings.

21 C 241/32, no. 303; C 241/34, no. 241.

22 *CCR 1296-1302*, 192, 376.

23 C 241/36, no. 316. Sevenak was later Bernewell's executor: *CCR 1302-7*, 192.

24 *CCR 1302-7*, 192.

In 1309 Roger owed £100 to William de Spanby, the Lincolnshire man who had custody of the lands of the Templars in that county on behalf of the crown, and £200 to the prior and convent of Thornholme, also in Lincolnshire, a debt contracted a year earlier. The first of these debts was registered in Lincoln, the second in London, but both were apparently secured against his Lincolnshire estate at Dunsby, because he is referred to as the lord of Dunsby in the proceedings.[25] These were large sums. By 1305-6 he was also borrowing in Nottingham from Sir Richard de Willoughby senior, the grandson of Ralph Bugge, the Nottingham merchant of the first half of the thirteenth century who had used his earnings from commerce to establish his family in landed society at Willoughby on the Wolds, the manor from whom his descendants chose to take their name.[26] From Willoughby Morteyn borrowed £25 6s. 8d. in August 1305, £130 in December that year, and a further £20 in January 1306.[27] Willoughby's own son, Richard de Willoughby the younger, married Morteyn's daughter Isabel in 1310, and he did not take legal action to call in these debts until December 1313, in the case of the £20, and April 1314, in the others. Morteyn's failure to repay debts began to cost him some of the land against which they had been secured; at least part of Eyam by 1307,[28] and of Walsall by 1311.[29] His financial relationship with Willoughby, his history of debt to others, and the marriage between their children, provided the background against which he lost his lordship and park of Wollaton.

A series of documents dated to late March and early April 1312 provide the first dateable evidence of the existence of Wollaton park. They are to be found among the Wollaton deeds in the Willoughby family archive, which forms part of the Middleton collection of manuscripts, held at the University of Nottingham, three of the most

---

25 C 241/68, no. 30; C 241/76, no. 114.

26 J.C. Holt, ed, 'Willoughby Deeds', in P.M. Barnes and C.F. Slade, eds, *A Medieval Miscellany for Doris Mary Stenton*, Pipe Roll Society, New Series 36 (1962), 167-87; *Report on the Manuscripts of Lord Middleton preserved at Wollaton Hall* (Cd. 5567, 1911).

27 C 241/79, nos. 59, 60, 63.

28 *Calendar of Patent Rolls 1301-7*, 516; *1307-13*, 31.

29 *Calendar of Patent Rolls 1307-13*, 401; *VCH Staffs*, 17, 169.

important of which for the history of the park are printed in the Appendix. One is the damaged deed of about March 1312 in which Morteyn granted the park, along with advowsons of the churches of Wollaton and Cossall, to Willoughby.[30] The link with Morteyn's debts is made clear by a slightly later deed, dated 23rd March 1312, which mentions that Willoughby already held the charter granting the park, and the pond and meadow next to it, together with the two advowsons.[31] In this deed, Willoughby bound himself to return to Morteyn a bond for a debt of £140 and seisin of the park and advowsons, if he or his representatives paid the debt at St Peter's church in Nottingham at two terms, £40 on 24th June 1312 and the remaining £100 on 11th November 1312. On 2nd April 1312 Morteyn quitclaimed to Richard de Willoughby senior and his heirs and assigns all his claims to the park and advowsons.[32] On the same day at Lenton they made a supplementary agreement, that if Morteyn were to pay £50 of the debt in St Peter's church on 11th November, Willoughby would not retain the quitclaim; if the £50 was not paid then, Willoughby would remain enfeoffed of the park and advowsons.[33] At about the same time, at Cossall, Morteyn gave power of attorney to Richard de Willoughby the younger and Robert de Sulby to put Sir Richard de Willoughby senior in possession of the park and advowsons.[34] These arrangements for the transfer of the property clearly took effect, since in a slightly later but undated grant by William son of Sir Roger de Morteyn to Sir Richard de Willoughby senior of twenty acres of arable land in Wollaton, the twenty acres were said to lie below Richard's park there.[35] When the elder Sir Richard de Willoughby died early in 1325, Wollaton park was mentioned in his inquisition post mortem, which mentions 'a certain park with herbage worth 6s. 8d. in the summer'.[36]

---

30 NUMD, MiD 1565; Appendix (1).

31 NUMD, MiD 1572.

32 NUMD, MiD 1571.

33 NUMD, MiD 1567, 1568.

34 NUMD, MiD 1570.

35 NUMD, MiD 1564: Appendix (2).

36 C 134/90, no. 15: Item est ibi quidem parcus cuius herbagio valet per annum in estate vj s. viij d. *Calendar of Inquisitions Post Mortem*, VI, no. 610 does not include this detail.

In the few years following 1312, the manor of Wollaton itself also passed from the Morteyns to the Willoughbys, already linked by marriage.[37] In 1314 Sir Roger de Morteyn granted to Sir Richard de Willoughby the elder the right to over eighty acres of woodland in Wollaton, for a fine of 40s., following an inquisition *ad quod dampnum* to establish whether such a transfer would damage crown rights.[38] Then Sir Richard the elder received the manor of Wollaton, with some exceptions, from William de Morteyn, Sir Roger's son, by a deed dated 7th April 1318.[39] The transaction was confirmed, after due allowance for the king's feudal rights, following the issue of a royal licence in October 1319, at the same time as Sir Roger de Morteyn enfeoffed his son-in-law Richard de Willoughby the younger with some of the remaining portion.[40] The manor was to be held of the king as of the honour of Peverel, for an eighth of a knight's fee. The inquisition which preceded the grant of the royal licence was held by the escheator Sir Ralph de Crophill, to whom Sir Roger de Morteyn later became heavily indebted and to whom he eventually also lost his Lincolnshire park at Dunsby, which may have been created at roughly the same time as the park at Wollaton.[41]

When he was in the process of handing over his land at Wollaton to the Willoughbys, Sir Roger de Morteyn seems to have turned to others for further loans. By 1313 he was in debt to Italian creditors, the Bardi of Florence, although only to the extent of £10.[42] Some other loans for much larger sums, secured against his lands in Lincolnshire or Nottinghamshire, were contracted, as well as smaller debts: £60 from John de Ousthorpe, clerk, in 1317; £600 from John de Ashby in 1318; 140 marks from the Chancery clerk William de Airmyn in the same year; £600 from Sir Ralph de Crophill in 1318; and £100 from Robert de Bristol, merchant of London, in 1320.[43] The two largest debts, both

---

37 An accurate early account of these matters is given in Thoroton, 222.

38 NUMD, MiD 1573; *Calendar of Patent Rolls 1313-17*, 197; C 143/100, no. 4.

39 NUMD, MiD 1577.

40 NUMD, MiD 1578; *Calendar of Patent Rolls 1317-21*, 393; Thoroton, 222.

41 See below; it is not mentioned in the 1283 extent of Dunsby.

42 *CCR 1307-13*, 584.

43 *CCR 1313-18*, 558, 590, 611, 618; *CCR 1318-23*, 107, 224, 693; *CCR 1323-7*, 125, 323.

of £600, were therefore made in the same year that the manor of Wollaton was given up. In March 1320 he borrowed £80 from Roger de Southcote, another London merchant, whose later attempts at recovery in 1322-3 led to the holding of two extents of his property at Dunsby in March and June 1323. The second of them stated that at the time of the loan he had held lands which had since come into the hands of Sir Richard de Willoughby, a total of thirty-eight acres sown with various specified crops, and a windmill.[44] His indebtedness to Sir Ralph de Crophill was doubtless the reason why he had to release Dunsby park and other property in Dunsby to Crophill early in 1325.[45]

As Thoroton so aptly put it, the first Sir Richard de Willoughby 'did increase his Patrimony very well in divers places, and [he] added to it much land, which he purchased of the Morteins'. The second Sir Richard, however, 'was the very great advancer of his family, being a judge' from 1328 to 1357.[46] Like his father, he was first a sergeant at law before becoming a judge, and then after a rapid rise up the legal hierarchy he was by 1338 the most senior judge in England, chief justice of the King's Bench. After only two years at the pinnacle of judicial power, his luck suddenly changed. Perhaps because of the killing of two Leicester men by members of his household, he had a spectacular fall from grace in the summer of 1340, and was tried for various offences early in 1341, before regaining the king's favour to some extent by the payment of a ransom. He returned to serve as an ordinary justice in a lesser court, the Common Bench, from 1343, until his eventual retirement in 1357. His disgrace may also have been to some extent connected with his reaction to a break-in at Wollaton park, which probably occurred in the spring of 1340. It was carried out by a group of twelve men, led by Hugh le Spicer, who became mayor of Nottingham in 1342-3 and twice more subsequently, and including other individuals from Nottingham and others of lesser consequence said to be from Lenton, Gamston and Kelham. Their precise motive is unclear, although the Nottingham men may have had some personal grudge against him. They were subsequently sued by Sir Richard de Willoughby through a writ of trespass, returned in the Court of King's

44 C 131/1, nos. 39, 40; C 131/171, no. 110; *CCR 1318-23*, 226.

45 *CCR 1323-7*, 342-3.

46 Thoroton, 222.

Bench, of which Sir Richard was himself the chief justice, about 3rd May 1340.[47] The description of the offence follows the normal formulae in such cases, stating that the defendants broke Richard's park with force and arms and hunted in it without licence and at their own will, taking and carrying away wild beasts and committing other enormities against Sir Richard de Willoughby and against the king's peace.[48] Sir Richard attempted to pursue the offenders with all the power and authority at his command, including not only his position as chief justice of King's Bench but also as the senior assize justice for Nottinghamshire. He continued to do so, through his attorneys, even when he was himself imprisoned and on trial in late 1340 and early 1341. He failed, however, to get any of the defendants into court, and apparently gave up the fruitless suit in the autumn of 1341.[49]

Wollaton park certainly survived the depredations of Spicer and his friends, and a document survives which shows Sir Richard, a few years later, making provision for the management of the park with the help of private contractors.[50] On Sunday 1st August 1344 he leased for sale to William le Warde of Hempshill (in Nuthall) and Richard de Gresley of Bilborough all his underwood within Wollaton park, except four perches around the inside of the park, which served to enclose it, if it was measured by Sir Richard's own men. The underwood was defined as including hazel, thorn, willow and a small amount of aspen. In return they agreed to pay twenty-four marks to him in four equal instalments, six marks in the week after Martinmas (11th November 1344), six in the week after Candlemas (2nd February 1345), six in the week after Easter (27th March 1345), and six in the week after St Peter ad vincula (1st August 1345). William and Richard were to pay for and make their profit in one year, before Michaelmas (29th September) 1345, and without any longer delay. They were also to protect and take care of

---

47 KB 27/320, rot. 5.

48 For the typical form of entries in King's Bench plea rolls in cases concerning illegal hunting in private parks using writs of trespass, see M.S. Arnold, ed., *Select Cases of Trespass from the King's Courts,* II, Selden Society, CIII (1987), 267-73, 367-98.

49 D. Crook, 'The disgrace of Sir Richard de Willoughby, chief justice of King's Bench', forthcoming in *Nottingham Medieval Studies.*

50 NUMD, MiD 1590; Appendix (3).

the remainder of the wood in the park without doing mischief or damage, and were to have free exit and entry through the gate of the park, and in no other part. If any mischief or damage were done in the park by them, or by any default in their guardianship of it, they were to answer to Sir Richard for the damage, and make other satisfaction for it. Warde and Gresley were to remain in the park no longer than specified in the agreement, except at a seasonable time if Sir Richard agreed, and when it would be to his profit. Both parties had, in turn, set their seals to the agreement. The copy which survives among the Willoughby deeds still bears a single seal, apparently that used by Warde and Gresley.

This deal probably represented good business to Sir Richard de Willoughby, since the underwood of Wollaton, which in 1283 and 1325 had been said to yield 6s. 8d. (half a mark) a year, was now to be leased for a return to him of £16 (twenty-four marks), forty-eight times greater in cash terms. The lease of 1344 mentions a gate to the park, through which the lessees were to enter and leave, but there is no specific mention of a pale to mark its boundary, or of parkers responsible for maintaining it. Indeed, the implication of the instruction not to take any of the four perches of underwood around the inside of the park suggests that there may as yet have been no pale but that the underwood, in octoconjunction with the old ditch or bank (*antiqua fossata*) mentioned in Sir Roger de Morteyn's charter, was sufficiently dense to enclose it.

Sir Richard de Willoughby's possession of Wollaton park was finally confirmed on 30th September 1355, when Thomas de Morteyn, son of William de Morteyn of Dunsby and presumably the grandson of Sir Roger, released to him in perpetuity all the claims he might have had to the manors, advowsons, woods, meadows, pastures and their appurtenances which had once belonged to Roger de Morteyn, William de Morteyn and Adam de Wellum, former parson of the church of Wollaton.[51] It is unfortunately impossible to give any information about the value of the park in 1362 when Sir Richard de Willoughby died,

---

51 NUMD, MiD 1591/1. Wellum was rector of Wollaton from 1291 to 1339: R. Brocklesby, ed, *The Register of William Melton, Archbishop of York, 1317-1340*, IV, Canterbury and York Society, vol. 85 (1997), no. 890. In 1319 he purchased land in Wollaton from Sir Roger and William de Morteyn: C 143/136, no. 4; *Notts IPM*, II, 289-90.

because his inquisition post mortem, which would certainly have included an extent, is now blind and almost completely illegible.[52] There is little reason, however, to doubt that, as it completed the first half century of its life, Wollaton park passed to its new lord as a mature component of the family estate.[53]

52 C 135/175, no. 15; *Calendar of Inquisitions Post Mortem*, XI, no. 459.

53 Wollaton and its park did not descend to the third Sir Richard de Willoughby (d. 1369), who inherited only Cossall of the Nottinghamshire estate: *Calendar of Inquisitions Post Mortem*, XII, no. 428. It was held by Hugh Willoughby, clerk, son of the second Sir Richard and brother of the third, who died on 1st September 1406: *CFR 1405-13*, 45-6; *Calendar of Inquisitions Post Mortem*, XIX, no. 112.

APPENDIX:
Early documents relating to Wollaton Park in the Middleton collection, University of Nottingham Manuscripts Department

Use of initial capitals has been modernised and punctuation inserted where appropriate. Also, *u* has been rendered as *v* where appropriate for conveying the sense of both the Latin and the French.

(1) NUMD, MiD 1565, grant by Sir Roger de Morteyn to Sir Richard de Willoughby senior of Wollaton park and the advowsons of the churches of Wollaton and Cossall, on or before 23rd March 1312. There is a tag for a seal, but the seal is missing. The right-hand margin of the charter is missing; the missing matter has been supplied in square brackets where possible, and the ends of the lines indicated.

Sciant presentes et futuri quod ego Rogerus de Morteyn miles dedi concessi et hac presenti carta mea confirmavi Ricardo [de Wylugby]/parcum meum de Wollaton' cum stangno et pastura predicto parco adiacente sicut per antiqua fossata solebat includi simul cum [advocationibus ecclesi]/arum de Wollaton' et de Cossale qui quidem ecclesia de Cossale Adam de Wellum tenet tamquam capella annexa ad ecclesiam de Wo[llaton'].. /persona habendum et tenendum totum predictum parcum cum stagno et pastura adiacente cum viis et semitis ad predictam pertinen[tibus].../vestrum ubicumque necessar' sunt cum advocationibus ecclesiarum predictarum predicto Ricardo heredibus et assignatis suis de capitalibus dominus feodi illius.../ad predictam parcam et pasturam et ad advocationes ecclesiarum predictarum pertinent imperpetuum. Et ego predictus Rogerus et heredibus mei totum predictum parc[um].../et pastura predicto parco adiacente cum viis et semitis ut predictum est simul cum advocationibus ecclesiarum predictarum contra omnes gen[tes].../gabimus acquietabimus et defendend[abim]us[54] inperpetuum. In cuius rei testimonium hinc presenti carte sigillum meum apposui. Hiis testibus Roberto de [Kymmarley][55],/Johanne de Aldesworth', Ricardo Martel de Chilwell', Willelmo Torcard' de eadem, Johanne de Stapelford', Ricardo de St..., [Rogero]/de Mamchaster de Beston' et aliis.

(2) NUMD, MiD 1564, grant by William son of Sir Roger de Morteyn to Richard de Willoughby senior of land in Wollaton, c. 1312 or later. The seal of William de Morteyn, in good condition, is attached by a tag. There is a complication in that 'Wollaton' is spelt 'Wollaston' in the deed, and the Willoughbys also held property in Wollaston, Northamptonshire, for which there are many deeds in the Middleton collection. Nevertheless the circumstances of the deed generally and the Nottinghamshire witness list mean that the deed must relate to Wollaton rather than Wollaston.

---

54 There is a hole in the parchment in the middle of this word.

55 Supplied from NUMD, MiD 1564.

Sciant presentes et futuri quod ego Willelmus filius domini Rogeri de Morteyn militis dedi concessi et hac presenti carta mea confirmavi Ricardo de Wyluby seniori viginti acras terre arrabilis cum pertinenciis in Wollaston quarum octodecim acre iacent in quadam cultura que vocatur Stokkyng sub parcum eiusdem Ricardi in eadem villa et due acre iacent en le Breche iuxta Stokkyng sub parcum predictum simul cum capitibus in Towilborn brok super predictam terram abutanttibus habenda et tenenda eidem Ricardo heredibus suis sive assingnatis totam predictam terram cum pertinenciis de capitalibus dominus feodi illius per servicia que ad illam terram pertinent imperpetuum. Et ego vero dictus Willelmus et heredes mei totam predictam terram cum pertinenciis ut supradictum est predicto Ricardo heredibus suis sive assingnatis contra omnes gentes warantizabimus imperpetuum. In cuius rei testimonium hunc presenti carte sigillum meum apposui. Hiis testibus Roberto de Kymmarleye, Ricardo Martel de Chilwelle, Johanne de Aldisworth', Roberto filius Galfridi de Streleye, Johanne de Brokylstowe, Rogero de Mamcestre de Bistun, Willelmo Torcard' de Chilwelle et aliis.

(3) NUMD, MiD 1590, indenture between Sir Richard de Willoughby and William le Warde of Hempshill and Richard de Gresley of Bilborough for the sale of the underwood in Wollaton Park, dated Wollaton 1st August 1344. A single seal, presumably of either Warde or Gresley, in good condition, is attached on a tag.

Ceste endenture tesmoigne qi monsere Richart de Wylughby chivaler leesnee ad vendu et graunte a William le Warde de Hempishil et a Richart de Gresseleye de Bylborw tot son soutz bois en le park' de Wolaton', forpris quatre perchis enviroun de deinz le dit park' pur le dit park' enclore, si on serra mesur' par les gentz le dit monsere Richart, cest asavoir coudre, espine, saus et menwis tremblers, si on serra liuer a eux par mesure pur vynt quatre mars a paier, cest a savoir sis mars ala feste de Seynt Martyn en iver procheyn avenir, et sis mars ala feste de la Chaundeleure proscheyn seuvant, et sis mars ala Pasch' proscheyn seuvaunt, et sis mars ala feste de Seynt Piere ad vincula proscheyn seuvant.[56] Et les ditz William et Richart conperunt et frunt lour proffit del soutz bois avant dite de vant la feste de Seint Michiel prochein avenir en un an sauns plus lunge de lai. Et les ditz William et Richart sauvorunt et garderunt le remenant del bois del dit park' sauns fere mal ou damage et averunt fraunche issewe et frauche entre a la porte del dit park', et en nule part ailours. Et si mal ou damage soit fest en le dit park' par eux ou par defaute de lour garde, les dites William et Richart respundrunt al dit monsere Richart del damage avant dite et ferrunt gre alium. Et les ditz William et Richart maynenorunt point en le dit park', fors qi en temps sesiunable si cum asiert et qi soit al proffit del dites monsere Richart. En tesmoinaunce de quel chose les parties avant ditz a ses escrips endentes entre chaniablement ount mis lours seals. Escript a Wolaton le Dymeynge en la feste de Seint Piere advincula lan de regne le roi Edward tierce apres le conqueste dys et ouitisme.

---

56 *Proscheyn seuvant* interlined.

2

Enclosure and the Depopulation of Stanton-on-the-Wolds

Alan Cameron

The Nottinghamshire village of Stanton-on-the-Wolds does not appear in a 1972 gazetteer of deserted medieval villages for the simple reason that it is a thriving and growing village of over 450 inhabitants.[1] Today, with the exception of Keyworth, it has a larger population than most of the neighbouring villages which overshadowed it for nearly a millennium. Yet it is a good example of a situation which detailed studies are showing to have been an equally common occurrence - a village which shrank to virtual extinction, but whose decline has been overlaid by subsequent re-population and new housing. In 1670 the fate of Stanton hung in the balance, and it is clear that at that time the village community so well described by W.G. Hoskins in Wigston Magna in Leicestershire had long since disappeared, leaving only a ruinous church with a non-resident vicar and two farms with their attendant cottages.[2] Robert Thoroton compiling his *Antiquities of Nottinghamshire* a few years later could only describe Stanton as ' a wholly enclosed and depopulated lordship'. This subjective statement can be tested against a number of mid-seventeenth-century measures of the state of Stanton - the Protestation returns of 1641/2 , the Hearth

---

1 Appendix to M. Beresford and J.G. Hurst, *Deserted Medieval Villages* (1972), see also note 13.

2 W.G. Hoskins, *The Midland Peasant* (1957).

Tax returns of 1664 and 1674, the Compton census of 1676, and accounts of the Clifton family estate. Apart from the church the Cliftons had been the only major landowners in the parish since the early sixteenth century.

In 1641 there were, including the rector David Chounan, twelve males over the age of eighteen, representing no more than eight families and suggesting a total population of around thirty.[3] A generation later the Hearth Tax return for 1674 indicates little change. Eight houses are recorded possessing between them seventeen hearths, of which seven belong to Mr. Henry Pate's house, four to the vicarage, and the remaining six to six cottages with one hearth apiece. Ten years earlier there had been two additional cottages, Mr. Pate's house had had an additional hearth, and the parish was still served by a resident rector, Mr. Lee.[4] The Compton census of 1676 recorded twelve communicants, no dissenters or Catholics, and also stated that Mr. Ousely the vicar was also rector of Keyworth, the neighbouring parish in which he lived.[5] Four cottager families can be identified as resident through the period 1640-1680; the Mees, the Flinders, the Shaws and the Flowers. Finally, the Clifton family estate accounts for 1675-7 reveal that Mr. Pate occupied Manor Farm, and was the only substantial resident tenant. Most of the rest of the estate was leased on terms of years to tenants who lived outwith the parish boundaries.[6] Again the figures point to a population of around the thirty mark. In 1603 a similar return had given the number of communicants as forty, and Professor Wood has suggested that this represented a population of about sixty-four.[7] Clearly in 1676 Stanton was at its lowest ebb, and was every bit as much a deserted village as its near neighbour, Thorpe in the Glebe.[8]

---

3 W.F. Webster, *Protestation Returns 1641/2-Notts./Derbys.* (1980), 83.

4 W.F. Webster, ed., *Nottinghamshire Hearth Tax 1664:1674*, TSRS 37 (1988), 61, 86.

5 E.L. Guilford, 'Nottinghamshire in 1676: A Transcript from the Tanner MSS. In the Bodleian Library, Oxford,' *TTS* 28 (1924), 106-113.

6 NUMD, Clifton MSS. Cl A 7.

7 A.C. Wood, 'An Archaepiscopal Visitation of 1603', *TTS* 46 (1942), 3-14.

8 Alan Cameron and Colm O'Brien, 'The Deserted Mediaeval Village of Thorpe-in-the-Glebe', *TTS* 85 (1981), 56-67.

Stanton's subsequent population history can be told briefly. During the eighteenth century the population grew, but not substantially. New families occupied the farms created out of land that had previously been waste. In general new houses were built in the centre of these enclosed holdings and not at the old village centre. In 1743 the parish contained thirteen families, making a total of fifty-nine souls of whom forty-four were communicants and fifteen were children under eight years of age. The rector, Charles Henchman was non-resident because he was a minor canon of Chester Cathedral, but a service was read each Sunday afternoon by one of the masters of the Free School in Nottingham for which he received £15 a year. It was also as a result of Archbishop Herring's 1743 Visitation that the parish registers began to be kept in a more consistent form.[9] John Throsby writing in 1797 observed that the village had eighteen houses, and a church in a condition which offended him. The land was sandy wet soil which let at 5s. – 7s. 6d. an acre a year, which he reckoned was dear even at that moderate price. He visited the church and village with a friend and his comments are not flattering: 'My friend, a reputable grazier who was with me observed at leaving this place that transportation from his native place would be preferable to him than be forced to earn his bread in this lordship.....'.[10] In the early nineteenth century most of the land passed to the Robinson family who were in the process of building up an estate centred on Widmerpool. It is from that period that agricultural improvement led to a growth in the number of inhabitants in Stanton. In 1853 the population was 177 in twenty-five dwellings scattered across the parish. There is no evidence of workshops in the village.[11] By 1921 the population had dwindled to ninety, which was maintained until after the war when new housing was built along the Nottingham-Melton Road (A606). More recently the development of Keyworth as a residential area dependent on Nottingham, has encouraged house building within the parish.[12]

---

9 S.L. Ollard and P.C. Walker, ed, 'Archbishop Herring's Visitation Returns, 1743, Volume 4', *Yorkshire Archaeological Society Record Series* 77 (1930), 133.

10 John Throsby, ed, *Robert Thoroton's History of Nottinghamshire,* I (1797), 80-81.

11 F. W. White and Co., *Nottinghamshire Directory* (1853), 404.

12 The 1991 census return gives Stanton 449 inhabitants in 150 households. Keyworth has a population of 7,467, Plumtree 181, Normanton 264.

The purpose of this essay is to attempt to reconstruct in as much detail as the evidence will permit the progress of Stanton from a medieval arable village to an enclosed parish dependent upon pasture by the mid-seventeenth century. The survival of a fifteenth-century law-suit relating to rights of pasture in the village sheds light on the progress towards enclosure. The story told here adds weight to the theory that has been discussed for a generation or more, that the greater part of the move towards enclosure in the Tudor period occurred before 1489. This was before governments of England began to be concerned with it as a social problem.[13] What is clear in Stanton is that by 1500 the village community had lost its collective control over its agricultural life, that enclosure was already well established, and that there was no longer a possibility of re-creating the older pattern of common field agriculture. The situation also contained within it the underlying dynamic for Stanton's decline towards depopulation and enclosure. This essay will concentrate on the written evidence, but in time this might be supplemened by field surveys or archaeological investigation. There is plenty of evidence of eroded ridge and furrow throughout the parish, and the old village centre near the church would appear to repay a detailed survey.

There is no reason to believe that the scale of Stanton's population decline in the later Middle Ages is unique, even within the region of the Wolds of Nottinghamshire and Leicestershire. The key differences seem to relate to the physical size of the parish, and the structure of lordship within which the agricultural system was developed. A working hypothesis is that a large parish of 1,000 plus hectares (2,200 acres) with a single lord is more likely to maintain its open-field system than a small parish with a divided lordship, or one whose agricultural system is intermingled with that of a bigger neighbour. A striking comparison may be made between Stanton and Wymeswold, also on the Wolds. Around 1412-15 it seems that Wymeswold's fields were re-organised to take account of population decline, re-allocated to the

---

13 R.H. Hilton, 'A Study in the Pre-History of English Enclosure in the Fifteenth Century', *Studi in Onore di Armando Sapori* (1957), 675-685. The difficulties of forcible enclosure in the early sixteenth century are the subject of Eric Kerridge, *Agrarian Problems in the Sixteenth Century and After* (1969). There is no entry for Stanton in the 1517 enclosure inquiry in Nottinghamshire. I.S.Leadam, ed., *Domesday of Inclosures for Nottinghamshire*, TSRS 2 (1930).

Stanton-on-the-Wolds Village.

tenants, and the field regulations recorded in writing.[14] Most of the parish of Stanton-on-the-Wolds lies above the seventy-six metre contour line, dipping by twenty metres where the watercourses cut through the clay. The village is situated towards the western boundary of the parish on sandy soil, but the greater part is strong boulder clay, which is difficult to drain. In the context of medieval arable agriculture this would have been labour intensive. The parish measures about 560 hectares (1,400 acres) but for most of its history was reckoned as a parish of 900 customary acres.

The Domesday return indicated that Stanton was a thriving place. The recorded tenant population is nineteen divided into socmen, villeins and borders, with a total of twelve ploughs. This would suggest a population of between 75-100 depending upon the multiplier used for family size. Perhaps the most significant feature of the return is that the parish appears already to have been divided between manors, and to have had significant external influences on its structure.[15] Three separate estates were recorded. The lands of the Count of Mortain, the major part of which was *socland* to Gotham, and the rest had belonged to a freeholder called Frane; Roger de Busli's estate which was dependent upon Plumtree; and, finally, William Peverel's estate which was *socland* but dependent upon Clifton.[16] It is important to note the pre-Conquest dependency on other villages which suggests comparatively late settlement, or at least strong Anglo-Danish traditions. The lack of any manor co-terminus with the village and its fields, and the fact that throughout its history Stanton's major landowners lived outwith the boundaries of the village, may go some way towards explaining the breakdown of a manorial system under the pressure of population decline.

---

14 Survey of Wymeswold. NUMD, Middleton MSS. 6/177/60. Agreement for the regulation of the Common Fields, Middleton MSS. Mi M 242. Logic would suggest that the re-organisation process would take place in each open field in turn over a 3-4 year period, to avoid disruption to the agricultural cycle.

15 There are problems of terminology. The 'parish' is taken to mean the area bounded by the modern parish boundaries, not that they existed in this form in 1085. There is more detailed work to be done on the intensification of ecclesiastical organisation in Nottinghamshire. It does seem likely that Stanton was served from the Plumtree hundred church at Flawford. No chapel is mentioned in the Domesday return.

16 John Morris, ed, *Domesday Book 28, Nottinghamshire* (1977), 4, 5-6, 9, 86.

The manorial history of the parish is briefly sketched by Thoroton, but the easiest part of the story is that relating to the land which was *soc* to Clifton.[17] This estate seems to have stayed intact down the centuries, and had absorbed most of the land held by the other Domesday tenants by 1520. Throughout it was held by military service by the family Nottinghamshire knows as the Cliftons, and it is from their estate papers that this story can be told. Part of the de Busli estate was inherited by Robert de Salcey around 1200. This, along with some of the estate built up by William Brito, plus a portion of Peverel estate, became part of the foundation endowment of St. John's hospital in Nottingham between 1222 and 1235. These gifts were recorded in the Nottingham Borough records, and at the dissolution of the order in 1536 became the property of the Mayor and Corporation.[18] By the end of the thirteenth century two other major estates can be identified, that of Nicholas of Widmerpool based on Widmerpool, and that of William Brito based on Normanton by Plumtree. The undated deeds of this period indicate ten resident freeholders qualified to serve as witnesses.[19] In 1327 the subsidy gives us eleven taxpayers between them finding £1 2s. 0½d.[20] In 1334 there were fourteen taxpayers finding £31 9s. 4¾d.[21] A best guess about the situation around 1340 is that there were two major manorial estates, and a number of small freeholdings.[22] The Clifton estate tenants held roughly 45 per cent of the parish, but this did not include the lordship of the manor or the advowson of the church, which seems to have gone with the other estate built up by Simon Sybthorpe and based on Plumtree. According to the Feudal Aid of 1346 both estates were held of the Honor of Peveril, the Clifton estate for a full knight's fee and the Sibthorpe estate by one-eighth of a knight's fee. There were also a number of small freeholders, many

---

17 Thoroton, 81.

18 *RBN,* 1 (1882), 16,18, 24, 26, 28; 4 (1889), 124.

19 NUMD, Clifton MSS. Cl D 333-337; ClD 334, which is undated, contains a reference to the grant of a piece of land in *Rielandes* 24ft x 24ft to build a windmill for corn grinding.

20 NUMD, PRO E 179/159/4.

21 PRO, E 179/159/5.

22 Between 1330 and 1390 there is a resident family whose surname is Frankleyn, which indicates a status above that of yeoman but not yet gentleman or esquire.

of whom were non-resident, and the estate of St. John's hospital in Nottingham.

Court Rolls of the Sibthorpe estate from early in Richard II's reign show the beginnings of changes - one or two empty crofts, some consolidation of holdings and the first mention of *terra frisca* (land abandoned and uncultivated).[23] The tax relief allowed against the 1334 assessment in Henry VI's reign was 60 per cent which is at the upper limit of the range of allowances for Rushcliffe *Wapentake.*[24] The *Inquisitio Post Mortem* on Joan Swillington who died in 1427 provides a graphic picture of the state of Stanton. She held two messuages and two virgates of land, the messuages were worth nothing because they were completely thrown down and lay in decay. The land was uncultivated 'for want of labour' and therefore worth nothing.[25]

An estate was built up during the 1420s and 1430s by Ralph, Lord Cromwell of Tattershall Castle, one of Henry VI's advisers, and Lord Treasurer 1433-1455.[26] This portion of the Cromwell inheritance descended to Maud one of his daughters and co-heiresses who married Sir Gervase Clifton, a very prominent Lancastrian, soldier and Treasurer of Calais from 1450-1460.[27] He was a younger son, and it seems probable that the portion of the Stanton estate, which was 'Clifton' was part of his inheritance and used to provide dower on his marriage to Maud. Sir Richard Illingworth, Chief Baron of the Exchequer (1415-1476) was one of the trustees of Lord Cromwell's will, one of the Trustees of Tattershall College and therefore one of the guarantors of the marriage.[28] Sir Gervase was on the 'wrong' side

---

23 NUMD, Clifton MSS. CL M 59-60, see also Clifton Deeds ClD 614, 615, 618, 631, 632.

24 PRO, E/179/159/66, 74.

25 K.S.S. Train, ed., *Abstracts of the Inquisitions Post Mortem relating to Nottinghamshire,1350-1436*, TSRS 12 (1950), 186-7.

26 Kent County Record Office, De L'Isle and Dudley MSS. U1475, M215.

27 An outline of Sir Gervaise Clifton's career can be found in J. Wedgewood, *History of Parliament, Vol. 1, Biographies of Members of Parliament* (1936) 194-5, but he appears in most of the general histories of the period.

28 He was a member of Lincoln's Inn, and was MP for Notts. 1447, 1449, 1455-6, and married Agnes the widow of Thomas Charlton Lord Mayor of London. In 1463 he acquired Bunny, Notts., and this probably explains the survival of papers in the Parkyns of Bunny MSS. in NUMD; Wedgewood, *Hist Parl.Vol.1;* HMC Reports 77, *De Lisle and Dudley MSS.* I, 174, 211.

at the Battle of Northampton (10th July 1460), and exempted from the King's (ie Edward IV's) general pardon. It is at this point that Sir Ralph Illingworth appears in a leading role in the story. The whole joint estate was conveyed by a feoffment to uses, the recipients being Thomas Tyrell, Thomas Bylling, and Richard Illingworth for the term of their joint lives.[29] This feoffment covered the whole of the Clifton estate in Stanton. In modern terms a trust was set up to provide for Maud in her widowhood, and their possible children. All three trustees were prominent lawyers of the time and in the event of Maud and Sir Gervase having no direct heirs the estate would revert to the main line of the Clifton family (that is to say to the heirs of his elder brother, Sir Robert Clifton of Clifton).

What seems to have happened is that between 1461 and 1463 Richard Illingworth bought out the interests of the other trustees, and also secured the rest of Gervaise Clifton's estate.[30] He had been active in Nottinghamshire as one of the two county MPs since 1447. He may have been profiting from his position as a lawyer. He bought an estate in Bunny in 1463 and built up an estate around Kirkby Woodhouse, Annesley Woodhouse, Broxtowe and Selston at this time.[31] In due course the latter estate descended to his son Ralph.

The political implications of the feoffment process are interesting, and conclusions are fairly clear. Sir Gervase Clifton had a difficult time during the 1460s. In November 1465 a Commission to inquire into treasons resulted in outlawry, and he was required to compound for a pardon. He was an uncompromising Lancastrian. He again served with Margaret of Anjou at the Battle of Tewkesbury in 1471, and in the aftermath of this battle was among those court-marshalled by Edward IV and executed. The obvious explanation is that Illingworth was working to protect the Cromwell inheritance from forfeiture, and Gervase Clifton needed cash to pay both fines and legal protection. A family trust of the type described was the only method of protecting a family's inheritance in fifteenth-century England when the head of the family found himself on the 'wrong' side of the political fence.

---

29 NUMD, Parkyns of Bunny MSS. Pa L 1.

30 NUMD, Parkyns of Bunny MSS. Pa D 49-51, the quitclaim from Clifton to Illyngworth is dated 1 March 1465, Pa D 52.

31 NAO, Portland of Welbeck: Cavendish Deeds 157 DD/P/CD/41: Deeds and Estate Papers 157DD/ P/15/2-3,6.

The other protagonist in the events to be described was Sir Richard Bingham, a Justice of King's Bench, and a man with strong local connections[32] who built up an estate by purchase of the other manor and holdings within Stanton.[33] What is clear is that he was on the opposite side of the political fence from Sir Gervase Clifton. He was associated as legal advisor to the Hastings family from at least the early 1450s, and in 1466/7 became a trustee of the will of William Lord Hastings, a strong supporter of Edward IV as Controller of the Royal Household.[34] A series of deeds and feoffments in 1468 show Bingham trying to raise his holdings into a fully fledged manor with exclusive rights over the whole area of the parish.[35]

The story of the next ten years can be followed in the records of the case, not merely in the Court of King's Bench where the case came to formal trial and verdict, but also in the preliminary and supplementary papers in the Clifton and Parkyns manuscript collections in Nottingham University Library.[36] This gives us an unusually complete picture, since witnesses' depositions survive with contemporary notes and comment about the situation. We can hear the voices of the village after 550 years, talking about their knowledge, or rather lack of knowledge about the situation. It is also interesting because both Illingworth and Bingham were learned senior judges, knowledgeable about the law, its processes and how they could be manipulated to favour one particular party. So far as one can tell at this distance the case was played 'by the book' without much of the violence or intimidation which was characteristic of the Wars of the Roses period. There are, however, indications of witnesses being bribed or rather persuaded to change their story, possibly in exchange for a promise of future benefits rather than an immediate cash reward. There are also oblique references to attempted intimidation of the parson and

32 Sir Richard Bingham was the second husband of Margaret Willoughby one of the daughters and co-heiresses of Baldwin Freville of Middleton in Warwickshire.

33 NUMD, Clifton MSS. Cl D 819-20.

34 HMC, 78, *Hastings 1,* 3, 295-6, 300.

35 NUMD, Clifton MSS. Cl D 788-791.

36 NUMD, Clifton MSS. Cl L 199/1-7, Cl D 821 Parkyns of Bunny MSS. Pa L 4/1-6.

bribery of Illingworth's tenants by Thomas Bingham,[37] Sir Richard Bingham's son.

A court roll of 1461 of the estate prior to the feoffment to Illingworth contains a chronicle of defective buildings and broken walls and fences, and therefore gives a fair indication of the general state of the village.[38] In the context of the quarrel which erupted within the next decade it is interesting to note that on this estate there were only six cattle to *gyst* on the common grazing.

By 1467 it is apparent that roughly one-third of the parish had gone out of cultivation completely. This was the major portion of the field in earlier deeds called the 'East Field' or 'Logge' Field in contrast to North and South fields. This 'grate waste' of 'nine score acres of arable land lieth ley and has time out of mind, and not *ered* or sown' lay between the Nottingham-Melton road and the Fosse Way towards Lodge-on-the-Wolds, and was the field furthest from the village centre. There is also evidence of furlong consolidation and enclosure in the other two fields, particularly in *Daleland* which seems to have been used as the 'outfield' when the village reverted from a three-field system to two-field arable agriculture. This is the agricultural background to the dispute between Illingworth and Bingham which seems to have started in 1467/8, when Bingham tried to assert his exclusive lordship of the manor by granting a lease of his land and the whole of this 'grate waste' and common grazings to a consortium of flock masters, James Banks, John Banks and John Hall. This trio then proceeded to exclude other tenants from the area, particularly those of Richard Illingworth by charging them with trespass and damage when they tried to exercise what they believed to be their grazing rights according to traditional village custom.

The dispute between Illingworth and Bingham rumbled on for two or three years without local resolution. Perhaps the most serious practical issue between them, or rather their respective tenants, was one of over-stocking the land with sheep. Around 1470 it seems likely that there was a total 900 sheep grazing in an area of roughly 300 modern acres. Even by modern standards that is a heavy stock rate for the area, particularly since they lacked the methods for providing extra winter feeding and therefore the land was not being permitted a

37 See note 43.

38 NUMD, Clifton MSS. Cl M 61.

period of time for recovery, and was likely to deteriorate further.

It is clear that Sir Richard Bingham was the aggressor and the timing of his legal assault is significant. The process was begun by Bill of Complaint with Answer, replication and Rejoinder. Internal evidence indicates that this process began in 1471/2 and both the timing and the method of proceeding are significant. In 1471 Ralph Illingworth was not re-appointed to the Exchequer, perhaps an indication of royal uncertainties about his loyalty. Sir Richard Bingham was a loyal Yorkist, and he might have hoped that this would bring a speedy judgement in his favour. We can presume that he had the full backing of William, Lord Hastings whose political star was dominant in Edward IV's Council.[39] Despite this, at no point is there any evidence of political interference in the case. It does appear to have been a genuine attempt to resolve conflicting rights of pasture which had become obscured by the passage of time and were almost beyond the human memory of those on the spot.

The form of procedure would seem to indicate that the case was dealt with at first either in Chancery or as a case in the King's Council. In neither case can it be traced, and it seems to have been referred to the Court of King's Bench in the Michaelmas term of 1475, where it was still under way in 1477.[40] While the phrase 'with force and arms' appears in the process of the case this should not be taken literally. While there probably were scuffles and perhaps the odd brawl between the tenants of the contestants, the prime purpose was to ensure that the case did come into the Court of King's Bench because it disturbed the king's peace.

The core of Bingham's complaint was that he 'was seized of the manor of Stanton-on the Wolds with appurtenances in his demesne as of fee', and that Richard Illingworth held certain tenements but no manor. The latter's tenants had pastured 400 sheep in the waste and other lands where 100 sheep would have been the amount sufficient to his holdings. Bingham also asserted that Illingworth owed suit of court but was a persistent non-attender.[41] Illingworth's complaint was a mirror image of these charges. The key legal matter was whether

---

39 William H. Dunham, Jr. *Lord Hastings Indentured Retainers, 1461-1483* (1954).

40 PRO, K.B. 27 Michaelmas, 15 Edward IV ro. 480 & 550.

41 NUMD, Clifton MSS. Cl L 199/1 also another copy at Cl L199/6.

Bingham or any other landowner could possibly have held all the furlongs within a single 300 acre field under an open field agricultural system, and therefore exclusive rights of pasture in a parish with a split lordship. Common sense suggested to the judges on the case that this was unlikely because it would have implied that Bingham had similar quantities of land in the other two fields, which he patently did not. The only solution was to examine witnesses on the spot, and attempt to evaluate the evidence before coming to a final judgement. One further twist in the story is that the Chief Justice of King's Bench who set up the inquiry was Sir Thomas Billyng, whom we have already met as one of the feoffees of the Cromwell inheritance in 1461. The examination of witnesses was taken by the William Prior of Lenton and Sir Robert Clifton of Clifton, both of whom were familiar with the situation in Stanton.[42] The full text is given in the Appendix. The logic of the evidence told against Sir Richard Bingham and was summarised as follows:-

> 'First as to the Common of Pasture
>
> It must be as the said Richard Illingworth alleges in his answer both on the waste and in the fields that is to say that he and all those etc. have had common in the waste and also on the land in the fields that lieth ley and have done time without mind. This matter needs no great examination for it is perfectly known both by the tenants and by the inhabitants, for if they had not had common for their beasts they might not have lived there.
>
> And As to the Gystement
>
> The gystement has been used by the farmers of those lands that Illingworth has in the manner and form as he alleged, and also the farmers of Bingham have. But the grudge that was between the said farmers there was because each one of them would take in as much gystement as he might get and so overcharge the common. And if it is true that Bingham is lord of the manor and so the soil and freehold of the waste were his, some men would think that he could gyste in the common field, because it is pasture

42 NUMD, Clifton MSS. Cl L 199/5.

> and has lain ley time without mind, which is in quantity four times the waste of the time. Therefore the said Bingham has no more cause to pasture nor gyste the soil and freehold of Illingworth, than has Illingworth to pasture in Bingham's freehold. Therefore Illingworth has as much right to pasture in Bingham's land as Bingham has to pasture in his, *and this is as it happened.*'[43]

There is also a comment on some of the undercurrents and personal difficulties in which some of the tenants found themselves.

> '....For William Hall which was born in the town and still lives there told Illingworth and Roger Brerely that Illingworth might close it and keep it several at all times of the year because he said that that had been the previous practice........But now the said Hall has become Bingham's tenant and so turned French, and therefore it is not wise to rely on him. And yet I would he were entreated in secret and granted a good reward upon my (presumably Illingworth's) purse to say the truth of all things...... for he is of great age and has lived there all his life......'

Although Sir Richard Illingworth died in 1476, judgement was given in the Michaelmas term of 1478 against Bingham which settled the legal niceties of the case, but the practical issues of pasture rights in Stanton, and its impact on both land and the social structure of the village remained unresolved.[44]

The story of the subsequent fifty years can be told very simply. In 1478 Sir Robert Clifton died and his son and heir was another Gervase (occasionally spelled Jarvis, which indicates local pronunciation). During the 1480s this Gervaise began the process of recovering the whole of the Clifton estate in Stanton and buying in the other freeholds

---

43 There is a good deal more in this document, but these clauses seem to be the most salient to the story NUMD, Clifton MSS. Cl L 199/6a.

44 Writ *diem clausum extremum* 3rd May 1476, *CFR* 1471-1485, 327; *Calendar of Inquisitions Post Mortem,* 1437-1485,74-75; Prerogative Court of Canterbury Wills, 1476, 25 Wattys. Will dated 1471 proved 15th July 1476. Sir Richard Illingworth's heir Ralph was formally admitted to his father's lands on 28th November 1476: see *CFR* 1476-1485, 392-3.

and interests.[45] This process was not completed until the 1540s. For much of the intervening period two families of flockmasters seem to have been involved in Stanton, the Banks family who have already figured in this story, and the Bradshawes, who dominate the sixteenth and early seventeenth centuries. The practice of leasing Stanton to a member of the Bradshawes for the term of a life is noted in 1504.[46] The final logical and irrevocable step occurred on 30th October 1540 when Christopher Bradshawe and Roger his son were granted the whole of the lordship of Stanton-on the-Wolds for a term of ninety years in return for a cash payment of £60 and an annual rent of £16 15s. 'without impeachment of waste in the town and fields of Stanton'. Two further conditions of the lease were: that the lessees should decay no more tenures in the village and its fields; and that they will supply an able man horsed and harnesses to serve the King under Sir Gervase Clifton and his successors, 'whenever the King shall require them for the wars'.[47]

There were modifications and adjustments to the lease during Queen Elizabeth's reign, but these were mostly in the direction of permitting the Bradshawes to demolish buildings, and make other changes in the direction of enclosing areas for pasturage.[48] During the 1560s the manor house appears to have been re-built and was let out as a country residence to a variety of tenants. The identification of the Bradshawe family with Stanton was completed by living in the village and being buried in the parish church.[49] It was only in the 1630s that there was a change of occupation when the Bradshawe family disappeared from the village, but by then Stanton had become the decayed lordship which Robert Thoroton found in 1676.[50]

---

45 *CCR* 1476-1485, 665; NUMD, Cl D 845.

46 *Calendar of Inquisitions Post Mortem,* Henry VII, Vol.3, 152.

47 NUMD, Clifton MSS. Cl D 1139/2.

48 NUMD, Clifton MSS. Cl D 1141-4.

49 NUMD, Clifton MSS. Cl D 1492 is the will of Roger Bradshawe of Stanton, yeoman dated 28th July 1566, and proved 10th October 1566.

50 NAO, Darwin of Elston Hall, DD. A 16/1-2.

Appendix
NUMD, Clifton MSS. Cl L 199/5.

This is the examination of certain persons taken before the Prior of Lenton and Sir Robert Clifton Kt. by virtue of a letter and schedule enclosed in the said letter and sent from Thomas Byllyng and Richard Cheke Kts.[51]

Certificate

In primis. We have examined the witnesses of the part of both Richard Bingham and Richard Illingworth and all say that all those whose estate the said Ralph Illingworth has in Stanton have been accustomed to pasture the waste and the other lands and tenements which have and now lie ley in the common field time without mind, with their own cattle and beasts at their pleasure. Also they say that Richard Bingham and his tenants have been accustomed to do likewise.

> Item. As to the article of gystement, the parson of Stanton being parson for nearly 40 years says that when the tenants and farmers have not had sufficient cattle in the same wastes and leys according to their tenure, they have taken in other men's. Four witnesses affirm this, but two witnesses of the party of the said Richard Bingham say that as far as they have knowledge that William Sibthorpe, whose estate Richard Bingham has, ordained farmers to take in gyste cattle and the money coming thereof divided in two, one half to himself and the other half to be divided between the tenants of the said Sibthorpe and Hopton, and others after the rate of their tenure. And another man dwelling in the next town says that in the time of William Sibthorpe certain tenants were wont to take in other men's cattle, and the money coming of the said gistement was divided in two, one half going to William Sibthorpe and the other to the tenants according to the quantity of their tenure.

Item. As to the nine score acres. The witnesses of both parties were examined whether Richard Bingham has nine score acres of several land lying together adjoining the waste or not. They say they know of no such thing. But one of the witnesses of the part of Sir Richard Bingham, Ralph Clerk says that in the nine score acres other men have had ground but now no man but the lord. William Hall of Stanton says that he has land of his own lying in the nine score acres, and the parson says that he was at the laying out of the lands of Henry Whetely within the supposed nine score acres. Also the parson says that Nicholas Widmerpool, Master of the House of St. John of Nottingham and other freeholders have land lying within the said nine score acres. Also Thomas Clerk of Wysowe (Wysall) says that William Hall late farmer to Richard Illingworth sold unto the said Thomas two loads of ferns growing upon two lands lying in the said supposed nine score acres, and William told Thomas that the two lands belonged to Richard Illingworth and were parcel of his farm.

---

51 This appears to be a summary in English of the detailed depositions recorded in Latin, which may be found at NUMD, Clifton MSS. Cl D 821.

As to the article whereby Richard Bingham reserved to himself in a lease to James Banks and others for a term of years of all the waste of commons in Stanton and the nine score acres of arable, there is no-one who can affirm the truth of the said lease or not. James Banks says that he occuppied and pastured all the above lands with five hundred sheep in the first year of taking up the lease. Also James says that he is not tenant for a term of years, but occupies the land from year to year. Also he says that this last year which is the second year of his occupation Richard Bingham charged him that he should not occupy the wates nor other lands contained in the supposed nine score acres and that he should take in no gyste of cattle. The parson says that James Banks and all the other farmers occupy the said wastes and all other lands with their cattle in all places as they did before any lease was made to them by Richard Bingham, to which several witnesses agree.
Item. As to the Dale land, several witnesses say that the Dale Land has been kept several at all times of the year until the time that James Banks was farmer, to Sir Richard Illingworth and those whose estates he has. But Ralph Clerk of Edwalton one of the witnesses of Richard Bingham says that the Dale land is not several, but should be divided with three fields that is to say two parts several and one part fallow. Also William Hall of Stanton one of the witnesses of the same party says that he farmed the Dale land for sixteen years, and says that he held it not severally.

On the dorse

And also John Mandeville of Keeworth (Keyworth) sometime farmer of the Dale land in Stanton under the said William Hall for three years together says that he held the said lands severally and it is now twelve years since he was farmer. Also the parson says that he heard an old man called Robert Davutre who said he was kinsman to Sir Richard Bingham, and died with him at Baseforthe (Baseford) told the parson and many other folks at divers times that whosoever was lord of Dale land might keep them severally at all times of the year, and other witnesses affirmed that they also heard the said Robert say this.

In the margin

This is the schedule enclosed in a letter sent from Thomas Byllyng

3

The Wages of Sin: Sex, Shame and Retribution in Nottinghamshire, 1560-1640

David Marcombe

In a well-known passage in *The Mayor of Casterbridge* Thomas Hardy vividly describes a skimmington, a 'Daemonic Sabbath' directed against two members of the local community whose morals were disapproved of. In this case the focus of public hostility was the adulterous relationship between Lucetta Farfrae and Michael Henchard, and such was the noise, trauma and sense of humiliation that Lucetta collapsed, miscarried of her child and eventually died.[1] By the Victorian period skimmingtons, or skimmity rides, were already very ancient, and they were effective because the whole community - or most of it - shared a clear-cut set of moral values which accepted that matters such as adultery or wife-beating were beyond the pale of acceptable social conduct. Though no Nottinghamshire examples readily come to light, Rex Russell has demonstrated that in neighbouring Lincolnshire 'rough music' and 'rantanning' were relatively common right up to the early-twentieth century, a means of taking action 'forcibly, noisily, and effectively' to ensure that 'certain social conventions would be upheld'.[2]

---

1 T. Hardy, *The Mayor of Casterbridge*, (Norton Critical Edition, 1977), 212-4.

2 R.C. Russell, *From Cock-Fighting to Chapel-building: changes in popular culture in eighteenth and nineteenth century Lincolnshire*, Lincolnshire Archaeology and Heritage Reports Series, 6 (2002), p.66.

It might be tempting to believe that all of this raucous excitement was part of a quaint and folkloric past beyond which we have now somehow 'progressed', but even a casual glance at modern society will prove that this is not the case. Today we still subject people to public ridicule and humiliation to try to influence their behaviour, upset them or just provide an outlet for our own anger and prejudice. Newspapers are fond of doing this, by 'outing' all manner of perceived deviants; and graffiti artists do it too, pronouncing on lavatory walls and other more public places what they consider to be inappropriate behaviour. What we are perhaps not so well aware of is that all of this – from Hardy through to the present – is a form of human behaviour which was exploited for centuries by the church as a means of controlling what it saw as vice and lewd living in society at large. Once it had become filtered through the bureaucratic procedures of the church courts, this deep-seated human impulse to 'name and shame' became an effective vehicle of social control which the ecclesiastical lawyers called penance. This essay explores how and why penance was used in the reformed Church of England, particularly in Nottinghamshire. It also asks how effective it was in achieving its objective of a moral reform of society.

The notion of deterrent in England was based on public punishment. Hanging, gibbeting, flogging and exposure in the pillory or stocks were all performed in front of whoever cared to come along and watch, the prevailing idea being that people would 'take warning' and amend their lives accordingly.[3] Writing in the early-nineteenth century, Mary Martha Sherwood drove home this message for the benefit of the young in her *History of the Fairchild Family* in which Mr Fairchild says to his wife: 'I will take the children this evening to Blackwood, and show them something there, which, I think, they will remember as long as they live; and I hope they will take warning from it and pray more earnestly for new hearts'.[4] Mr Fairchild's place of enlightenment was a gibbet, where the mouldering remains of condemned criminals were hanged in chains for the edification of passers-by, and, good father that he was, 'He refuses to let his children leave this place of horror until he tells the whole story which led up to the execution'.[5] In the context

---

3 J.A. Sharpe, *Judicial Punishment in England* (London, 1990), 6-9.

4 Quoted in Russell, *Cock-fighting*, 7-8.

5 *Ibid*, 8.

of moral crime penance performed precisely the same function as the gallows and the gibbet did in the secular sphere. It also embodied some of the risks noted by Gatrell in his recent seminal study of public executions in England. So long as there was broad agreement between governors and governed as to what constituted a suitable case for punishment, these public deterrents could work well. When that consensus broke down, however, public punishment ran the risk of discrediting those who imposed it, a feature which Gatrell highlights in the context of certain eighteenth- and nineteenth-century capital crimes and which is equally true for penance.[6]

Corporal penance as an antidote to moral crime rested on Old Testament precedent endorsed by the writings of St Paul. The pre-Reformation church believed that penance was essential for the forgiveness of sin and that it should be imposed by a priest in his role as 'physician of the soul'. Repentance, confirmed by some outward acknowledgement of guilt, was required 'to preserve the holiness of the Church, but also to awaken wholesome fear and sorrow in the heart of the offender while there is yet time'.[7] Thus the sacrament of penance was critical to the whole Catholic doctrine of salvation. It reduced the time spent in purgatory and was comparable to actions such as going on a pilgrimage, or purchasing an indulgence, in terms of its overall efficacy. Its public aspect also provided a useful bonus in terms of its contribution to social control within the local community. In the early Church public penance was deemed appropriate only for the crimes of idolatry, murder and adultery and was performed before the congregation lying prostrate on sackcloth and ashes. By the Middle Ages the catalogue of 'mortal sins' had been greatly expanded and several distinct grades of penance had been differentiated, imposed for offences such as fornication and disrespect of the Sabbath and Holy Days. Medieval penitents were often expected to walk in parochial processions, barefoot, wearing appropriate dress and carrying candles,

---

6 V.A.C. Gatrell, *The Hanging Tree: execution and the English people, 1770-1868* (1994), 1-25, 56-89.

7 W.E. Addis and T. Arnold, *A Catholic Dictionary: containing some account of the doctrine, disciplines, rites, ceremonies, councils and religious orders of the Catholic Church* (1893), 646-54.

but quite commonly whippings were also employed, as late as the fifteenth century.[8]

All of this, like so much else of the Roman Catholic tradition, was absorbed lock-stock-and-barrel into the Church of England at the Reformation, despite the fact that the primary purpose of penance - the salvation of the offender's soul from the flames of hell - had been undermined by the advent of Protestant doctrine. Tudor and Stuart English people, in obedience to the prayer book and the thirty-nine articles, believed that man's salvation was pre-ordained by God and, of course, in this context, the ancient theological justification for penance was largely irrelevant.[9] The *Book of Homilies*, first published in 1562, stated that repentance was a worthy act which could make a person 'clean changed and altered', but unless that person was *chosen of God* – one of the elect – it would lack true spiritual efficacy.[10] Corporal penance, therefore, counted for little when it came to redemption, and even less in the journey through purgatory which was no longer believed to exist. However, this doctrinal revolution did not mean that penance wilted and died in the reformed Church of England. On the contrary, it survived, and its use may well have expanded, though its *raison d'être* changed. In the seventeenth century penance came to be regarded not so much as a vehicle of personal salvation, as a means of enforcing the broader spiritual integrity of the community and conformity to the generally accepted standards of 'good neighbourhood'. In other words, it became a social device more than a spiritual one.

Though penance had arguably always had this function, there was now a new emphasis which was rooted in two important shifts in the English mentality initiated by the Reformation and the economic upheavals of the sixteenth century. First, the theories of community and divine retribution developed by the early Protestant theologians, particularly the idea that evil actions on the part of individuals were likely to bring down divine wrath on the community at large. Second,

---

8 P. Hair, ed, *Before the Bawdy Court* (1972), 127, 142.

9 *The Thirty Nine Articles and the Constitutions and Canons of the Church of England* (1724), 7.

10 *Certain Sermons, or Homilies, appointed to be read in Churches in the time of the late Queen Elizabeth of famous memory* (1852), 508-9.

the understanding, on the part of most people, that immoral and antisocial activity not only offended God, but could also cause distress and damage to one's neighbours, a mode of thinking that had particular relevance in periods of severe economic depression such as the 1580s and 1590s, and 1620s. Fornication potentially gave rise to bastards which could easily become a burden on the poor rates; adulterous wives or husbands caused upheaval within the community; and those who kept alehouses on the Sabbath encouraged disorder and detracted from the proper duty owed to God. Public penance was a means by which these faults, and others like them, could be acknowledged and advertised to others. It was at one and the same time a punishment for the transgressor, a deterrent to the uncommitted majority and a statement of intent by the church and godly village hierarchs. The language of penances bears out all of these points very clearly. I desire 'God principally… and lastly all you my good neighbours whom I have offended to forgive me'; 'take example by my punishment to live a chaste and godly life'; 'learn by my punishment to know and reverence them that are in any authority over us'.[11] So as a means of buttressing the social order and ensuring that the community lived at peace with God and itself, penance lived on as a sanction in the reformed church despite the doctrinal inconsistencies implicit in its retention.

It would be wrong to conclude from this, as some historians have done, that penance was some heavy-handed form of 'social control' imposed from above. The situation was more subtle and complicated. As we have seen, left to its own devices the local community set limits on the sort of behaviour it would tolerate, and it had ways and means of making known its disapproval of persistent or notorious moral offenders. Such events could easily get out of hand, as in the case of Lucetta Farfrae's death or when Lord Latimer, a notorious lecher and abuser of his wife, was tied back-to-front on his horse and paraded around the streets of Snape, naked, during the Northern Rebellion of 1569.[12] The authorities could not be seen to approve of such actions on the part of plebeians, however noble the moral code they professed to be upholding. Thus, in order to prevent tumult or the overthrow of the established social order, it was highly desirable that the punishment

11 NUMD, AN/PN/352.

12 H. Aveling, *Northern Catholics* (1966), 68.

of moral crime be put on a regular, structured, and controlled footing. Consequently the church courts professed to serve the local community rather than to terrorise it; indeed, without a measure of co-operation between church and people the whole system would have fallen flat on its face. The courts depended on churchwardens for the presentment of offenders, dealt with malefactors in the name of the community, and sometimes even handed over potential penitents for punishment by local gentlemen or parochial authorities.[13] The extent of this co-operation was to prove to be the limit of penance as an effective sanction, because once the broad consensus as to what constituted a deserving case broke down, so did the ability of the courts to pursue the prosecution of an offender with any effectiveness. As we shall see, the effective imposition of penance – like all aspects of criminal justice in pre-industrial England – was heavily dependant on co-operation between the governors and the governed.

All church courts were empowered to use penance, but it was used most commonly in Nottinghamshire, both in *ex officio* and instance cases, by the high commission which met from time to time at Southwell; by the archdeacon's court which covered most of the county in terms of regular ecclesiastical jurisdiction; and the court of the peculiar of Southwell. Even then it was only employed as a sanction in the most serious cases, which in the sixteenth and seventeenth centuries generally meant offences such as incontinence, adultery and fornication before marriage. In 1602 and 1608 almost all of the penances imposed in the archdeaconry were for sexual misbehaviour.[14] However, Nottingham penances were not exclusively directed against this sort of offence and one of the trends noticeable in the early-seventeenth century is the rise in the number of penances given out for non-sexual misdemeanours. Out of a total of seventy-two penances imposed in 1609, for example, twenty-four were for crimes such as non-observance of the Sabbath by playing cards, football or drinking in alehouses.[15] There is some evidence to suggest that, whereas people

---

13 For example, see D. Marcombe, *English Small Town Life: Retford, 1520-1642* (1993), 138.

14 Unpublished figures from the work of the A(rchdeaconry) R(esearch) U(nit), C(entre for) L(ocal) H(istory), University of Nottingham.

15 Ibid.

readily accepted penance as a 'traditional' penalty for fornication and incontinence, they were less likely to countenance its use to help enforce some of the more 'secular' or 'new-fangled' preoccupations of early Stuart government, a small manifestation of a larger crisis of confidence which was to spill over into civil war in 1642.

As in the Middle Ages, the most common form of penance was the single public act imposed for incontinence or fornication and performed in the parish church during morning prayer on Sunday, traditionally the best attended service of the week. The offender was supposed to wear 'penitential habit' which in Nottinghamshire meant that he or she had to appear with bare head, legs and feet, wrapped in a white sheet, and sometimes holding a white rod, the symbol of chastisement. In 1564 the Southwell court specified precisely how Stephen Luxton and Elizabeth Massey of Oxton were to be reduced to their undergarments, 'he bareheaded, barelegged and barefooted in his shirt only and a sheet about his middle; and she barelegged and barefooted in a petticoat and a sheet about her middle'.[16] The penitent having been symbolically separated from the main body of the parish in this way, the performance of the act of penance was carefully stage-managed. The offender was to kneel in the sight of the congregation during the reading of the gospel and a sermon or homily directed against fornication or adultery. Then, standing 'on some form or desk' and 'in most view of the people', the penitent was to repeat 'in an audible voice' the words of a confession read by the minister, acknowledging his sin, naming the co-respondent and requesting the congregation 'to take example by my punishment to lead a chaste and godly life'.[17] The performance of penance was then to be certified to the court under the hands of the minister and churchwardens. So concerned were ecclesiastical judges that penances should be performed and certified 'in due order and reverence', they sometimes wrote to parish clergy with detailed instructions about how the event should be handled.[18] It is surprising that given the drama and pathos

16 S(outhwell) M(inster) L(ibrary), Act Book 21, f.3.

17 NUMD, AN/PN/352.

18 For an example from the diocese of Durham, see Durham Cathedral Library, Raine MS 124, f.172a.

implicit in such events no English artist felt inclined to record them for posterity. Only David Allan's eighteenth-century depiction of the Scottish 'stool of repentance' gives any impression of the mixed emotions – distress, anger, mirth and indifference – which broke through the surface on these occasions.[19]

For more serious transgressions the number of penances could be multiplied and the court could order them to be performed in more than one place to maximise the humiliation of the offender. Apart from churches, the most usual place of exposure was the market place of the nearest town, either at the market cross or 'upon some barrel or other thing in most view of the people'.[20] On these occasions a placard was sometimes attached to the penitent. This was a large piece of paper or card fixed to the breast and back bearing a description of the offence 'in great letters'. A woman who left her husband and unlawfully married a clergyman carried the words 'FOR SHAMEFUL ADULTERY' at the Malt Cross in Nottingham.[21] These placards were considered suitable for penances performed in places where long statements of guilt were not appropriate in view of the general bustle and noise. Another system sometimes employed in public places was to precede the offender by a court official as a sort of herald. Joan Harwood was expected to perform her penance in the market places of Southwell and Newark:

> and there to go about the market barelegged in her petticoat and a sheet about her middle and a kerchief cast loose upon her head... and William Garland, the apparitor, to go before her with a white rod in his hand to show the people why she doth the same.[22]

Joan Harwood at least had the concession of being allowed to wear her shoes, but in the year of her sentence, 1564, attitudes were harsh. In the 1560s and 1570s Archdeacon Louth would quite frequently order penances to be repeated four, or even six times, but along with the

---

19 Hair, *Bawdy Court*, p.101.

20 NUMD, AN/PN/352.

21 Ibid.

22 SML, Act Book 21, f.27.

David Allan, The Stool of Repentance.

use of the placard and the apparitor-herald this severity seems to have been dying out in the seventeenth century. Then, even a notorious offender, guilty of incest or unrepentant adultery, would be sentenced to three penances at the most.

The severity of public penance could be mitigated in several ways, notably by allowing the victim to perform it in his or her ordinary clothes or by authorising the ceremony to take place on Wednesdays or Fridays when fewer people were present in church. For less serious offences, private penance was becoming the norm by the early-seventeenth century, performed before or after divine service usually in the vestry in front of the minister, churchwardens and a number of 'honest men' to be determined by the court. In these circumstances the penitent was permitted to wear his own clothes and bore no special distinguishing marks. Certainly this mode of penance could not have held the same terrors as public disgrace before the congregation or in the market place, and as the seventeenth century progressed the trend was towards greater use of these private, or at least semi-public, acts. The last penance to be performed in Nottingham market place was in 1667 and thereafter all public penances took place in church until they finally ceased in the county in 1794. Even in private the 'honest men' tended to be phased out, and in the late-eighteenth century declarations were more often read in the privacy of the parson's house without even the churchwardens being present.[23] The last public penances took place in England in the nineteenth century, but by then, ironically, they had become such curiosities that people flocked to them in large numbers. In a case in Liverpool in 1840:

> an immense number entered the church in order to have a glimpse of the degrading ceremony... The whole of Church Street was... literally crammed with spectators, so much so that it was with difficulty that either a coach or cart could pass.[24]

There were many variants of the basic types of penance described above. In civil suits, generally for defamation, penitents were often expected to make their declarations outside the house of the person slandered. The aggrieved party was entitled to bring along witnesses to see justice done. In more unusual cases ecclesiastical judges could rarely resist the temptation to make a morality tale out of the penance, explaining in detail the nature of the offence and how it gave 'evil example' to others. The case of Stephen Shepherd of Whatton, 'a grievous offender', shows the lengths to which a determined official might go:

> I heretofore... was a suitor in the way of marriage to Agnes Barrow and after that did privately contract matrimony with her and then had carnal knowledge of her and beget her with child. After which I left her and did not only contract matrimony with one Emot Robinson but proceeded further and married her... and by carnal knowledge did indeed consummate the same matrimony

---

23 A.C. Wood, 'Nottinghamshire Penances (1590-1794)', *TTS* 48 (1944), 61-2.

24 Hair, *Bawdy Court*, 228.

> or rather commit most foul and detestable adultery with the said Emot... And further whereas not content with my said evil and ungodly doings, but heaping one sin and wickedness upon another, since I was so married have left the company of the said Emot... and have divers and sundry times known the said Agnes Barrow to the manifest contempt of God and of the good laws in this behalf provided, the great danger of my soul and evil example of others.[25]

These lurid stories were couched in homely language and probably did as much to stoke the fires of village gossip as they did to lead people along the paths of righteousness. Indeed, a legitimate criticism of the penance system might be that it gave perfectly innocent people encouragement to live an evil life by putting salacious ideas into their minds in the first place. The same reservation is frequently expressed about sex and violence on television today.

Penance could also be used in a practical way, particularly to extract open confessions of paternity that might be of use to churchwardens, overseers and other parish officials. In 1592 William Askewe of Nottingham stated that 'if I had to do with the said Isabel [Dobbes] it was in time of my sickness and if the child come between Palm Sunday and Low Sunday I will father the child'.[26] The Southwell court saw another practical benefit when it sentenced Elizabeth Danke, a widow guilty of adultery and evidently a person of some means, in 1564:

> That upon Saturday next she shall come unto the cross standing nigh the sign of the Saracen's Head in Southwell and then and there shall distribute unto certain of the poorest people of the same town 12d showing them why and wherefore she doth give the same unto them and desiring them to pray for her and exhorting them all that be then there present to take heed that they fall not in the like offence and to let her be a warning an exemplar unto them.[27]

---

25 NUMD, AN/PN/352.

26 Ibid.

27 SML, Act Book 21, f.28.

Similarly, in 1572, following his penance for adultery, Humphrey Stafford of Dunham 'shall deliver to the curate there in the presence of the said people 6s. 8d. to be dealt unto the poor of the parish'.[28] Financial penalties of this sort, linked to penances, were quite common in the Southwell peculiar but do not appear to have been widely used in the archdeaconry, an illustration of how penitential practice could vary within a comparatively small area.

From time to time experiments were attempted, other than payments to the poor, to make penance more effective or more terrifying, often harking back to the medieval precedents of corporal punishment. The late-1560s seem to have been a period of real severity, perhaps encouraged by an injunction of the Council of the North to tighten up on licentious living.[29] In 1567 John Caton and Joan Warren of Bleasby were sentenced to kneel in the choir of the church 'bareheaded and naked from the middle upwards with sheets about the nether parts of their bodies' while the homily against adultery was read: 'and when the homily is done William Garland shall be ready with a birch rod and shall give either of the parties three strokes upon the bare shoulders and then they shall go up and kneel where they kneeled before until the service is done'.[30] In 1570 John Bradshaw, a convicted bigamist, was made to process around the market place at Nottingham in penitential garb with a placard declaring his offence and his two wives following him 'in like manner'.[31] Most severe of all, perhaps, the Southwell court ordered a number of women to be 'carted' by local constables in 1568, one of them, Alice Bradshaw of Dunham, to be deported 'over the water into Lincolnshire again from whence she came'.[32]

The Armenians could be equally imaginative, though with less emphasis on the corporal aspect of punishment. In 1638 Robert Smith of Granby, convicted of adultery, was ordered to stand in the church

---

28 Ibid, f.17.

29 D. Marcombe, ed, *The Last Principality: politics, religion and society in the Bishopric of Durham, 1494-1660* (1987), 132-3.

30 SML, Act Book 21, f.49.

31 NUMD, AN/PN/352.

32 SML, Act Book 21, f.53.

porch in penitential garb as the bell tolled for morning service, 'asking and entreating of such people as pass by him unto the church to pray to God to forgive him'.[33] After the reading of the second lesson the minister was to lead him into the church as the psalm *Miserere Mei* was sung in English and place him in the middle alley 'far apart from all other people'. There he was to recite his confession. As a group the Laudians were very keen on penance, and its strict enforcement, and this example shows how some of them were closely in touch with the precedents of the early church, especially the symbolic exclusion of the penitent from the congregation prior to his 'readmission' through confession. All of this underlines the great flexibility of penance as a sanction. Clearly the courts had absolute discretion to award a form of penance which fitted the circumstances of the offender and which they believed was appropriate to the crime. The flexibility of the system is further illustrated by the fact that quite often the courts were prepared to countenance mitigation of some aspect of penance in response to a specific request. Sometimes this was done on the grounds of health. A man from Greasley, not too incapacitated to have sex with a servant, was permitted to keep his hose and shoes on during penance 'in regard of his age'; and Widow Cleter was given a similar dispensation 'in respect of her weakness'.[34] Joan Cowper of Dunham was permitted to do penance 'in her clothes as she goeth... with a kerchief cast loose about her head and a sheet about her middle' because 'she is with child'.[35]

Dispensations were not always made just on humanitarian grounds. Occasionally cryptic notes are to be found on schedules of penance. 'Memorandum, that the woman is alone to do this penance for the man is for special respects deferred and respited till the coming of Mr Archdeacon'.[36] Notes such as these generally imply that a commutation of penance for a cash payment is at least under consideration. Commutations dated back to the Middle Ages when a whole range of

---

33 Wood, 'Nottinghamshire Penances', 56.

34 NUMD, AN/PN/352.

35 SML, Act Book 21, f.17.

36 NUMD, AN/PN/352.

activities, and especially the giving of alms for pious uses, were considered appropriate for the mitigation of corporal penance. Commutations were unpopular, partly because of the unfair advantage they gave to the wealthy and partly because there was a suspicion that not all of the money collected was put to 'good and godly uses' as was intended. In Nottinghamshire commutations could certainly be bought during the Tudor and Stuart period and although the cost was linked to the culprit's ability to pay, overall figures tend to indicate a sharp rise in the price of the service over the period 1560-1610. In the 1570s, for example, a commutation could cost 10s. or 13s. 4d., but by the first decade of the seventeenth century this same service might set a sinner back £4 13s. 4d. or £5 6s. 8d. The sources on which this money was bestowed are illustrated by the case of Robert Walker of Mansfield who bought a commutation of his penance for incontinence in 1565: 6s. 8d. went to the poor of Mansfield, 3s. 4d. to the prisoners in Nottingham gaol, and 3s. 4d. to the poor of Blyth Hospital.[37] Other good causes included the repair of roads and bridges, the maintenance of poor scholars at Oxford and Cambridge, and even a payment of £10 7s. 8d. to defend the judge against an accusation in Star Chamber. Sadly, the records of commutation are not all we would wish them to be. Although some are recorded in the Act Books, there is always a suspicion that many more were granted than were recorded. Certainly the concern shown in Visitation Articles about the whole question of unlawful commutation implies that an underground traffic was rife.

Who, then, actually performed penances? Gentlemen, of course, were well able to buy commutations or to use their local influence to prevent their misdemeanours coming to light in the first place. Nevertheless, Thomas Sturton of Sturton paid £5 in 1592 rather than do penance in his own parish and the court even accepted payment by instalments from embarrassed gentlefolk who did not have the ready cash to hand.[38] Clergymen occasionally did penance before their parishioners, although this was more often imposed on curates than upon the more prestigious rectors and vicars. Clergymen were

---

37 NAO, DDTS 1, ff.2, 6.

38 Ibid, ff.166-7; 4, ff.44, 53, 88, 98; NUMD, AN/PN/352.

sometimes permitted to make their declarations before other clergy at a visitation or synod, thus protecting the integrity of the clerical profession, so it is perhaps surprising to see how often they were disgraced in just the same way as the laity. It must have been an occasion of special note when an incumbent did penance in front of his flock, since it was he who was responsible for guiding it in the ways of true Christian morality. Hugh Hole, vicar of Caunton, found guilty of incontinence in 1570, was invited to conclude his declaration by asking his parishioners to pray for him 'that he may become a new man towards God and amend his former naughty life and that they will take no evil example of him'.[39] The fear of 'evil example' was indeed a major preoccupation when the morality of the gentry and clergy was under the microscope; yet the paradox was that there were real difficulties in imposing penance on *élite* groups in society who were expected to represent 'authority'. For these reasons such exercises might be considered to have been less frequent than they would have been had wholly objective criteria been employed.

Apart from these two possible exceptions, penance was likely to be performed by people from all levels of society, the only *caveat* being that it became increasingly more frequent further down the social scale because of the growing inability of offenders to buy commutations. Although penitents were thus a mixed bag, there was a tendency for more women to do penance than men. This is interesting when we remember that men invariably outnumbered women in church court presentments and that, generally speaking, more men than women were sentenced. The point is that there was a greater likelihood of women actually completing their penances. In 1608 and 1609 just under half of the women sentenced to do penance in the archdeaconry performed it, while amongst men the figure was between a quarter and a third.[40] The specific example of Retford bears out the general trend. Between 1565 and 1610, out of seventy-six recorded penances in the town, 47 per cent of people sentenced were male compared with 53 per cent female, yet 40 per cent of women certified their penances as opposed

39 SML, Act Book 21, f.67.

40 Unpublished figures from the work of the ARU, CLH, University of Nottingham.

to 33 per cent of men.[41] It is not difficult to postulate reasons for this gender-based imbalance. Women were less mobile, especially at a time when they might have been pregnant or there was a baby to consider. They were probably more vulnerable than men to the pressures of village gossip, urging them to conform. Women were certainly less able to buy commutations unless they had a wealthy relative or protector in the background. For these reasons penance became, in practice, lopsided in its implementation both in social and gender terms.

How effective was penance as a sanction? William Harrison in his *Description of England* spoke of 'penance in sheets' as 'no punishment at all… but smally regarded of the offenders'. 'For what great smart is to be turned out of a hot sheet into a cold, or after a little washing in the water to be let loose again onto their former trades?'[42] As an archdeacon's official himself we must assume that Harrison knew what he was talking about, and certainly he felt that some sharper sanction was needed to bring recalcitrant offenders back into line. Philip Stubbs, a puritan, took a similar view:

> the punishment appointed for whoredom now is so light that they esteem not of it; they fear it not, they make but a jest of it. For what great thing is it to go two or three days in a white sheet before the congregation… in so much as I have heard some miscreants impudently say, that he is but a beast that for such a white liveried punishment would abstain from such gallant pastime.[43]

Though these opinions are confirmed by some contemporary records, Houlbrooke is of the view that penance could be 'a humiliating experience' and Trotha Walker of Selston would, no doubt, have agreed

---

41 Marcombe, *Small Town Life*, 138-40, 277.

42 W. Harrison, *Elizabethan England*, Scott Library (nd), 242.

43 Quoted in Hair, *Bawdy Court*, 57.

with him.[44] In 1608 her brother offered the archdeacon's official the considerable sum of £20 if she was relieved from penance for fornication, suggesting it was not a penalty to be trifled with.[45] It seems that much depended on the personalities of the people involved and the nature of the communities in which they were expected to perform penance. In an urban setting or in one of the loose-knit parishes of Sherwood Forest, penance might not have been regarded with the seriousness that it was in a 'closed' agricultural parish, dominated by a resident lord or a caucus of moralistic yeomen. These variable factors make generalisations extremely difficult.

It is only by looking at specific local examples that we are able to build up an impression of the way in which penance was performed and the effect or non-effect it had on the people involved. The archdeaconry records provide some contrasting examples. At Burton Joyce Richard Dawson and his wife did penance 'very penitently confessing their offence sorrowfully and also requesting us all there to pray for them'; and at East Markham John Coup 'performed with such repentance as was to the great good liking of the congregation and hope of their more honest life hereafter'.[46] In 1602 the vicar of Gedling went into raptures over the 'penitent manner' in which Joan Arnoll had performed her punishment 'the salt tears distilling down both her cheeks very copiously so that the people then and there assembled... were very sorry for her'.[47] This reaction was probably common enough and hardly surprising when we remember that we are dealing mostly with poor and vulnerable young women, and that seventeenth-century people were not always the heartless and moralistic bigots of popular imagination. Ministers and local gentlemen occasionally wrote to the court asking it to show clemency with regard to fees or subsequent performances of penance. In 1595, Peter Roos, a Laxton gentleman, pleaded for Margaret Lane who had recently done

---

44 R. Houlbrooke, *Church Courts and the People during the English Reformation, 1520-1570* (1979), 47.

45 NAO, DDTS 11, ff.91, 92, 95, 148, 154, 164, 181, 184. Eventually she performed her penance 'penitently', so the offer must have been refused. NUMD, AN/PN/355.

46 Ibid, AN/PN/352.

47 Ibid, AN/PN/354.

penance for fornication: 'she is utterly undone by the evil fortune that she had in the matter wherein she was troubled and in the suit about the same and being a poor servant… she hath nor can have no more to pay… than that she hath paid'.[48]

If in these instances penance matched up to what it should have been, a communal exercise of self-examination and forgiveness, on other occasions it fell far short of that mark because of disobedience, contempt or fear. Sometimes people had to be virtually forced to speak 'with much calling upon' or 'with much ado'; then they mumbled their penances with little show of contrition. In 1592 at Radford 'David Lloyd scarcely say some of the words… but kept up a scolding and unreverently behaviour'.[49] In the neighbouring parish of Basford, Edward Stephenson was appointed to do a double penance for adultery in 1618. First, he turned up on Sunday wearing his hose and shoes and without a white rod or sheet. Turned away by the vicar, he reappeared on Michaelmas Day with a sheet but still without a rod and still wearing shoes and hose.[50] Sometimes the whole occasion degenerated into farce. When the parish clerk of St Nicholas's, Nottingham, was asked to stand in and supervise a penance for the vicar in 1609, things went badly awry. The penitent, Thomas Fairforth, was being punished for slander, uttering 'certain words too foul to be rehearsed here'. He proved a tough nut to crack. 'What he liked not to speak that he left out [said the bemused clerk] and charged me I put it in myself, in a very disgraceful manner and not without offence to all that did behold it'.[51] Since clergy were reluctant to admit to their superiors if things got badly out of hand in this way, this was probably a more common occurrence than is evident from the records.

The people who performed their penances, either willingly or reluctantly, were always a minority of those actually sentenced. Some offenders tried, successfully or unsuccessfully, to obtain fraudulent certificates to say that they had complied with the order of the court. Adam Gower of Gretton was one such person trapped for dishonest certification in 1592, being forced to confess the whole sorry business

48 Ibid, AN/PN/352.

49 Ibid.

50 Wood, 'Nottinghamshire Penances', 57.

51 NUMD, AN/PN/355.

in another penance.[52] But the most intractable problem was disobedience: people who were sentenced to do penance and then simply ignored the order of the court. Out of 214 archdeaconry penances analysed between 1607 and 1609 only 34 per cent were ever certified, and the 37 per cent of certified penances in Retford between 1565 and 1610 was only slightly better.[53] Some of these outstanding penances may well have been commuted, but the fact that a high proportion of offenders were excommunicated indicates that disobedience was rife. Many people certainly treated excommunication with scant respect. The courts neither had the time, the manpower, nor the inclination to follow up these recalcitrants, even though the powers of compulsion were there to be used if officials felt so inclined.

Sometimes, therefore, an example just had to be made, and two case histories serve to illustrate the mechanics employed. In August 1605 Anthony Kerchivall of Nottingham was cited for fornication with Elizabeth Metcalfe. Following an unsuccessful attempt to purge himself, he was sentenced to do penance in September, but was excommunicated when he failed to certify. Nearly three years then elapsed, during which time the archdeacon's official complained to the High Commission about Kerchivall's contumacy and the High Commission responded by ordering him to perform his penance on 1st May 1608. He still proved reluctant to comply and went to St Peter's church three times before he eventually did as he was ordered, 'penitently', on 22nd May.[54] Henry Parr, a Nottingham tanner, was forced into submission in another way. Having stood excommunicate for several months following his failure to perform a penance for fornication, the court applied for a writ *pro captione* in January 1606. This was a device by which the ecclesiastical courts appealed to the secular arm for support, and following the issue of such a writ an offender could be arrested and imprisoned by the sheriff and only released when he agreed to conform. The application had the desired effect. In April Parr was absolved from his excommunication and on

52 Ibid, AN/PN/352.

53 Marcombe, *Small Town Life*, 277.

54 NAO, DDTS 10, ff.88, 91, 97, 103; NUMD, AN/PN/355.

3rd May he certified that he had performed his penance according to the order of the court.[55] These cases prove that when there was determination penances could be enforced, but it is significant that both Kerchivall and Parr were established citizens of Nottingham and that their contumacy was taking place under the very nose of the court. For those who simply moved on to find work or residence elsewhere, or just kept a low profile, there was little hope of ever catching up with them. Certainly Wood is incorrect in his belief that the failure to perform penance was an eighteenth-century phenomenon.[56] Although a comparatively high proportion of penances was still being certified in Nottinghamshire in the early-1590s, the situation had changed dramatically by 1610 and in these twenty years we may well be dealing with a critical turning point, not only locally, but also with regard to the whole history of penance in England.

In theory, penance was a means of controlling moral disorder within local communities by mobilising communal opinion as the principal sanction against it. In practice, it was a punishment of very variable effectiveness depending on who performed it and where it was performed. In the early-seventeenth century extreme puritans could look north to Scotland and across the seas to America and see in action there forms of public penance much more draconian than those imposed in their homeland.[57] But at a time when these same individuals were making representations to Parliament for harsh new legislation to control fornication and adultery, the church courts, it seems, were moving towards a closer *modus vivendi* with the parishes they served and penance was becoming noticeably *less* severe in tone. Ironically, when that new legislation was finally introduced during the Commonwealth and the church courts were temporarily abolished, the statutes against fornication and adultery demanded such stringent proofs that few convictions were forthcoming; certainly many fewer sexual offenders were punished in the 1650s than in the 1630s, one of the more unexpected ironies of the 'puritan revolution'. After the Restoration the liberalisation of penance continued until its eventual

---

55 NAO, DDTS 10, ff.23, 28, 37, 128, 160, 162.

56 Wood, 'Nottinghamshire Penances', 62.

57 Hair, *Bawdy Court*, 257.

collapse in the Victorian era, by which time it was an anachronism enforced, at best, half-heartedly by the courts. Once the ecclesiastical authorities had abandoned penance, moral control was left entirely in the hands of local communities — arguably a much more volatile scenario, as is proved by the death of Lucetta Farfrae and the recent burning to death of a suspected paedophile in Hull.

4

Emma Child, née Barnard, formerly Willughby (1644–1725): records of the life of a gentlewoman

Dorothy Johnston

On 16th October 1725 Emma, Lady Child, died in London. She was, as so many of her contemporaries, a woman defined by her relationship with men: father, husbands, sons, and even son-in-law. The shadowy reflection of her life and personality is all the more frustrating when one considers the rank and reputation of these men. Her father, Henry Barnard (c.1614-1680), a merchant of the Turkey Company, was knighted on 5th March 1676/7. Francis Willughby (1635-1672) of Middleton and Wollaton, her first husband, was not only a substantial midlands landowner but a well-regarded mathematician and natural historian.[1] The wealth and influence of her second husband, Josiah Child (1630-1699), Governor of the East India Company, was recognized by a baronetcy in 1678. The Willoughby baronetcy was created in 1677 for her eldest son Francis Willoughby, then only nine. His brother, Thomas Willoughby, the second baronet, became first Lord Middleton in 1712. Richard Child, the surviving son of her second marriage, who succeeded to the Child baronetcy in 1704 after the death of his step-brother, was created Viscount Castlemaine in 1718

1 During the lives of Francis and Emma Willughby, the usual form of their surname was 'Willughby'. This is followed in reference works and is therefore used here, although from his children's generation the form 'Willoughby' was used.

and Earl Tylney in 1731. Her links with men of rank was extended through her daughter, Cassandra, who in 1713 married her cousin James Brydges, subsequently ennobled as the Earl of Caernarvon (1714) and Duke of Chandos (1719).

For the most part, historical references to Emma concern the lives and actions of these men. Her relationship with them ensures at least a passing mention in their biographies. At times their ambitions and preoccupations directly concerned her. Her marriages, and the death of her first husband leaving her with infant children, made inevitable a number of arrangements involving money and property – arrangements closely affecting the estates and financial interests of the Barnard, Willoughby and Child families. This was the normal position of many young wives, but in Emma's case a complication arose from the disputed executorship of her first husband's will, giving rise to acrimonious complaints and litigation between her Willoughby children and their step-father. Even more unusual, there is a contemporary account of the difficulties by her own daughter, Cassandra Willoughby, whose history of the Willoughby family is still the most readily available and frequently quoted source for the story of Francis Willughby, his children, and their quarrel with Sir Josiah Child.[2] Her account is concerned primarily with estates and inheritance; the emotional dilemma for Emma, caught between husband and children, is only briefly mentioned.

This essay examines the story of Emma's long life in its own right, through a brief review of the biographical sources. Investigation reveals a wealth of evidence from different periods in her life. We see her not only as daughter, wife, and mother, but as employer, householder and the purchaser of goods and services. Interpretation of some of the evidence calls for further study of Willoughby estate and legal affairs in the late-seventeenth century. The sources lie largely – though not exclusively – within the Middleton Collection at the University of Nottingham. They include legal and financial papers, vouchers relating

---

2 Her writings survive in several sources. Drafts are included in the Brydges papers within the Stowe Collection in the Huntington Library and in the Stoneleigh MSS at the Shakespeare Birthplace Trust. Two volumes contain fair copies; NUMD, Mi LM 24, 25. The second volume is cited here, from A.C.Wood, ed., *The Continuation of the History of the Willoughby Family, by Cassandra Duchess of Chandos* (1958).

to estate business and routine household administration, and both private and official correspondence. Very few of the papers are entirely personal to Emma. The majority concern business, her agents, or family affairs. Some have been used before, but with other objectives. Looking at them from the perspective of Emma not only tells her story and reveals something of her personality and opinions, but also adds to our understanding of her more famous relatives. In a wider context, they reveal a subject of possible interest to the growing number of historians who study either the financial and property aspects of marriage or the personal lives of women in the late-seventeenth century.[3]

Emma Barnard was born in Shropshire in 1644, the younger daughter of a prosperous merchant, Henry Barnard. His two daughters Elizabeth and Emma were co-heiresses. Although later correspondence indicates a close and affectionate family, virtually nothing is known of her early life. Emma's mother, also Emma, was a Charlton; her uncle, Sir Job Charlton of Ludford, Shropshire, remained an important contact throughout her life. It seems likely that religious observance and devotional study were important to the Barnard household. Two small notebooks of theological commentary survive among her papers, both bearing her autograph 'Em Barnard'.[4] With them is the copy of a sermon preached by Mr George Antrobus, a prayer on behalf of her fatherless children, and a notebook dated 1675 containing a collection of prayers, apparently associated with a personal servant of Emma's.[5] A further hint of her own family's traditions of religious expression can perhaps be seen in the unusually full expression of faith and confidence in the 'Kingdom of Glory' in her father's will of 1678.[6] Whatever the extent of Emma's own religious convictions, she appears to have fitted well into the household of her first husband, Francis Willughby, at Middleton Hall, Warwickshire, with its emphasis on regular household prayers, hard work and modest living.[7]

---

3 The approach taken in S. Staves, *Married Women's Separate Property in England, 1660-1833* (1990) and E. Spring, *Law, Land and Family* (1993) can be contrasted with, for example, E. Graham, H. Hinds, E. Hobby and H. Wilcox, *Her own life. Autobiographical writings by seventeenth-century Englishwomen* (1989).

4 NUMD, Mi A 143/27/12, 13.

5 NUMD, Mi A 143/27/12, 7, 11.

6 PRO, PROB/11/363; copy at NUMD, Mi 1/13/21.

7 Wood, 110-11.

A hint of the circumstances leading to the marriage of Emma to Francis Willughby is given in the later account by Cassandra, who had access to family letters since lost. She was able to record at least six occasions when Francis's friends and relatives identified a possible bride and urged the thirty-year old to marry.[8] Perhaps from delicacy, she does not mention who introduced him to the Barnards or what advantages were argued for the match. On 9th January 1667/8 the marriage took place at the Bridgnorth home of the Barnards.

It is fortunate that both the pre-nuptial marriage articles of 8th January 1667/8 and the post-nuptial marriage settlement of 29th September 1668 survive, as the terms of the contract were subsequently to cause dissent.[9] Under the articles a marriage portion of £6,000 was provided for Emma, to be paid in instalments; £4,000 by Christmas 1668, and the final third secured in land for payment in full after ten years. Willughby was to provide a landed settlement worth £600 a year for Emma as jointure in lieu of dower, and promised a similar income of £600 a year for their male heirs. A daughter stood to inherit £6,000 on her marriage day, to be increased to £8,000 for division with any second daughter. Once the £6,000 was paid, Willughby was to sign a release of all claims on Barnard's estate. These provisions were further worked out by the terms of the September settlement, which identified the Willoughby estates, making separate landed provision for both the first and second son of the marriage. Sir Job Charlton and Sir James Brydges were named as trustees, together with the groom's uncle by marriage, Sir Thomas Wendy. Willughby's own situation changed substantially in 1671, when he inherited estates at South Muskham and South Carlton from Sir William Willoughby of Selston.[10] His will of 1672 took account of this in settling separate estates for his two sons while making arrangements to protect the jointures of his mother and wife. He gave Emma the option, should she outlive his mother, to exchange her jointure lands at Wollaton for his mother's at Middleton.[11]

From copies of letters which Cassandra subsequently found among family papers, we know that Emma's marriage settlement caused

---

8 Wood, 108-10.

9 NUMD, Mi 1/7/15; Mi 1/9/1.

10 For a summary of the bequest and ensuing litigation see Wood, 112-15.

11 NUMD, Mi 4/149/5.

family disagreement.[12] Barnard, apparently on hearing that Cassandra Willoughby, Francis's mother, thought the £6,000 too little, attempted to change arrangements so that Emma might retain an interest in his estate. This however affected the interests of his elder daughter, Elizabeth and her husband, Sir James Brydges, who strongly opposed the idea that the provision in their marriage articles be now altered. Brydges corresponded directly with Francis Willughby about this in November 1668, at the same time expressing his hope that the matter would not prejudice their friendship. In the following April Barnard informed Willughby that his dispute with Sir James was preventing him from completing arrangements about the landed security for the final £2,000 due under the articles. Barnard still wished to nominate Emma and Francis to inherit in the event of his elder daughter dying without children. The matter was unresolved a year later when, on 2nd May 1670, Willughby made it clear to Sir James that he would prefer to let the subject drop but that he – and Emma herself – felt they should clarify some misapprehensions. Emma, he wrote, 'utterly disclames y^{t} ever she went or was sent a begin for £1000'. His mother's initial unease about the settlement concerned only the question of reversion, once it was clear that the marriage portion would be secured in land rather than stock. He shared her feeling of injury, however, about the limited opportunity to negotiate the marriage articles: 'there being hardly any match y^{t} is fairly made but ye young Wooer has liberty to goe back & consult wth his Friends'. He regretted that the terms had been fixed 'without the consent of her [Emma] whom it most concerned', and added that 'I should have thought my self bound in conscience to have disputed it a little more before our Marriage but y^{t} my Mistress absolutely forbad me the making any disturbance, wch seeing w^{t} has followed, she repents she did'. Despite these reservations, Francis urged his brother-in-law to resolve the difference with Barnard. Their last recorded exchange on the subject was a full year later, in March-April 1671. Brydges thanked Willughby for mentioning his interests recently to John Wilkins, Bishop of Chester – a favour which Brydges in the circumstances found 'unexpected'. Willughby replied that he was no party to the differences between Brydges and Barnard and advised him frankly to put the matter aside. For our purposes,

12 Cassandra's copies of the correspondence are in the Huntington Library, Stowe Collection, STB Box 2, Folder 1, 1-3.

the most interesting aspect of these exchanges is the role of Emma herself – apparently fully informed and able to influence Francis in his opinions and actions. This is in contrast to the usual picture we have of women as voiceless in the arrangements of their marriage settlements.[13] His last comment on the subject was fifteen months later, in his will, which granted Emma on certain conditions the final £2,000 of her marriage portion, 'to make her some compensation for my too rashly accepting conditions to her disadvantage at marriage'.[14]

As a new bride, Emma did not join a young bachelor's establishment in need of domestic management. Middleton Hall was her husband's mother's home. Lady Willoughby, still an active and able woman, continued the running of the household. Francis himself was in his thirties, and had for the previous ten years been engaged in scientific study, involving natural history field trips in England and Wales, an extended tour on the Continent and close association with the activities of the young Royal Society.[15] These interests influenced the pattern of life at Middleton. The eminent natural historian John Ray (1627-1705) was a close friend who in the 1660s made his home at Middleton. A part of each day was spent in study or in scientific observation of the natural world; trees, plants, animals, birds and insects. In addition, Francis had extensive estates to manage, in Nottinghamshire as well as Warwickshire. For Emma, maternity came quickly. Pregnancy and the care of three children absorbed her time and energies in the brief four and a half years of her marriage.[16]

Emma subsequently described their life at Middleton to her daughter Cassandra, who wove the account into her history of the family.[17] An

---

13 See for example A. Laurence, *Women in England 1500-1760* (1884) 232. Recent research suggests that in the course of the eighteenth century this world was changing: Sandra Dunster, 'Women of the Nottinghamshire Elite c.1720-1820' (Ph.D thesis, University of Nottingham, 2003)

14 NUMD, Mi 4/149/5.

15 Biographical accounts of Willughby have already drawn attention to Emma, usually in connection with the departure of John Ray from the Willughby household. See *DNB* and D. Cram, J.L. Forgeng and D. Johnston, *Francis Willughby's Book of Games* (in press, 2003).

16 Francis, born 13th September 1668, Cassandra, born 23th April 1670, and Thomas, born 9th April 1672: Wood, xiii, 129-30.

17 Wood, 94-141 *passim*.

even more vivid picture is portrayed by the letters Emma as a young bride received from her sisters-in-law, Lettice Wendy (1628-97) and Catherine Winstanley (1630-94). Catherine was frequently resident with her mother at Middleton, where her only son was born in March 1667/8. Perhaps because they were often in the same house, only two letters from Catherine to Emma survive. In the first, in November 1668, Catherine wrote affectionately, thanking Emma for the happiness she had brought to her brother and revealing her acquaintance with Emma's parents.[18]

There survives also a series of twenty-four letters from Francis's elder sister, Lettice Wendy, who lived at Haslingfield in Cambridgeshire.[19] The year of writing was not usually given, and must be estimated from internal evidence. They began in February 1667/8, immediately after Emma's marriage. Lettice was pleased that her brother had 'pitcht on one soe suteing to him' and looked forward to meeting Emma. The subsequent correspondence demonstrated how closely knit the wider family was, keeping in touch through both letters and visits. There was regular reference to Emma's parents, often apparently at Middleton, where Lettice met them, and to the Charltons in Shropshire. The letters mention gifts or commissions to send clothes and food, and are full of news of friends and their activities. Lettice thanked Emma for her 'Rare Gosipping Stuff wch is a further testimony...of y^{r} exquisitnes in all things; Indeede all is done wth as g^{rt} Art as is Possible'. In a rare personal comment she observed: 'I p[er]ceive by my Bro[ther] you are very vertuous, too much for ye time'.[20] Later, after Francis's death, she reassured Emma: 'y^{u} wrong y^{r} selfe much in saying y^{u} are a sorry scribe; for wtho^{t} flattery, in that and in all things els y^{u} undertake, few I think comes neere y^{u}'.[21]

The growing family at Middleton was a topic of conversation. In July 1669 Emma and Francis set out for Sir Job Charlton's to take the waters, leaving their recently weaned son ('dear Jewel Frank') in the care of his grandmother at Middleton; Lettice hoped he would be

---

18 NUMD, Mi Av 143/35/1.

19 NUMD, Mi Av 143/36/1-24.

20 NUMD, Mi Av 143/36/3.

21 NUMD, Mi Av 143/36/18.

walking by the time they returned.[22] On 5th May 1670 she wrote to congratulate Emma on the birth of her daughter, news she had heard from her brother who called briefly at Haslingfield on his journey from Bedford to London. She told Emma of her surprise that Francis should have left her at such a time: 'but y^{u} now know him soe well y^{t} I hope y^{u} neither doe nor ever will have any cause to censure any of his acttions to p[ro]ceede from want of affection'.[23] In an undated letter, apparently of December 1669, she referred to a recent visit to Haslingfield, and warned Emma of being rash in travelling in her condition: 'pray be wary for good folks are every day more scarse y^{n} others'.[24] Illness and health were regular themes, especially in the case of Emma's husband Francis. The litigation following his inheritance from Sir William Willoughby necessitated frequent journeys to London and elsewhere, despite regular alarms about his health. In February 1671/2 Lettice sent word to her sister-in-law about his appearance, adding 'tis pitty his Dear Nourse & he should ever be p[ar]ted'.[25] In fact, Emma did occasionally accompany him on his journeys, leaving the children at Middleton with their grandmother. One of these visits occurred when she was pregnant, and she confided in Lettice that she feared the baby had turned in her womb, as the result of some mishap in London. Emma did not want to worry Francis with this knowledge, but Lettice later informed him, in her anxiety for Emma's health.[26]

Emma's brief marriage to Francis ended with his death on 3rd July 1672, aged only 36. It was a difficult time for the entire family. Catherine Winstanley was also widowed, and there was a need to settle her affairs as well as the inheritance from Sir William and the trust established by Francis Willughby's will. Emma felt the loss of her husband keenly. The force of the shock to her is illustrated in a note she made on 5th June 1707, thirty-five years later, when she recorded an upsetting exchange with her step-son adding: 'This cut me to ye heart, & cannot but note ye day it having been very fatale to me, it

---

22 NUMD, Mi Av 143/36/2.

23 NUMD, Mi Av 143/36/3.

24 NUMD, Mi Av 143/36/7.

25 NUMD, Mi Av 143/36/14.

26 NUMD, Mi Av 143/37/1.

was ye day my dear Mr Willoughby was seised with that violent fevour of which he died'.[27] Her sister-in-law, writing in August 1672, was concerned that she might be giving way to excessive grief: 'take heede you provoke not God to goe further on in smiteing; and though you have lost ye greatest losse yet doe not think you have lost all'. She reminds her of the much worse plight facing Catherine Winstanley, whose married life had not been the happy experience enjoyed by Emma and Lettice.[28] Her words may have seemed prophetic when, the following spring, young Cassandra fell dangerously ill.[29] In the event Cassandra recovered, and the few remaining letters were more concerned with Lettice's own dilemma, as her husband fell ill and died late in 1673. Lettice's affection for her nephews and niece is demonstrated at this difficult time in her offer of a tame Magpie which could speak a few words.[30]

It is not easy to judge the frequency of the correspondence or the significance of its falling off. The few letters between 1672 and Emma's second marriage do not suggest any lessening of affection. The health of the elderly Lady Willoughby was increasingly a concern and legal affairs were still burdensome, but the deaths of their husbands reduced the opportunity for family business letters. On at least one occasion, Lettice appears to have stayed with Emma's parents the Barnards in Shropshire.[31] In the last in this sequence, of May 1676, she mentioned 'a late proposal' which she believes that Emma was being encouraged to accept for herself and her children. Although she believed that 'being in ye floure of your age tis pitty if God pleased you should passe ye remainder of your dayes in solitude', Lettice urged Emma to consider the matter very seriously.[32] We do not know Emma's reaction to this advice. The decision may already have been made, for Emma's marriage to Josiah Child took place on 22nd August 1676. Although we know that occasional correspondence continued between Lettice and Emma, the only further surviving letter in the series dates

27 NUMD, Mi Av 143/27/5.

28 NUMD, Mi Av 143/36/16.

29 NUMD, Mi Av 143/36/15.

30 NUMD, Mi Av 143/36/17, 20, 21.

31 NUMD, Mi Av 143/36/22.

32 NUMD, Mi Av 143/36/23.

from more than twenty years later, when Lettice responded to an enquiry from Emma about news from Wollaton and discussed a possible match for her daughter Cassandra.[33]

It is quite possible that Emma was encouraged to marry again. She and her children were indeed provided for, but Francis Willughby's death had left a volume of legal affairs, and the death of Sir Thomas Wendy removed one of the trustees of both the will and Emma's marriage contract. The other executors of Willughby's will were Sir Henry Barnard, and three of Willughby's friends, John Ray, Philip Skippon and Francis Jessop. Neither Skippon nor Jessop was involved in proving the will and Barnard undertook the bulk of the business, compiling the executory accounts and working with Sir Thomas and with Ray to oversee estate affairs and the expensive chancery litigation concerning the inheritance from Sir William Willoughby of Selston.[34] An added anxiety for Emma's parents in the first year of her widowhood came from her low spirits. On 15th January 1672/3, Barnard referred to her 'melancholy humour', which has meant that 'you hath little mind of doeing anything but what of necessity compells you'; he reminded her of the young children left in her care, and urged her to 'cheer up' her spirits.[35] Barnard needed Emma's practical assistance at Middleton; his letters involved her in discussions about the legal affairs he and Ray were conducting in London and gave instructions about business matters to be undertaken in Warwickshire.[36]

As was common for widows with such responsibilities, Emma made a will, on 1st October 1674.[37] She made charitable provision for the poor of Wollaton and Middleton and neighbouring parishes. Her gold was divided equally between her children. After settlement of her debts, any remaining money was left to her second son Thomas, together with any profit which might accrue from the posthumous publication of Francis Willughby's study of birds, a work which was to appear two

33 Wood, 119-23, 131; NUMD, Mi Av 143/36/24.

34 NUMD, Mi A 102 . The Middleton Collection contains extensive evidence of litigation concerning Francis Willughby's will and the Willoughby of Selston inheritance; see in particular NUMD, Mi A 101-20, Mi C 34, Mi E 3/1-2, and Mi L 30, 53-56.

35 NUMD, Mi Av 143/39/1.

36 NUMD, Mi Av 143/39/1-9.

37 NUMD, Mi 1/13/24/2.

years later, supported by her funding of the illustrative plates.[38] Jewels and furniture of value were mentioned individually. The family of her sister Elizabeth Brydges stood to inherit should her own family die before her. Her mother, together with Catherine Winstanley, witnessed the will. It seems that her parents spent lengthy periods at Middleton, where a late-1676 inventory specified quarters both for Lady Barnard and for John Ray.[39]

Sir Henry was still actively engaged on the Willoughby trust when, now resident with the Childs at Wanstead in Essex, he made his will on 11th April 1678. He left £2,000 for Thomas Willoughby on his majority, provided he did not inherit the Willoughby estates, in which case the sum should instead go to his grand-daughter Cassandra. An interesting condition, token perhaps of anticipated disputes, required that his heirs should 'in no sort be troubled or molested by any vexational or misguided pretences of my Grandchildren' regarding his actions as trustee.[40] It was in fact after Barnard's death on 25th April 1680 that the difficulties always present in the Willughby trust became insurmountable. The story, which deserves a full study, concerns both legal aspects of the trust and the domestic tension caused by a growing rift between Willughby's children and their step-father. The legal side came to focus on the role of John Ray, variously described as 'a meere Schollar' and one 'not very inclinable to business of that nature',[41] and on the choice of further trustees to fill the place of Wendy and Barnard. It is difficult to say what Emma thought of the affair, although letters received by her – such as those from John Ray – indicate that she fully supported her husband's wish to recruit new trustees outside the terms of the will.[42] Indeed, Sir Josiah explains on 16th July 1680 that since her father's death Emma had 'concern'd herselfe more than formerly...in her childrens affaires and had desired my assistance'.[43]

---

38 *Francisci Willughbeii ...Ornithologiæ libri tres* (1676). John Ray, the editor, acknowledged her generosity in his foreword.

39 NUMD, Mi R 322/18; undated, but must be post-August 1676, as it includes reference to 'Lady Child's Chamber'.

40 NUMD, Mi 1/13/21; probate granted 15th June 1680: PRO, PROB/11/363.

41 NUMD, Mi L 53/62; Mi L 30/15.

42 NUMD, Mi E 4/29-32.

43 NUMD, Mi L 30/15.

Correspondence of this time from Edward Dovey at Wollaton to Emma, Lady Child, and from John Wilkinson at South Muskham, show us something of Emma's personal involvement in business affairs. Dovey wrote to her in May 1680, offering condolences on her father's death and promising to serve her. He was also in correspondence with James Brydges, now Lord Chandos, who as her brother-in-law was a trustee for her jointure settlement. The letters give many details about Wollaton and Middleton, both economic and social. The state of the coal pits, the decay of buildings and roofs at Wollaton, the extent of unemployment, and estate matters including poor harvests, the deer, the fishponds and the orchards, were all touched upon. Response was expected, and a gap in her replies caused complaint. The correspondence implies that Emma was familiar with Dovey's business, and with his family: he thanked her for treatment for his 'dropsical distemper'; he asked her to break the news to his daughter, who is in her service, of the death of her mother; he commented on the difficulty of removing moths from the furnishings at Wollaton. Wilkinson from Muskham likewise offered local news, referring to rentals for young Thomas Willoughby's estate, and mentioning bridges, militia demands, and the school.[44]

Although Sir Josiah succeeded in winning control of the trust, he was to face more serious opposition and criticism from his step-children. The legal case brought against Child for his actions in the trust has yet to receive detailed historical treatment, but a summary of the episode is familiar through Cassandra's later account.[45] The young Francis felt keenly that he was not receiving an adequate education at Wanstead. Desperate to leave Child's household, he first sought support from his uncle, the Duke of Chandos, who urged by him to stay with his mother. Francis refused, and although he was only twelve escaped from Wanstead and took refuge with Lettice Wendy. He never returned, and, in their turn, his younger brother Thomas and their sister Cassandra also left, the latter at the age of seventeen, to join her eldest brother at Wollaton. In the subsequent legal case Child was accused of taking £60,000 from the estate. This was never proven. Child defended himself strongly against the charges of waste and

44 NUMD, Mi E 4/1-65 *passim* and Mi L 53/37.

45 Wood, 118-20, 132-6.

misappropriation of funds, referring to the debts which burdened Francis Willughby's estates and justifying as legitimate, for instance, his right to take money for the children's maintenance and education. He was clearly an unyielding opponent; his refusal to allow Francis to take goods from Middleton in order to set up home in Wollaton was typical of a man who allowed no compromise. The crisis in the family ultimately centred on Emma. Child was acting in her name and the children knew that she would not oppose her husband to support them. Concern about the distress caused to her by the legal action finally prompted Thomas to drop his suit. A poignant record of the hurt caused to Emma by her sons' actions survives in a paper bearing the precise dates on which Frank and Tom and her daughter Cass 'went away'.[46] Cassandra later looked back with pity on the position of Emma, 'who was indeed a very tender mother'.[47]

Emma meantime had the cares of a second family to attend to. Sir Josiah had been married twice before, and had four living children. Emma gave him two more sons, Barnard (b.1677) and Richard (b.1680). The evidence of her personal life at Wanstead during the 1680s and 1690s is slim; little apparently survives beyond a few vouchers recording personal expenditure.[48] A study of the career of Sir Josiah Child would certainly add to the picture of their life style at Wanstead. From Cassandra Willoughby we know that in 1690 Emma enjoyed a visit to her children at Wollaton.[49] In her notes and journals Cassandra implies frequent visits to Wanstead, where she seems to have spent winters with her mother during the early 1690s. Cassandra's life is unusually well recorded for a woman of her period, and further work on her archival remains would amplify the account of her mother's life.[50] She mentioned regular visits between Wanstead and Canons, the home of Emma's sister, Lady Chandos. She recorded the death of her grandmother Emma Barnard in 1696, and the smallpox attack

46 NUMD, Mi Av 143/27/2, 2nd June 1681; 2nd May 1685 and 20th July 1687.

47 Wood, 121.

48 E.g. NUMD, Mi Av 143/3, 5.

49 Wood, 138.

50 J. Johnson, *Excellent Cassandra. The life and times of the Duchess of Chandos* (1981) introduces Cassandra, the Chandos circle, and the sources for such a study.

which in 1698 killed her step-brother Barnard and made both Richard and Cassandra herself dangerously ill.[51]

Sir Josiah's death on 22 June 1699 left Emma once more a widow, but this time with adult children to support her. The terms and conditions of his will (made before his son Barnard died, although the event was noted in a codicil) reveal much about the man and his family. He asked for a quiet night-time funeral, costing no more than £50. The sixty recipients of his charitable bequest of £300 were to be chosen for their merit, without reference to their religious persuasion. He left Barnard and Richard the use of Wanstead until his eldest son and heir Josiah, on whom the bulk of the estate was settled, paid an agreed sum of £20,000. His unforgiving nature is shown in remarks about both his son Josiah and his daughter Mary. He left the latter only £5 'because she hath married not only without my consent but expressly against my command and contrary to her own repeated promisses and lett others learne by her example'. Sir Josiah's own sense of family ensured the naming of all his children as beneficiaries should Barnard and Richard both die, although he notes that 'Josiah and my said daughter Mary have both of them behaved themselves undutifully to me and broake many promises made to me in a high and ungrateful contempt of me their father who have bin to kinde to them'.

Emma, 'my deare and loving wife', was made guardian of his sons Barnard and Richard: 'I have greate experience of her care and kindness of them'. Should she die or marry again, he appoints Sir Thomas Willoughby of Wollaton as one of their guardians, adding pointedly: 'in confidence that the said Sir Thomas Willoughby will be ayding and assisting to my said two younger sons as I have bin to him his brother and sister'. A further direct reference to his involvement in the Willoughby trust lay in his allowance of a fixed sum each year for the maintenance of the children. Perhaps even more extraordinary is his reference to Emma's jointure estate at Middleton. Her marriage articles had specified a jointure from Child of £6,000.[52] He now raised this to £10,000, referring to his profitable management of her money

51 E. Hagglund, '"An Account of the Journeys I have taken ..": The travel journal of Cassandra Willoughby', (M.A. thesis, University of Birmingham, 1996), 9, 36, 51-2.

52 Draft copy survives; NUMD, Mi L 53/68.

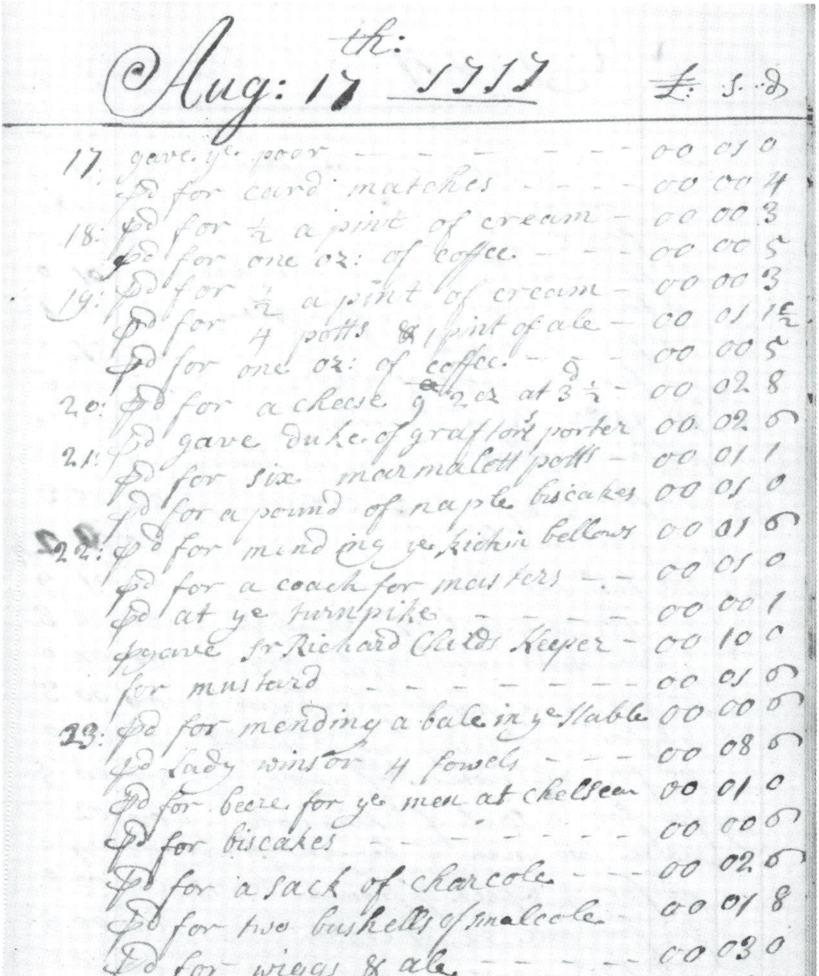

Aug: 17th: 1717

		£	s	d
17.	gave ye poor	00	01	0
	pd for card matches	00	00	4
18:	pd for ½ a pint of cream	00	00	3
	pd for one oz: of coffee	00	00	5
19:	pd for ½ a pint of cream	00	00	3
	pd for 4 potts & 1 pint of ale	00	01	1½
	pd for one oz: of coffee	00	00	5
20:	pd for a cheese 9 [illegible] 2 oz at 3½	00	02	8
	pd gave duke of graftons porter	00	02	6
21:	pd for six marmalett potts	00	01	1
	pd for a pound of naple biscakes	00	01	0
22:	pd for mending ye kichin bellows	00	01	6
	pd for a coach for masters	00	01	0
	pd at ye turnpike	00	00	1
	gave Sr Richard Childs keeper	00	10	0
	for mustard	00	01	6
23:	pd for mending a bale in ye stable	00	00	6
	pd Lady winsor 4 fowels	00	08	6
	pd for beere for ye men at chelsea	00	01	0
	pd for biscakes	00	00	6
	pd for a sack of charcole	00	02	6
	pd for two bushells of smalcole	00	01	8
	pd for wiggs & ale	00	03	0

Accounts of Lady Child, 1717 (NUMD, M: A 128).

and Willoughby jointure estate. He requested that she honour his wish to pass this sum to her Child sons before or at her death, reminding her that: 'that honourable gentleman Mr Willoughby now with God left estate enough and left sufficient for his own children whose estate was faithfully administered and advanced greatly whilst I had the charge of it and beyond his hopes and expectations in his life time'.[53]

As executor of Emma's will in 1725, her son Thomas Willoughby retained accounts recording her personal expenditure as well as correspondence concerning her jointure estate at Middleton.[54] Evidence concerning her final years of widowhood thus survives, providing ample proof that she enjoyed her jointure settlements.[55] This shows her continued residence at Wanstead for some years, paying her son Richard the expenses of her household. In 1711 Emma purchased the lease of a property in Soho Square, to be her home for the remainder of her life. Extensive building work was set in hand, but was not well supervised; litigation about its quality and about payment continued until 1719, providing evidence about the refurbishment of the property.[56] Correspondence from her agent Thomas Holt at Middleton supplemented other financial accounts, with details of income from the sale of stock at Smithfield a regular item. Fresh produce was regularly sent from Middleton to London. Her principal source of income was the interest on East India stock. Records of her expenditure are for some years extremely detailed, providing the names and wages of servants, the provisions for the kitchen, household and clothing items and significant sums spent on horses, coaches, and livery. Family members were mentioned regularly; from 1716 to 1720, for example, she was apparently paying for dancing lessons for her Willoughby grandsons.[57]

The most obvious indication in the vouchers of Emma's increasing age lies in the detail of the apothecary bills. In the year of her death, for instance, she purchased pectoral draughts, cordial powders, melilot

---

53 NUMD, Mi 1/13/38; will was proved 6 July 1699, PRO, PROB/11/451.

54 See in particular NUMD, Mi Av 143; Mi E 4; Mi A 128.

55 See Staves, *Married Women's Separate Property*, 96, for a cautionary note about the effectiveness of jointure settlements.

56 NUMD, Mi Av 143/2, 13,16.

57 NUMD, Mi Av 143/17/26-30.

plasters and vesicatories for shoulders, arms and legs, while at the same time she continued to have dressmaker and upholstery expenses.[58] In her final illness she made notes to supplement the content of her will. One reads: 'The picture of Wollaton is Lady Dutcheses own Pickture which I desire she may have', signed 'Em: Child'.[59] The 'Dutchess' was her own daughter, Cassandra, married in 1713 at the age of 43 to her cousin James Brydges, now Duke of Chandos. He suffered heavily at the collapse of the South Sea Company in 1720, and it is possible that Emma gave him financial assistance.[60] In her final will, made on 8th July 1725, she transferred to Cassandra her interest in a £2,000 bond due to her by Chandos. The will, a brief document, makes no mention of transferring her £10,000 jointure to her son Richard – perhaps this had already happened. His only formal legacy was release from a bond for £2,000, of which she wished that part should go to her grand-daughter. Other bequests were for small amounts. Mary, the disobedient daughter of Josiah Child, was remembered, and there were legacies for her servants. The poor of the parishes of Wanstead in Essex, St Anne's in London, Middleton in Warwickshire and Wollaton in Nottinghamshire in each case received £10. Her son Thomas Willoughby, now Lord Middleton, was executor and received the residue of her estate.[61]

Emma Child's long life followed an essentially familiar course for women of her period. It is perhaps in its account of the typical that her story will have widest appeal. She may not have left a journal in the style of Abigail Gawthern,[62] but her personal voice is certainly

58 NUMD, Mi Av 143/18/1-16.

59 NUMD, Mi Av 143/18/6.

60 P.G.M. Dickson and J.V. Beckett, 'The Finances of the Dukes of Chandos: Aristocratic Inheritance, Marriage, and Debt in Eighteenth-Century England', *Huntington Library Quarterly*, 53 (2001, published 2003), 309-55.

61 PRO, PROB/11/606.

62 A. Henstock, ed., *The Diary of Abigail Gawthern of Nottingham, 1751-1810*, TSRS, XXXIII (1980).

present in the record. She was a dutiful daughter, a loyal wife and loving mother. Although she appears as passive in the Willoughby/ Child disputes, there are indications that she could speak her mind. The value of her story lies, however, not only in the pattern of a woman's life or even in elucidating the personalities involved, but in the wider historiography of women and marriage in the late-seventeenth century. She was an example, of which there were many, of a woman whose marriages brought different worlds together – the City context of the merchants, the country estates of the gentry and aristocracy, and the potentially classless world of the new scientists in the Royal Society.

5

'The pleasant and glorious condition of this noble forest' - mapping Sherwood Forest before 1800

Steph Mastoris

Writing on 24th May 1675, Robert Thoroton used his position as the author of the first published history of Nottinghamshire to highlight the important part played by Sherwood Forest in the county's past. However, the concluding comments of his section on Sherwood was to bewail the declined state of forest. After sketching the history of Sherwood as a royal forest from the twelfth century he commented, 'But I shall not be further particular in exhibiting any further collections on this subject, because the pleasant and glorious condition of this noble forest is now wonderfully declined'.[1] Although Thoroton was largely correct in considering the high days of the forest were over, such pessimism was to some extent ill-founded. Sherwood Forest survived well into the eighteenth century as an important landscape feature, and until the early nineteenth century as a legal entity.[2] This imprecision was due in part to the different ways in which the Forest was viewed by inhabitants, landowners, administrators and the

---

1 Thoroton, 507.

2 J.C. Cox, *The royal forests of England* (1905), 204-222; J.C. Cox, 'The forest of Sherwood', in E.L. Guilford, ed., *Memorials of old Nottinghamshire* (1912), 106-123; R.M. Butler, 'Sherwood Forest', *TTS*, 50 (1946), 36-51.

monarchy. For each interest, Sherwood, like other royal forests, could be seen not only as a legal entity but also as a working landscape for hunting, agriculture, displays of wealth and power, and a locale for raising Crown revenues. In this way the main imperative for the forest was changing frequently and, combined with its sheer size (around 100,000 acres), resulted in a steady stream for maps of all or part of the forest from the fourteenth century (when map-making was in its infancy), to the end of the eighteenth century when state-sponsored cartography by the Ordnance Survey started to reduce the need for specially-commissioned maps and plans of the area.[3] In all, around 115 manuscript maps dating from before 1800 have survived that depict a portion or all of Sherwood Forest. The key aim of this essay is to contextualise these maps by relating them to their original purpose and demonstrate how their utility defined their characteristics. No map is created without a specific purpose, and its purpose determines the form and content of the cartography. The sheer variety of interests stimulated by the workings of Sherwood as a royal forest resulted in the creation of maps of greatly differing style.[4]

Since its creation in the eleventh century, Sherwood Forest had been recognised as one of the more significant of the seventy or so royal forests that existed in England by the end of the middle ages. The forest occupied approximately 100,000 acres of central Nottinghamshire (about 20 per cent of the county's area) in an area shaped like a lop-sided hourglass. Many of its boundaries were formed by rivers: the Trent to the south, the Meden to the north, the Leen to the south-west and the Doverbeck to the south-east. The extent of the forest was closely related to the acid, thirsty soils which overlay a belt of sandstone running north to south down the centre and west of the county. The poverty of this land and its designation as royal forest resulted in a landscape with large tracts of scrubland (termed 'waste') interspersed with woodland and a number of parks in addition to almost fifty small nucleated villages, the town of Mansfield and the borough of Nottingham. In the early seventeenth century the Crown was still

---

3 C. Delano-Smith & R. Kain, *English Maps* (1999), 118-135; Sarah Bendall, *Dictionary of land surveyors and local map-makers, 1530-1850*, vol. 1 (1997), 4-66; W.A. Seymour, ed., *A history of the Ordnance Survey* (1981).

4 G.J. Turner, *Select pleas of the Forest,* Selden Society, xiii (1899); Cox (1905).

the largest landowner in the forest, with holdings concentrated in the woodlands of Birklands and Bilhaugh, north of Edwinstowe, and the extensive parks of Bestwood, Clipstone and Nottingham. However, during the later seventeenth and eighteenth centuries the Crown's interests in Sherwood Forest declined as several extensive estates were extended or created by members of the nobility, such as Welbeck and Clumber (the Dukes of Newcastle) and Thoresby (the Earls of Kingston). The establishment of these 'Dukery' estates not only transferred land out of royal hands, it extinguished forestal rights over them. The parliamentary enclosure of many forest parishes in the latter part of this period completed the process, and by the early nineteenth century the Crown exerted hardly any traditional rights over Sherwood Forest. As a legal entity it therefore ceased to exist.[5]

There are extant around 470 manuscript maps of places in Nottinghamshire, dating between the fifteenth century and 1800. Just around a quarter of these delineate either all or part of Sherwood Forest and they afford a wide range of cartographic styles and purposes. Virtually all are listed in Harold Nichols' inventory of Nottinghamshire local maps.[6] Many of these maps were a result either directly or indirectly of the special legal and agrarian conditions present within the forest's bounds. A small number were commissioned directly by the Crown or Commonwealth, while the remainder were commissioned either by local forest officials or private landowners. In general, the maps were drawn for one of three reasons: to show the location of the forest and define its boundaries, as an aid to hunting within the forest, or as a means of demonstrating land ownership, occupation and use (or misuse). The last of these accounts for the vast majority of the surviving maps.

---

5 H. Boulton, ed., *The Sherwood Forest Book,* TSRS, XXIII (1965); S Mastoris and S Groves, eds., *Sherwood Forest in 1609, a Crown survey by Richard Bankes*, TSRS, XL (1997), fig.1; J.D. Chambers, *Nottinghamshire in the eighteenth century* (London, 1932), 145; Butler, 36-51; S. Seymour, 'The Dukeries Estates: improving land and landscape in the later eighteenth century', *TTS*, 97 (1993), 117-128; Crown Commissioners, 'The fourteenth report of the Commissioners appointed to enquire into the state and condition of the woods, forests and land revenues of the Crown..., 28th March 1793', *Lords' Papers* (1793).

6 H. Nichols, *Local maps of Nottinghamshire to 1800: an inventory* (1987).

The need to define the overall extent of a royal forest was fundamental to its effective administration, and from at least the early thirteenth until the seventeenth century written perambulations of their outer boundaries were produced regularly as part of the process of administering forest law.[7] It is only towards the end of this period that maps were created to record the forest boundary. In overall style, these boundary maps are drawn at a small scale and lack much topographical detail. The cartography concentrates on delineating the boundary and locating the traditional merepoints (waymarkers) that were used by those undertaking regular perambulations of the forest.

For Sherwood two maps dating from the late sixteenth- or early seventeenth- century depict the course of the forest perambulation as established in the 1230s. The more detailed and significant of these perambulation maps came to light only a few years ago and has only recently been acquired by the British Library.[8] It shows the full extent of the forest at a very approximate scale of about one inch to one and a third miles (1:85722). It is not dated and there is no indication of its cartographer, although it is attractively drawn in ink and colour washes on paper. Both the style of lettering and the watermarks in the paper suggest that the map was created during the first quarter of the seventeenth century. The second map is held in the archives of the Dukes of Rutland at Belvoir Castle and is more mundane and less formally laid out than the British Library map.[9] Also drawn on paper in ink at about the same scale it too is undated, although inscriptions written at the top left hand side of the map suggest that it was produced at about the beginning of the seventeenth century.

On both maps the boundary of the forest is clearly delineated and its course plotted by the nominal identification of most villages and major watercourses within and immediately outside Sherwood. A wide variety of topographical features are located in words and symbols

---

7 D. Crook, 'The struggle over forest boundaries in Nottinghamshire, 1218-1227', *TTS*, 83 (1979), 35-45; David Crook, 'The archbishopric of York and the boundaries of the forest in Nottinghamshire in the twelfth century', in G. Garnett & J. Hudson, eds., *Law and government in medieval England and Normandy* (1994), 324-340.

8 BL, Additional MSS, 74,219.

9 Photograph in BL (maps), 4640(1), and illustrated in D. Price, 'Medieval land surveying and topographical maps', *Geographical Journal*, 121 (1955), plate 3.

along the course of the boundary line. Many of these natural and man-made features are the standard locations referred to time and again in the written perambulations recorded by forest officials from the thirteenth to the seventeenth centuries. On both maps, there are few additional topographical details within the forest, other than several landscape features and concentrations of woodland. However, the British Library map shows a number of major roads traversing the forest, crudely drawn possibly by a second, later hand. Not only would this unusual detail have helped define the forest's boundary, but it may have assisted in the collection of *chimminage* (payment due for passage through a forest).[10]

The need to draw up such maps was probably created by a decline in the practice of perambulating the forest's bounds in the late sixteenth and early seventeenth centuries, and the consequent shortage of communal memory to identify the boundary's course conclusively. Furthermore, the last part of this period witnessed a revival of activity by the forest administration, and this too would have fostered a need for maps of the boundary. Certainly, the fact that at least two such maps were produced points to some sort of need by forest administrators.[11] The publication of the earliest printed county atlases around this time seems to have greatly assisted in this mapping exercise, for the overall layout and design of the two perambulation maps is certainly influenced heavily by the way in which Christopher Saxton and John Speed depicted Sherwood Forest in their maps of Nottinghamshire of 1576 and 1610. Although the legal boundary of the forest is not shown in the county maps, its rough extent is shown through a cluster of standard tree symbols and the major forest parks are shown and captioned.[12]

Topographical features along the course of the forest's boundary which are additional to those in the standard perambulation text were

---

10 Both maps are compared in S. Mastoris, 'A newly-discovered perambulation map of Sherwood Forest in the early seventeenth century', *TTS*, 102 (1998).

11 P.R. Seddon, 'The application of forest law in Sherwood Forest, *c.*1630-1680', *TTS*, 82 (1978), 37-44.

12 W. Ravenhill, ed., *Christopher Saxton's 16th century maps* (1992). J. Speed, *The theatre of the empire of Great Britain* (1611, *recte* 1612); a modern reproduction published as N. Nicholson & A. Hawkyard, eds., *The counties of Britain, a Tudor atlas by John Speed* (1988).

added by the two anonymous map-makers. Ironically this exercise influenced the nature of the last written perambulation of Sherwood which was undertaken in 1662. This included almost every feature on the perambulation route shown on both the British Library and the Belvoir maps, and thereby greatly increased the number of boundary reference points compared to any of its predecessors. Comparison of boundary points given in the written perambulations and the British Library map shows such a close correlation that it seems very probable that this map (or a copy) was used by the forest officers in 1662.[13]

The prime purpose of royal forests was to provide an area in which beasts of the chase (*venison*) could be fostered and hunted by the monarch and his favoured retainers.[14] For this a detailed knowledge of the terrain of the forest's 100,000 acres would be required by huntsmen and other forest officials and topographical maps would be of great assistance in this work. It is therefore surprising that very few maps designed for this purpose are extant, although this could be due to the fact that they may have been more frequently used in the field than other types of map, and that their subject matter meant that they would not have been retained by those office-based officials concerned with the niceties of the legal administration of forests. The general approach used to create maps for hunting was to provide a view of the terrain where the deer can be located, the chase pursued and a kill made. An understanding of the whereabouts of coverts, valleys, and open spaces is far more important than defining the location of settlements or property boundaries.

The only extant map for Sherwood Forest that seems to be specifically designed for use as an aid to hunting is also the earliest of the whole *corpus* of pre-1800 Nottinghamshire maps.[15] Again it forms part of the archives of the Dukes of Rutland at Belvoir Castle and was created in the late fourteenth or early fifteenth century, possibly about 1437 when Ralph Cromwell was appointed Warden of the Forest and Constable of Nottingham Castle. Drawn in red and brown ink on a single skin of parchment, it gives a highly stylised representation of

---

13 A. Stapleton, *The last perambulation of Sherwood Forest* [1662] (1893).

14 J. Birrell, 'Deer and deer farming in medieval England', *Agricultural History Review*, 40 (1992).

15 Photograph in BL (maps) 4640(2).

Sherwood Forest's topography, based upon a square sub-divided into eight triangles by diagonal, vertical and horizontal parallel lines. As a result, the map provides a plan of the forest that is quite skewed with each quarter representing areas at different scales.[16]

The few topographical features shown on the map include a number of water courses as red lines, and Nottingham town and Lenton Priory as stylised pictorial sketches. The rest of the map is used to show the relative positions of over three hundred named locations. These help identify a fair proportion of villages within the forest along with many of the perambulation reference points along the forest boundary. Two of the royal parks (Bestwood and Clipstone) are clearly identified, as are most of the *hayes* (game preserves) within the forest. The majority of place names refer to landscape features in the open country, especially river-cut valleys and dales, woods and meadows. In this way the map would have provided a huntsman with a useful list of the sequence of the most likely places to find, chase, corner and kill deer.

The Crown's right to hunt extended over all freehold and tenanted land within a royal forest. Despite this blanket liberty, forest administrators were very keen to understand who held what land in order to prosecute any agricultural activity that contravened the forest laws protecting the *vert* (trees and ground cover). During the medieval period, when the use of forests for hunting was at its height, the main motivation for such control was based on a genuine desire not to reduce or restrict the extent of the chase. The forest courts were kept busy with presentments of those landowners found to be restricting the vert through assarts or purprestures.[17]

By the early seventeenth century royal hunting in the forests was declining and the local forest administration was becoming anachronistic. Even so, central government officials redoubled their efforts to enforce forest laws for fiscal reasons, in an attempt to increase revenue from Crown estates. Such action coincided with a more general desire on the part of landowners to improve their property through

---

16 M.W. Barley, 'Sherwood Forest', in R.A. Skelton & P.D.A. Harvey, eds., *Local maps and plans from medieval England* (1986). I am grateful to Alan MacCormick for his observations on the topography shown in this map.

17 David Crook, 'The development of private hunting rights in Nottinghamshire, *c.*1100-1258', *TTS*, 105 (2001), 101-109.

enclosure, drainage, woodland management, and even proto-industrial activity. This, in turn, helped to foster the new profession of estate surveyor.[18] As a result a considerable body of maps was produced to support a variety of written surveys, which sought either to assist in the improvement of land or to provide evidence in the prosecution of those who contravened forests laws by such action.

For Sherwood, maps defining land ownership and land use constitute a large majority of those extant. The general approach to designing maps for these purposes was to survey property boundaries at a sufficiently large scale to be able to delineate individual fields and curtilages. As a result the maps deal with much smaller areas of land, compared with the maps drawn up to define overall forest boundaries or assist the huntsman. In all, there are over 100 maps surviving from before 1800 which deal with land ownership or land use in Sherwood Forest.[19] For analysis they are best grouped according to four main motives that caused them to be created, namely official surveys, settlement of disputes, private estate management and enclosure of commonable land.

Seven maps survive that were directly produced by Crown officials. By far the most important of these arose from the survey by Richard Bankes between 1608 and 1609.[20] The map depicts the southern third of the forest extending from the river Trent in the south to the top of Bestwood Park, Arnold and Calverton parishes in the north. A written survey was also drawn up by Bankes providing sometimes fuller descriptions of the owners, occupiers, agricultural use, name and acreage of each parcel of land. As this written survey covers the whole of Sherwood Forest, it seems likely that Bankes originally produced maps of the area not shown on his extant map. Annotations on the written survey, together with references to this work in contemporary administrative records, reveal that Bankes' map was commissioned by Crown officials as preparation for a major campaign to detect and

18 J. Thirsk, 'The Crown as projector on its own estates, from Elizabeth I to Charles I', in R. Hoyle, ed., *The estates of the English Crown, 1558-1640* (Cambridge, 1992), 297-352.

19 Nichols.

20 PRO, MR 1142; for a transcription of this map together with an edition of the accompanying survey see Mastoris and Groves.

prosecute those landholders who had *assarted* land in Sherwood Forest. Within a few months of the completion of the map and written survey, a number of landowners were being summoned before royal commissions for defective titles to answer cases of asserting forest land without adequate permission to do so. The resulting litigation resulted in a considerable amount of new revenue for the Crown, as well as directly and indirectly motivating private landowners to commission map surveys of their estates.

Twenty or so years later the Crown was once more attempting to raise revenue by reviving forest law, and in Sherwood a number of special commissions of enquiry were set up to investigate local cases of assarting.[21] Three fragments of the maps produced by one of these special commissions in about 1630 illuminate the way in which cartography was used in the service of the maintenance of forest law. Of the three maps, one is a general sketch plan of Perlethorpe in the north-eastern corner of the forest.[22] The second, though much mutilated, shows Edwinstowe in a much finer style which is somewhat akin to that of Richard Bankes.[23] The third shows Thoresby lordship in a similar style to the second and again is mutilated.[24]

The first of these maps seems more concerned with delineating which parts of the parish are within or outside the forest boundary, while the latter two maps delineate areas of freehold land and give acreages and some indication of land use, especially where *brecks* (temporary enclosures of forest waste for arable cultivation) had been established.[25] Two out of the three maps are endorsed to show that they were shown to a number of local landowners, and these people were then asked to sign a deposition of some sort, witnessed by two county legal officers (one of which was Gilbert Boun, sergeant at law and foedary for Nottinghamshire).[26] Such use of local knowledge was

21 Thirsk.

22 PRO, MPB 63(1).

23 PRO, MPB 63(2).

24 PRO, MPB 63(3).

25 D.V. Fowkes, 'The Breck system of Sherwood Forest', *TTS*, 81 (1977), 55-61.

26 Adrian Henstock, 'Robert Thoroton: Nottinghamshire antiquary, 1623-1678' *TTS*, 81 (1977), 15.

standard practice when drawing up written estate surveys long before this time, but it is interesting to find cartographic information being used in this way.

At the conclusion of the English civil war the estates of the Crown passed into the hands of Parliament to be sold off. Prior to these sales detailed written surveys were commissioned by Parliament, and these naturally included the Crown lands within royal forests such as Sherwood.[27] Only one map seems to have been produced of royal land-holdings in Sherwood and this accompanied a written survey of Bestwood Park, the largest of the three royal parks within the Forest, and then consisting of over 3,600 acres.[28] The map is rather sketchily drawn in ink on paper. The anonymous surveyor does not seem to have consulted the portion of Richard Bankes' map dealing with this area and the plan is far more crudely drawn. However it does show a number of lodges, pools and park 'compartments' not recorded by Bankes. As a major concentration of Crown land in the county, the Commonwealth commissioners no doubt saw the park as a discrete estate which could be easily sold. However, it is unclear why maps were not created for other sizeable portions of royal property of a more complex shape and nature (such as the woods of Birklands and Bilhaugh north of Edwinstowe). Indeed, there are very few maps surviving for the Parliamentary surveys in general and it is not clear whether many were originally created.

After the civil war another official survey of part of the forest produced a map whose purpose is not clear.[29] The map shows the northernmost portion of the royal wood of Bilhaugh and the two townships of Thoresby and Perlethorpe further to the north. The map is unsigned and attractively drawn in ink and bright colourwashes on vellum. It seems to date from the later seventeenth century and was probably produced by either the Surveyor General of Woods, Forests, Parks and Chases or the Auditors of the Land Revenue to define the extent of Crown property before its sale to William Pierrepont, fourth

---

27 S. Madge, *The domesday of crown lands* (1938, reprinted 1968).

28 PRO, E 317/Notts/10A, illustrated in Madge, 336, and re-drawn and discussed in S. Gillott, 'Bestwood: a Sherwood Forest park in the seventeenth century', *TTS*, 89 (1985), 57-75.

29 PRO, MPE 1467.

Earl of Kingston in 1683. Pierrepont paid Charles II £7,100 for 1,370 acres of land here to create a formal park around his house at Thoresby. He then had his home re-modelled between 1685 and 1687 to create a grand, Italianate mansion. In this way one of the most important of the Dukery estates was created out of a portion of Sherwood Forest.[30]

The last official map of a part of the forest was created in 1791 at the behest of the Royal Commission to enquire into the state of woods, forests and land revenues of the Crown, established in 1786. The Commissioners' *Fourteenth Report* of 1793 contains much important historical information about Sherwood and its administration as well as suggesting ways in which the small amount of Crown land left in the forest could be best managed. The map depicts Birklands and Bilhaugh, which were by this time the only sizeable pieces of forest land still in royal ownership. The quality of the surveying and cartography is very high, and the draftsmanship akin to that found in early Ordnance Survey maps.[31]

Nine maps have survived that were directly created to assist in the settlement of disputes over land or rights of way in the forest. The earliest was created in the early 1590s, and depicts a portion of the river Trent between Stoke Bardolph and Shelford, an area on the extreme southern edge of Sherwood.[32] It was used as evidence brought before both the Privy Council and Star Chamber in 1592, to resolve a dispute between Francis Fletcher and Sir Thomas Stanhope over the latter's construction of a weir and locks on the Trent to help feed water to a mill in Shelford. The map is drawn on paper in ink and colour wash at a scale of approximately 1:5000, and shows Stoke Bardolph, the Trent, a number of roads, and the old course of the river on which Stanhope's mills had been built. All of this topographical detail is directed at helping members of the court locate the point on the river which was affected by the weir, and the map makes no pretence at being a more general plan of the area.

---

30 D.V. Fowkes, 'Nottinghamshire parks in the eighteenth and nineteenth centuries', *TTS*, 71 (1967), 72-89.

31 PRO, MPE 340 & 547 (photographic copy in NAO, ED 4 L); Crown Commissioners.

32 PRO, MPF 10, illustrated in S. Revill, 'A 16th century map of the river Trent at Shelford', *TTS*, 75 (1971), 81-90.

A map dated 1606 shows the conjunction of the boundaries of the lordships of Warsop, Clipstone and Birklands wood.[33] The original is now lost but a number of good quality photographic copies were made in 1934 and these are preserved in the three main Nottinghamshire record repositories. This area appears to have been very open at the time and lacking clear topographical waymarkers. The map seems to have been created to define more clearly the course of parish boundaries where they intersected. The need to define such boundaries was especially important at this time as the Crown had alienated Clipstone manor and park in October 1603 to Lord Mountjoy, who sold the estate to the Earl of Shrewsbury in 1604. Following this transaction legal disputes over the property took place and it seems likely that the map was produced to help clarify a point of the argument.[34]

Four maps are directly related to the work of the commission for defective titles which was active in Sherwood Forest between 1610 and 1616, and used the survey by Richard Bankes as a means to seek out those who had created assarts and purprestures on their own land. One of the first to be accused was Sir John Byron, for land on the southeast of his estate at Newstead, acquired from the Crown in 1540. In April 1614 he was summoned to an inquisition held by the commission in Papplewick. In preparation for this Byron commissioned Thomas Langdon to survey and create a map of Kighill and Ravenshead wastes in May 1613.[35] This is still at Newstead Abbey and is a very elegant production drawn in ink and paint on parchment. Despite the quality of his cartographic evidence, Byron was forced to pay £500 to compound for his 'crime' in June 1615, by dint of not having specific reference to an area of old assart land in his title deeds.[36]

An even bigger 'catch' for the commission was Sir Charles Cavendish, son of Bess of Hardwick and part of the most powerful landowning family in north and central Nottinghamshire. The commission identified a number of undocumented assarts within the portion of Cavendish's estate that lay within Sherwood Forest. True to his aggressive character Cavendish fought the issue all the way

33 NAO, WP 5 S.

34 D. Crook, 'Clipstone Park and "peel"', *TTS*, 80 (1976), 35-46.

35 Nottingham City Museums, Fraser 262.

36 V. Walker & M. Howell, *The house of Byron* (1988). CSPD, 1623-25, addenda.

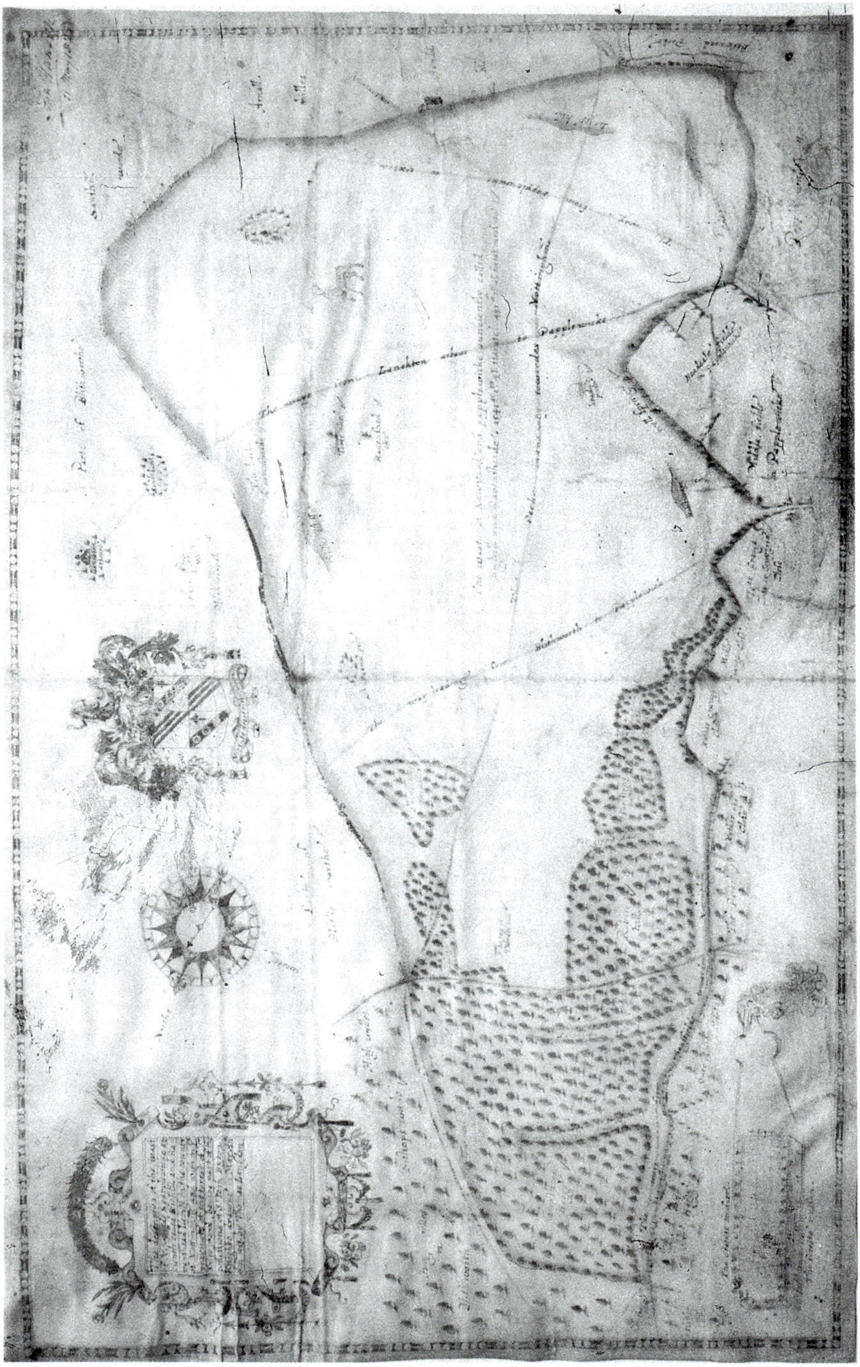

Thomas Langdon's map of part of Kighill & Ravenshead, Newstead, 1613. (Nottingham Museums, Fraser 262)
Reproduced courtesy of Nottingham City Museums

through the commission's system of inquisition. An offer to compound followed (if no deal could be struck) by prosecution in the Exchequer Court. However, Cavendish died in April 1617, before the case was resolved, but not before three pieces of cartographic evidence were created by the prosecution apparently copied from the Crown survey by Richard Bankes.[37]

The three maps depict Carburton, Gleadthorpe and the waste to the east of Kirkby in Ashfield.[38] All are drawn with ink on paper with certain areas highlighted with colour wash. The information written upon the maps corresponds exactly to the written survey undertaken by Richard Bankes and the style of the draughtsmanship is very close to Bankes' cartographic survey of 1609. What is particularly tantalising is that as only his map of the south of the forest survives, these three plans provide the only glimpse of the two huge maps of the north and middle portions of Sherwood Forest that Bankes must have produced.

It seems very likely that two further sketch maps of an area to the east of Blidworth are also the result of litigation arising out of forest law. Both maps are in a late seventeenth century hand and one can be dated with certainty to after 1660.[39] Both are drawn in ink on paper and are quite schematic in style and show the location of brecks in Allamore, an area of commonable land to the east of Blidworth, adjoining the parish of Farnsfield. Both maps were found within the parochial papers of Blidworth church and deal with a dispute over a number of brecks which had been established in Allamore over a number of decades.

Although these maps have much of the appearance of evidences in a local squabble, their date and location suggests that they might have been produced during the long-running sequence of sessions of the last forest court for Sherwood, overseen between 1663 and 1669 by the Duke of Newcastle in his guise of chief justice in eyre north of the Trent as part of a final attempt by the monarchy to revive the rule of forest law. The court heard many pleas including some from the men of Blidworth and Farnsfield concerning communal land. The outcome of the plea is not known.[40]

---

37 CSPD, 1611-18, 1623-25.

38 PRO, MR 429(1), MPF 295, MR 4298(2).

39 NAO, BD 4 S, BD 6 S.

40 Seddon, 37-44.

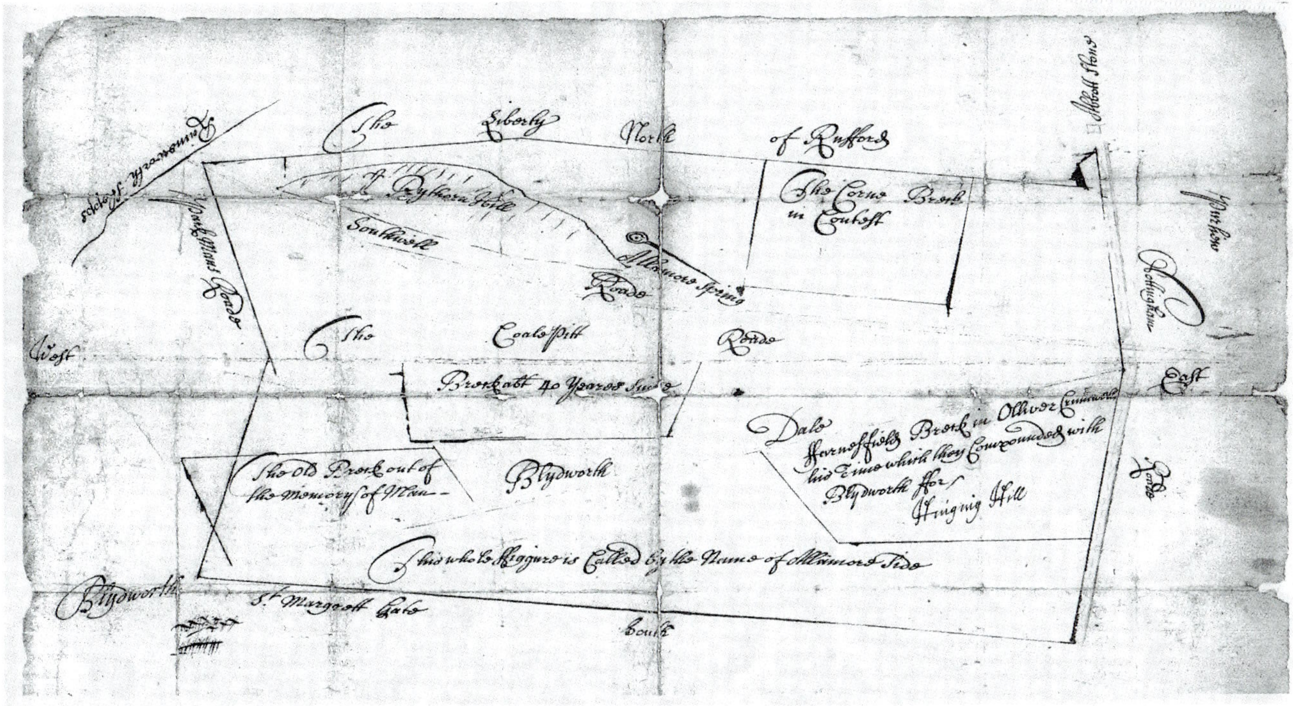

A sketch map showing brecks in Allamore Side, Blidworth, late 17th century. (NAO, BD 6 S)
Reproduced courtesy of Nottinghamshire Archives

The final example of a map produced to resolve a dispute dates from 1764.[41] Some years before the introduction of the Blidworth enclosure bill in 1769, the inhabitants seem to have been making preparations for this major alteration to the physical and tenurial landscape by clarifying an unclear boundary on the eastern border of the parish. In 1764 they undertook an extensive exercise to establish the boundary between Blidworth and Farnsfield, where it ran through Blidworth Forest. Appended to the two-membrane formal agreement and verbal description of this boundary is a brightly coloured but rather crudely-drawn plan of the disputed area. Both the bold use of colour washes to denote the area being discussed and the fairly sketchy cartography suggest that this map was drawn up to be exhibited in parish meetings. In this its design echoes the style of maps created in the sixteenth century and surviving in central judicial records. The purpose of the map is even further highlighted by the depiction of a line of stone boundary markers bisecting Blidworth Forest.

Around two-thirds of all the surviving maps depicting land in Sherwood Forest were commissioned by private individuals to further the management of their estates. The rather unfair litigation against landholders who had made assarts in the forest that took place following the Richard Bankes' survey of 1609 seems to have fostered the first major phase of private estate mapping in Nottinghamshire. As discussed above, Sir John Byron commissioned Thomas Langdon to survey a part of his estate, albeit more to provide evidence in court than to give an overview of the Newstead estate. However it is clear from annotations and corrections in a later hand that Langdon's map was used in the management of the Byron lands during the following two centuries.

Two far more sustained and impressive estate surveys also seem to have originated from the fear of the Crown survey of 1609. Just as Richard Bankes was completing his work, William Senior was beginning both a written and cartographic survey of the estates of William Cavendish (brother of Charles Cavendish), just across the border in Derbyshire. The following year Senior surveyed and mapped Sutton in Ashfield, the only property belonging to Cavendish within Sherwood Forest, and continued in his work until early 1614. He was

41 NAO, BD 5 L.

re-employed between 1616 and 1619, and 1626 and 1628, when William inherited more land. The book of written surveys and the Chatsworth Atlas which contains his cartographic work is a fine example of a systematic approach to surveying a large private estate.[42] This achievement was then repeated for the Nottinghamshire branch of the Cavendish family between 1629 to 1640 when Senior compiled what is now known as the Welbeck Atlas.[43] Sadly, the book of written surveys for this work is lost. In all, Senior produced nineteen maps of estates in Nottinghamshire for this atlas, ten of which lay within Sherwood Forest. Senior's surveying was fairly accurate and drawn up on a grand scale in ink and colour wash on vellum sheets measuring about 25inches x 15 inches, with often a map occupying a double page spread. The overall composition is good and the range and quality of colour superb.

It is hard not to see the original impulse for this sustained exercise in estate mapping as an attempt by wealthy landowners to fight the Crown's campaign of map making to identify property of questionable legal status within the area subject to forest law. The Crown's campaign to enforce these rights became discredited in the early 1620s, but was revived again in the early 1630s under Charles I.[44] Once again there were a number of estate and parish maps created around this time (both within and outside the forest), and it is possible that the surveys of the forest parishes of Lenton and Radford by Richard Smythe in July 1632, and Rufford lordship by John Bunting in December 1637 were undertaken with this in mind, especially when both lordships lay partially outside the bounds of the forest.[45] In the case of the map of Lenton and Radford there is nothing to indicate the way in which the forest boundary divided the area in half, but in the map of Rufford a

---

42 Devonshire Collections, Chatsworth (photographic copies maps in NUMD). An edition of the survey text is printed in D.V. Fowkes and G.R. Potter, eds., *William Senior's survey of the estates of the first and second Earls of Devonshire, c.1600-28*, Derbyshire Record Society, 13 (1988); G. and J.M. Scurfield, 'To be as a looking glass to their estates: the early 17th century surveys of William Senior', *The Cartographic Journal,* 33(2) (1996), 149-156.

43 P[ortland] E[state] O[ffice, Welbeck] (photographic copies of maps in NAO).

44 Thirsk.

45 NAO, RD 3 L, and NAO, RF, 4 L.

concerted effort was made by John Bunting to show forest perambulation and merepoints where they lay within the estate. In contrast he provides no associated identification points along the outer limits of the estate where it lay in the forest purlieu.

Once the process of estate mapping was started, of course, the owners also would have readily recognised the other benefits of having their estates recorded in this way, especially where improvements were being undertaken on the poor, sandy soils of the forest wastes. This was the motivation for so many of the assarts, especially those of a short term nature, known as *brecks*. The need to map these to clarify the extent of the agricultural improvement and the often-associated conversion of rights of common must have been strong. As a result a number of small sized sketch plans of brecks and enclosures of commons survive. The most interesting and earliest of these was undertaken in 1608 by John Smythson wherein Sir Charles Cavendish recorded the agreement of the men of Carburton to his enclosure of a portion of the parish common.[46] A second plan of part of this area was created in 1610 and both were later tipped into William Senior's Welbeck Atlas by Charles' son.[47] Later examples of this type of map include the two late seventeenth-century maps of brecks in Blidworth, mentioned above, a map of 1771 for Calverton and six for Carburton, created between 1775 and 1777.[48] In the same way that most brecks existed for only a limited period of time, the plans depicting them are usually extremely 'casual' pieces of cartography, drawn roughly with only the minimum amount of information. Orientation, a key landmark and the names of owners or places abutting the breck form the key data, along with the acreage taken in to temporary cultivation. These maps served as *aides memoir* of a temporary piece of agricultural management. They are sometimes annotated with details of the creators and duration of the breck. The Calverton map records that the breck was requested by Calverton residents who were tenants of the proprietor (Archbishop of York) and that it would begin on Lady Day 1772 and last for seven years.

---

46 PEO (photographic copy in NAO, CA 1 S); A. Woodhouse, 'A newly-identified estate plan by John Smithson, 1608', *TTS*, 103 (1999), 125-29.

47 PEO (photographic copy NAO, CO 2 S).

48 NAO, DD M 10/13; PEO, map 55.

Although there was a renewed attempt to restore the rule of forest law immediately after the restoration of the monarchy in 1660, it was soon clear that the Crown no longer had need of Sherwood Forest as a place for the chase or as a status symbol. During the later part of the seventeenth century therefore the Crown sold off substantial tracts of land in the middle and north of the forest to a number of aristocrats, and although this sounded the death knell of the forest in all but name, it fostered a new period of official and private estate mapping. Whereas the estate maps of the first half of the seventeenth century sought in the main to record what was and had been on the ground for some time before, the maps of the later seventeenth century and eighteenth century sought to depict major improvements. This was the era when the large 'Dukery' estates at Clumber, Thoresby, Welbeck and Rufford were being developed by the leading aristocrats of the county.[49]

Forest matters impinged upon at least one Dukery estate in the early eighteenth century. At Clumber two maps record the creation of a new deer park in 1709. This was the result of a joint venture between the Crown and the third Duke of Newcastle. Although the land was owned by Newcastle, Queen Anne could use the park to protect and control her red deer until her death (in 1714). The immediate aim was to provide a method of containing the large numbers of feral deer still roaming the forest. These were becoming a nuisance in an area where increasing amounts of land were being turned over to long and short term arable. A longer-term aim of this agreement was to enhance the Clumber estate with a private deer park, mimicking the medieval royal parks at Bestwood and Clipstone. The maps recording the creation of this park are quite contrasting in execution and show nicely the way in which cartography changed to supply the needs of the user. The earlier was drawn up in about 1706 and is quite sketchy in execution. It seems to be a working document for the laying out of the park, akin to the sketch plans drawn up for the creation of brecks. The map provides an indication of the location of the new park within the existing field boundaries, roads and the river, and provides calculations of the park's overall acreage. Other topographical detail is sparse and roughly drawn. The later map was drawn up in about 1710 when the deer park was nearing completion. This is a more formal document,

---

49 Seymour, 117-128.

in keeping with the estate plan tradition, designed to show a new feature in the landscape. The detail is elegantly drawn with all topography outside the park pale absent, and apart from the scale bar there are no calculations of acreages or distances included. The map is titled with flourishing gothic script, 'A Mapp Of Her Majesties Park Att Clumber' and everything is contained within a double-ruled border.[50]

Throughout Nottinghamshire the process of enclosure of commonable land to create discrete fields had been going on from the late fifteenth century. This was undertaken in a piecemeal fashion until the mid-eighteenth century when large-scale enclosure of whole or significant portions of parishes was achieved through private acts of parliament. In Sherwood Forest the pattern of enclosure took two forms, influenced by soil conditions. On the sandy soils that comprised the majority of the forest large-scale fenced deer parks (Bestwood and Clipstone) were created out of the extensive scrubland, first by the Crown and then in the later seventeenth century by the leading aristocratic land owners. In the eighteenth century these landowners also used sizeable areas of land to create plantations. On a less dramatic level, the much smaller, temporary enclosures (*brecks*) noted above were created for immediate agricultural needs, and these tended to be located in closer proximity to settlements. As a result there was far less large-scale parliamentary enclosure to be undertaken within the heartlands of the forest in the latter part of the eighteenth century. However, on the more fertile soils of the southern part of the forest early enclosure had been focused on the creation of small closes for pasture, often on the fringe of villages.[51] The 1609 map of the south part of the forest shows that by this date considerable areas of land had been re-ordered in this way.[52] As the higher quality of the land precluded the creation of large deer parks and plantations there remained far more arable commonable land in this area by the eighteenth century. Towards the end of this century the drive for enclosure by act of parliament gathered pace, and by the early 1800s

---

50 Both maps are illustrated and discussed in S. Morrison, 'The creation of Clumber Park, 1709-14: the last royal park of Sherwood Forest', *TTS,* 106 (2002), 103-117.

51 W.E. Tate, *Parliamentary land enclosure in the county of Nottingham during the 18th and 19th centuries*, TSRS, V (1935).

52 Mastoris and Groves.

many parishes in the south-eastern forest had undergone Parliamentary enclosure. Most of remaining forestal rights and privileges were extinguished by these enclosure acts.[53]

Maps created for large-scale enclosure account for only about 15 per cent of all known maps of forest lands, and the majority of these were located on the more fertile land in central and southern part of Sherwood. Parliamentary enclosure of a parish was a considerable undertaking, requiring accurate surveys of the land and its holders both before and after the implementation of the act. Besides defining the boundaries and acreage of all parcels of land dealt with by the act, the maps usually give the names of people and institutions to whom land was awarded and a reference number linking map with books of reference. The resulting maps are therefore very detailed, quite accurate and well known to local historians as often the earliest cartographic representation of a parish's landscape. At Blidworth three acts of parliament were required to complete the enclosure of the parish, and the two surviving plans (for 1770 and 1812) demonstrate how drawn out the process could be. The earlier map not only locates the land to be enclosed under the 1770 act (to the south, east and north-west of the village), but also indicates roughly the proximity of 'old [pre-parliamentary] enclosures' nearby. All remaining commonable land within the parish apart from Heywood Manor was enclosed under the act of 1805/12.[54]

The surviving *corpus* of manuscript maps of Sherwood Forest described here is extensive and this seems to have been the result of the interaction of a number of factors. Most fundamental was the special agrarian, legal and administrative workings of the royal forest. These not only required the extent of Sherwood to be defined for huntsmen and administrators alike, but also attracted the attention of revenue-hungry Crown officials as a place where detailed changes to land use could generate income for the monarch. Such needs created a vast body of written records and, when necessary to clarify a difficult point, quite detailed maps. Two other factors are the poor quality of forest soils and the strong aristocratic tenurial presence within Sherwood. The need to improve the yield of estates came early to the

53 Tate.

54 NAO, EA 14/2, EA 15/2.

forest, and the quantity of major landholders brought about the wherewithal to undertake considerable early enclosure of wastes and commons and the creation of brecks and ornamental parks. Again, where necessary, maps were commissioned to record these improvements, and in at least two cases more extensive and systematic cartographic surveys of estates were initiated not only as landed wealth increased, but also as a precaution against further attacks on assarts by Crown officials. Furthermore, the large, open tracts of waste that made up the heart of the forest were difficult to define in words, so once again maps were necessary to record boundary disputes adequately.

Sherwood was not alone of all the royal forests in England in this respect, but from a brief survey of other royal forests it seems that the survival rate of maps in Nottinghamshire is significantly greater.[55] This may not be solely the result of chance. From the post-medieval period substantial aristocratic estates have existed within Sherwood Forest, and their owners not only had the financial resources to commission maps, but also preserved them in muniment rooms. Furthermore the Crown's interest in Sherwood was long-term, if fluctuating, in intensity, and this too acted as a spur to the use of maps and other forms of survey of land in the forest. Indeed, it could be argued that much private estate mapping was inspired by the need to respond to state initiatives. In many ways, therefore, contention and necessity can be seen to have been the mothers of cartographic invention in Sherwood Forest, with the strong presence of both the Crown and wealthy private landowners providing the financial wherewithal to commission surveyors of varying ability. Their legacy provides an unusual insight into the landscape and topography of this famous royal forest.[56]

---

55 The forests of Rockingham, Dean and Needwood. I am grateful to Sarah Bendall for letting me read an early draft of her paper on the mapping of Needwood Forest.

56 I am grateful to Catherine Delano-Smith for encouraging me to undertake this survey and commenting upon an earlier draft of this essay. As always, great assistance has been given by the staff of the Nottinghamshire Archives, the Local Studies Library, Nottingham Central Library, and the University of Nottingham Manuscripts Department. I am also grateful to Derek Adlam for providing access to the Welbeck Atlas of William Senior. Help and support have also been given by Peter Barber, Sarah Bendall, Lynne Mastoris and Sue Sharman. As well as honouring the work of Adrian Henstock I should like this essay to be in memory of my dear friend Julia Milne (1959-2000), someone for whom Nottinghamshire was always a special place.

6

'The Warmest I have': Henry, second Duke of Newcastle, and Nottingham Castle

Trevor Foulds

William Cavendish first Duke of Newcastle-upon-Tyne died on Christmas Day 1676 in his eighty-fourth year. Despite his age his 'sudden death' caught everyone unawares. Henry (1630-91), his only surviving son and heir, had just received letters which Thomas Osborne, first Earl of Danby, presented to King Charles II. Danby hurried back to the king on 29th December with the news. The king was 'most sorry to hear for the death of my old friend': William had been his governor and surrogate father for three years (1638-41) and a loyal supporter.[1] Henry, a Gentleman of the Bedchamber to the king and now second Duke of Newcastle, left London for Welbeck Abbey. He and his wife, Frances, did not attend William's funeral, which was held in Westminster Abbey on 22nd January 1677. William's body was buried under the marble tomb in the abbey's north transept in which his beloved second wife Margaret Lucas (1623-73) already lay. The new duke remained at Welbeck taking stock, for here were personal things that he had not seen for many years. Because of 'y[e] unkindness to us at Wellbeck' he had avoided living with William and Margaret and resided chiefly at Glentworth (Lincs.) and Worksop Manor or in London. He had loved his father but the first duke was so dominant a character that his son's love and duty had been severely tested at times.

1 *CSPD 1677-8*, 545; HMC, *Manuscripts of His Grace the Duke of Portland* ii (1891), 152; *CSPD 1637-8*, 361.

Henry was married to Frances (1630-95) daughter of William Pierrepont (1607-78), second son of Robert Pierrepont, first Earl of Kingston-upon-Hull, a close neighbour in Nottinghamshire with a house at Thoresby.[2] In 1677 the family, 'our little selves', consisted of Henry (1663-80), Elizabeth (1655-1734) married (30th December 1669) to Christopher Monck (1653-88), second Duke of Albemarle, Frances (1660-90), Margaret (1661-1716), Katherine (1665-1712) and Arabella (1673-98). The daughters had to be provided for and at his death the first duke left heavy debts. And then there was William's ultimate grand design, that rising monument to his *gloire*, the celebration in stone of the dynasty and his achievements, Nottingham Castle. This essay examines the second Duke of Newcastle's completion and subsequent occupation of the Ducal Palace.

William Cavendish bought the medieval castle of Nottingham, its park and lands in 1663 from George Villiers, second Duke of Buckingham, for £4,400. He did not start building until 1674 but thereafter progress was rapid.[3] By his will (4th October 1676) the first duke, described as *potentissimus princeps*, bound Henry as his sole executor to complete the building, for which he assigned £2,000 per annum.[4] Whatever Henry's misgivings about this project and the drain on his income he understood his father's aims and objectives. He dutifully completed the building and, with his wife, undertook its interior decoration and furnishing.

Detailed accounts for the building of the Ducal Palace have not survived. However, a volume in the hand of Thomas Farr, the second duke's steward, entitled 'A booke of Thomas Farrs' weekly disburstments for the use of his Grace Henry duke of Newcastle' lists payments for the Ducal Palace from October 1677 to December 1683.[5] There are no details concerning the building but it is clear that large sums of money (£200-£300) were being regularly paid to Mr Neale, one of the trustees of the first duke's will, which must have included payments to the various building contractors. By 1679 building work

---

2 NAO, DDP8/131: marriage settlement, 10th-12th May 1653.

3 T. Foulds, '"This greate house, so lately begun and all of freestone": William Cavendish's Italianate *palazzo* called Nottingham Castle', *TTS* 106 (2002), 81-102.

4 PRO, PROB 11/353 fos. 173-4.

5 NAO, DDP6/7/2/238 (unfoliated).

had tailed off and by 1680 had virtually ceased. What Farr's accounts show thereafter is the fitting out of the Ducal Palace. A peak was reached in 1681 that indicates the decorating and furnishing was at its height, and another lesser peak was in 1683 probably for similar reasons. Farr's accounts suggest that the total amount spent on fitting out the Ducal Palace was £6,378 12s. 2d.

Mention of architectural fittings for the Ducal Palace are few but between 22nd September and 29th December 1677 'Mr Hall', probably Richard Hall, tombmaker and stonecarver with a workshop near Stoney Street in Nottingham, had supplied eight 'chimny peeces' at a cost of £52. In November 1678 Farr accounted for two more (cost £18) and in February 1681 Mr Richard Wright was paid £52 for marble chimneys which Frances in her weekly household book numbered as six.[6] This makes a total of sixteen chimney pieces which altogether cost £122.

From Farr's accounts fifty-five workmen, tradesmen and suppliers can be identified as involved with the Ducal Palace: masons (ten) with two brickmakers, joiners and carpenters (ten), smiths (nine), upholsterers and more specialised craftsmen (twelve), suppliers of deals (four), two painters (Mr Gibbs, Samuel Rose), two glaziers (Mr Bunney, William Chappell), and one plasterer (Mr Smith).

The masons worked on the East Front stairs, the terrace wall and paving outside and inside. Of this group Joseph Jackson was long serving. He had played an important role in building work at Bolsover in the 1660s and was still working for the family at Nottingham with his son, Joseph Jackson the younger, and probably a close relation, Peter Jackson. Another mason, Matthew Porter, was working at Welbeck in the 1690s.[7]

Of the smiths, William Booth was paid £25 for the 'Iron Rayles for Stairs' (3rd February 1682/3), probably the banister or handrail of the internal staircase marvelled at by visitors because it was a cantilevered one. John France, locksmith, made keys, locks and firegrates. Booth, Mr Wright and John Pearson, smiths, were working at Welbeck in the 1690s.[8] Joiners and carpenters undertook a wide

6 NAO, DDP6/7/2/237.

7 NUMD, Pw1 624; NA, DD4P/58/79a/21.

8 NAO, DD4P/58/75a/50, 52-3.

range of work. Robert Rose made bedsteads and Joseph Gale carved cedar frames. Richard Marples, 'joyner', who lived in Worksop, worked on the chapel at Welbeck (1677), made beds, picture frames and a 'bilyard table'.[9] Perhaps the most skilled joiner or carpenter was Jonathan Lucas described as 'ceder joyner' or 'working with cedar'. Between July 1681 and May 1683 he was paid £181 16s. for 'cedar work' of which £7 was for a cedar floor (5th May 1683). Between March and May 1682 Lucas wainscoted the dining and drawing rooms in deal which cost £69 14s. 11d. The floor of the state bedroom (approximately 66½ square yards) was inlaid with the ciphers and ducal coronet in a white wood, possibly white ebony, that may have resembled the contemporary inlaid floor of the 'Queen's Closet', Ham House, created by Henry Harlow for the Duke and Duchess of Lauderdale. Comparisons between the Ducal Palace and Ham House are not altogether invalid as Frances and Elizabeth Dysart, Duchess of Lauderdale, corresponded.[10]

Lucas's total bill for two years was £251 10s. 11d. In addition he worked at Welbeck January to December 1682 wainscoting and making sash windows. The earliest mention of cedar was on 16th June 1677 when Mr Yates was paid £1 12s. 6d. for cedar boards but for where was not stated. For the Ducal Palace Richard Wright was paid £120 for cedar on 5th February 1680/1 and he also sawed it. Cedar was carried by Jeremiah Browne who was paid £100 on 4th February 1680/1. This was transported by Myles Walker from 'Lond[on] to Gainsbrow' at a cost of £7 10s. (11th February 1681/2). Thus the load was brought by sea and was then picked up by Browne who was paid for 'Ceder by water carried from Gainsborough to Nottingh[am]' on 18th and 25th February 1681/2.

A final group made or supplied a number of disparate items. It included amongst others James Burdin for bedding, John Kilby, glassman, Mr Peach, pewterer, Mr Starkey for glass candlesticks, Ralph Bigges for cane chairs, and two cabinet-makers, Mr Wiseham and Mr

---

9 W.F. Webster, ed., *Nottinghamshire Hearth Tax 1664:1674* TSRS, 37 (1988), 133.

10 J. Hicklin, *The History of Nottingham Castle* (1836), 78, 81; J.G. Dunbar, 'The Building-activities of the Duke and Duchess of Lauderdale, 1670-82', *Archaeological Journal* 132 (1975), 221-5; HMC, 152.

Pistor. Caleb Wilkinson, a young Nottingham cabinet-maker, made or supplied a looking glass. With Thomas Barnes, carpenter, he occupied two messuages in Bridlesmith Gate, Nottingham, in 1709.[11] The most prevalent name in this group is 'Mr Putnam ye upholster'. He can be identified as John Putnam. Between 4th May 1678 and 15th December 1683 he was paid altogether £856 10s. 4d., and the highest single bill was £250 'Furniture pro [for] Nott[ingham] Castle' (24th February 1682/3). Putnam became a man of substance in Mansfield Woodhouse and with his wife Jane leased land in Sherwood Forest in 1699. What exactly his position was is unclear but by the 1690s he and Jane were household officials at Welbeck. Jane bought a wide range of goods such as linen, apples, 'Bookes for ye Chappell', flint sweetmeat 'glassis', and made payments to tradespersons and other visitors that she claimed from Thomas Farr. John was equally involved in miscellaneous petty items but also was paid 10s. 'for Stuffing his G^s^ Chaire', and he supplied matting for the library, drawing and dining rooms at Welbeck. John Wright charged 2d. 'for a loc mendin for Mr Putman [*sic*] candle kubard' (18th May 1691).[12]

Celia Fiennes visited in 1694 and was impressed:

> ... the roomes are very lofty and large, 6 or 7 state roomes, and a long gallery hung with fine Pictures of the family, the wanscoate is most of Cedar; some roomes are hung with good tapistry, the Chamber of State is hung with very rich tapistry so much silver and gold in it that the 3 pieces that hung the roome cost 1500£; the bed was rail'd in as the presence chamber used to be – the bed was damaske; the floore of the roome was inlay'd with Cyphers and the Corronet ...[13]

Fiennes was describing the state apartments. This sequence of rooms included the whole of the east front (dining room, hall, state chamber, withdrawing room), the south front (gallery) and south west wing (state bedroom and closets) at Principal (first) storey level. Their furnishings continued to impress visitors well into the eighteenth century for they

11 NAO, DDCH/2/5.

12 NAO, DD563/7-8; DD4P/58/75a/10, 16, 54, 63, 69, 78.

13 C. Fiennes, *The Journeys of Celia Fiennes* (1947 edn.), 72-3.

remained untouched for at least forty years if not longer. The magnificent State Bed of 'Rich Crimson Genoa Velvet lined with white Indian Sattin Compleat, a red Persian false Case and Rod …', surrounded on three sides by its rail remained until 1770 and the seventeenth-century tapestries were still in place when they were looted by rioters in 1831. The earliest extant inventory (1717) appears to reveal an interior 'frozen in time' from the 1680s so that the rooms described were as furnished by the second duke.[14] The inventory clearly shows that the opulent effect of the Ducal Palace's interior decoration was largely achieved by the extensive use of sumptuous and expensive materials and textiles.

Tapestries were a particular decorative feature and found in the state chamber (five pieces), state withdrawing room (three pieces) and three very fine 'architect tapestry hangings' in the state bedroom. They were found also in lesser rooms. The subjects of the pieces were said to be Old Testament ones or the evangelists and martyrs. Contemporary visitors were informed that the tapestries depicting the four evangelists were 'bought by the Duke [William] when he fled wth Prince Rupert to Antwerp, & cost 2000^li^'.[15] 'Mr Allen upholster' was paid £35 for 'Tapstrey hangings' in January 1680/1. In the State Chamber was the state canopy 'embroider'd with Gold and Gold Fringe'. Perhaps this was what the 'gould and silver twist' costing £32 15s. 4d. was for, supplied by Mr Henry Southouse 'a Londoner' in November 1681. Under the canopy were two elbow chairs and two footstools with a 'fine Turky work carpet'.

Above the cedar wainscotting in the state gallery the walls were covered by magnificent gilt-impressed leather hangings, fragments of which survive in Nottingham Castle Museum.[16] Over the gilt-impressed leather were twenty whole length portraits in cedar frames with thirty others 'of severall sorts', a total of fifty pictures, which Fiennes noted were family portraits. Altogether the 1717 inventory lists 142 pictures, many of which were then damaged, like the ten whole lengths in the

---

14 NAO, DD4P/39/55 mm40-51.

15 M.R. Wagner, *The English Travels of Sir John Percival and William Byrd II: The Percival Diary of 1701* (1989), 96-8.

16 N(ottingham) C(ity) M(useums and) G(alleries) 1893-26.

Elizabeth Cavendish eldest daughter of Henry 2nd Duke of Newcastle, wife of Christopher Monck, second Duke of Albemarle. Artist: Thomas Murrey. Commissioned for the state gallery, Nottingham Castle. Source: NAO, DDP6/19/18/105 (glassplate).

state chamber and seventy-five 'pictures great and small several rotten and all very much decayed' stored in the kitchen. Only one of the pictures was described, that of 'King Charles the Second when a youth' hung in the state bedroom. Two full lengths in the State Gallery of Henry's eldest daughter Elizabeth and her husband Christopher Monck, second Duke of Albemarle, were commissioned from the portrait painter Thomas Murrey (1663-1734), for Frances wrote to Elizabeth from Welbeck, 1st April 1682, 'I give my Lord Duke and you a 1000 thanks that your Pictures from head to foote are doeing for Nottingham Galery'.[17] According to Farr's accounts between September 1677 and October 1683 £246 13s. 6d. was spent on pictures, The two largest single payments (1683) of £50 and £114 were to 'Mr Comer Limmner', who was of York (*c.* 1620-*c.* 1700). This was sufficient to have paid for nine full lengths. Other artists paid were 'Mrs Baker' for 'his Graces picture' (£6 15s.) on 'moehaire' (£7 14s.), 'Mr Byrne ye Limbner' £36 1s. 6d. for drawing eight pictures, Mr Daniel (£3), and 'the Pictur Drawer [for] 2 Picturs' (£21). Amongst other contemporary artists patronised were Mary Beale (1632-97), Francis Elliott, Garret Morphy (died 1715/16), and Mr Pole. It is possible that many of the portraits of dukes William and Henry, their wives, children and ancestors that are now at Welbeck were removed from Welbeck and Bolsover to the Ducal Palace and others were commissioned especially for display there.

On 10th February 1690/1 John Putnam submitted his bill: 'for oyle and cullers for the peeces at Notingham Castle 1s. for help to take them downe and put them up and prime the back side 5s. for a lining and tacks 1s. 4d.[18] Pictures only ten years old would not need cleaning or touching up with colour or to be re-lined but older, ancestral portraits by Adriaen Hanneman (1601-71), Daniel Mytens (1590-1642), Gerard Soest (1602-81), Hendrik Van Steenwyck the younger (1580-1649), and Paul Van Somer (1576-1621) amongst others, might have needed this attention. The south-facing State Gallery with its gilt-impressed leather hangings and pictures in gilt cedar frames must have been stupendous in sunlight and candlelight. The whole was a powerful dynastic statement and complemented that of the East Front.

---

17 R.W. Goulding, comp., and C.K. Adams, ed., *Catalogue of the pictures belonging to His Grace the Duke of Portland* (1936), nos. 98, 415, 417.

18 NAO, DD4P/58/75a/54.

A major question about the Ducal Palace is how frequently did the second duke and his wife live in it? There is little documentary evidence beyond Farr's account book that ends in 1683. Farr's accounts show that Newcastle's first visit was in August 1678. On 27th September 1679 Newcastle requested a friend, Sir John Reresby (1634-89), 'to bear him company to Nottingham to see his castle there, which was almost finished' and he arrived on 29th September.[19] This visit is not reflected in Farr's accounts so that they cannot be an infallible guide to frequency of residence. In 1680 Newcastle was there in August and his daughters only are mentioned in October that year. In August 1681 the duchess and her daughters were there probably in preparation for Newcastle who stayed for the week of 1st-8th October which the duchess noted was the 'first weeke my Lord lived att Nottingham Castle'.[20] Again this is not reflected in Farr's accounts but there was a burst of activity afterwards down to 5th November 1681. It was in November 1681 that the duke and duchess with their unmarried daughters formally and ceremonially took up residence in the Ducal Palace. Their daughter Elizabeth, Duchess of Albemarle, was to join them, for Newcastle wrote to Danby from the Ducal Palace on 14th November: 'My Wife went erly this day to Wellbeck retorning to day to order our little Building there so y^{t} we may goe there 3 weeks hence, wee are certaine God willing to have my Daughter Albermarle here a thorsday [17th November]'.[21] Since the duchess went to supervise the new building work at Welbeck and had, according to Farr's accounts, done the same at the London home in Clerkenwell, and since she spent time on her own at the Ducal Palace, it seems probable that she was largely responsible for the opulent interior.

Once in residence the family spent time visiting and receiving distinguished neighbours, as Newcastle informed Danby on 22nd November 1681:

> I have done my duty to your Lo^{p} relations wayted upon my Lord of Ruttland at Belvoir Castle and my Daughters wayted of my

---

19 A. Browning, ed., *Memoirs of Sir John Reresby* (2nd ed., 1991), 189.

20 NAO, DDP6/7/2/237.

21 NUMD, Pwl 543.

> Lady Ruttland when I did not goe and her La^{p} was pleased to acsept of y^{m} very kindly and has been pleased to condesend soe much as to come here since … I acquante your Lo^{p} y^{t} my Daughter Albermarle is here and in good health …[22]

The mayor and corporation of Nottingham ceremonially paid their respects and £50 was given 'To Mr Mayor of Nottingham to Buy a piece of Plate for ye use of that Corporacion' on 17th December 1681. With this the corporation bought a loving cup and two quart tankards that bear the London assay mark for 1681 and remain in the possession of Nottingham City Council. The pieces are decorated with acanthus leaves and inscribed *Ex Dono Hen. Ducis Novi Castri Anno Dom. 1681. Gervasio Wylde Majore.*

Although the interior was still unfinished, Newcastle was pleased with the Ducal Palace at least on one point: it was warmer than Welbeck, as he informed Danby when back at Welbeck on 22nd December 1681:

> I receved the Honnor of your Lo^{p} of ye 14th at Nottingham upon ye 17th but I hope your Lo^{p} will pardon me I did not pres^{t} my many thankes to your Lo^{p} from thence, for it tooke me some time in making visits to ye Mayor and Aldermen before I came here … To give your Lo^{p} an account of our little selves we came here a tusday [20th December] having been seven weekes at Nottingham and this House [Welbeck] is soe un reddy for us y^{t} it is very cold in comparrison of our House at Nottingham for y^{t} is really ye Warmest I have …[23]

Newcastle's daughters resided at the Ducal Palace in May 1682 and the family may have been there in early September when corn was bought (£8 4s.) at Nottingham for horses. Reresby was staying at Welbeck when Newcastle, as lord lieutenant of Nottinghamshire and recorder of Nottingham, received directions from the king, dated 26th September 1682, 'that you remove to your castle at Nottingham till the disorder be over'. Like many other corporations Nottingham was

---

22 NUMD, Pw1 544.

23 NUMD, Pw1 545.

required to surrender its charter for a new one, and the Tories, with Newcastle's encouragement, had complied. Riots broke out in September. Attended by baronets, knights, and forty squires and gentlemen, Newcastle took up residence in the Ducal Palace. He was never comfortable in awkward political situations but his presence had some effect and he feasted the Corporation (£13 4s. 8d.) possibly at the Ducal Palace on 14th October. Charles II thanked him 'for composing the distempers at Nottingham'.[24] Newcastle and his family are not known to have been in Nottingham in 1683, although a visit in early October may be indicated by Farr's accounts.

Newcastle was at the Ducal Palace on 9th August 1684 to obtain a marriage licence for his daughter Katherine to marry Thomas Tufton, sixth Earl of Thanet. The license was issued on 12th August at Nottingham. Newcastle decided that there was insufficient accommodation for wedding guests: 'We shall move to Welbeck in three or four days, where we shall have house room and more privacy to accommodate your Lordship'.[25] The wedding took place at Welbeck on 14th August. Afterwards the family returned to the Ducal Palace to entertain George Villiers, second Duke of Buckingham, and 'all the nobility and gentry of that and the nighbouring countys had met there at this time upon occasion of a hors-race, most of which his Grace entertained one night at supper and a ball'. Reresby was thrilled on 4th September to stay at the Ducal Palace 'though all visiters except near relations laid in the town'.[26]

In May 1686 Louis de Duras, second Earl of Feversham, Marquis de Blanquefort, was negotiating for the hand of Newcastle's daughter Margaret, with Reresby acting as a marriage broker. Margaret's sisters were against it and both the duke and duchess were unfavourable, Duras 'being a Frenchman and of very little certain estate'. King James II applied pressure. Duras, a Protestant, was 'a fyne gentlemen of his person and a good soldier', nephew of Henri de la Tour d'Auvergne, Maréchal de Turenne, and was James II's commander in chief against Monmouth's rebellion (1685). On 4th November 1686 Reresby arrived at Welbeck 'to find a great disorder in the family by reason of soe

24 *Reresby*, 277; *CSPD 1682*, 432, 459, 477; *CSPD 1683*, 6.

25 HMC, 157.

26 *Reresby*, 344-5.

great a falling out between the Duke and Duchesse that they were parted from bed and board', and that Newcastle had vowed never to sleep with his wife again. The duchess was angry over the proposals for Margaret and incandescent that Newcastle, under pressure from the king, was in favour of marrying another of their daughters, Arabella, to Colonel James Fitz James (1670-1734), the king's illegitimate son. Fitz James, later created Duke of Berwick (1687), was to become a renowned commander in the French army.[27] 'A papist and a bastard' the duchess railed, and departed to live in another part of Welbeck with her daughters, while Newcastle burnt his will and made a new one disadvantaging his daughters.[28] Newcastle poured out his grief in letters. The poet Thomas Shadwell, his father's protégé, though 'layd up with a fitt of Gout so violent', was surprised by the tale of woe. Nevertheless he rallied to reply with soothing elegance.[29]

Newcastle thanked his neighbour at Rufford Abbey George Savile, first Marquess of Halifax, for:

> thinking of my poore selfe, and truly my Lord I doe not expect to live halfe a yeare … As your L^{p} old serv^{t} my Father sayd often to me there was noe happiness to living quietly and dieing quietly … for as long as I have a Crust to eate of and a sell to go to to be free from Company I shall Compass y^{t} happiness … Your L^{p} must heare of ye difference between my wife and I … I will not be hectored … for I am not ashamed of my proseedings.[30]

Some days later Halifax was bothered again:

> … truly my Lord I could not presume to troble your L^{p} againe soe soon wth my scribble but y^{t} it is a great releefe to me in my greefe to impart my selfe to soe noble a frend. It is very well known in my Family I beleeve in ye Countrey wth w^{t} scorns and slight my Wife and my Daughter Margrett proseed towards me

---

27 *CSPD 1686-7*, 359.

28 *Reresby,* 425, 437-9.

29 NUMD, Pw1 248.

30 NUMD, Pw1 641 (8th January 1686/7); *Reresby*, 211.

> and they Publish me to be ye very roge in ye World because I desire ye like of y^{m} I did in Feb: last to wch thay submitted and now they refuse. It is 14 weekes since I had patience in this matter, butt I am resolved not [to] live longer in a House wth my Wife then to ye 4th of Feb: and y^{t} is ye time she sett severall months since to goe to Nottingham … I can give my Esstate to whom I please and I will keepe up ye memory of my Father in spite of my Wife …[31]

On 4th February 1686/7 the fragmentary accounts for Frances's and Margaret's stay, without Arabella, at the Ducal Palace begin.[32]

What is clear from these accounts is that much had to be bought in. Bridget Seyliard and John Newton supplied groceries, Mrs Mary Greathead livery stable and servants' quarters, Joseph Newsome household bread and 'roles', Elizabeth Barker milk and cream, Mrs Mary Wright brooms, mops and skeps, and Mrs Mary Drury substantial quantities of meat. All these were Nottingham people and they were probably established suppliers when the family was in residence.

Robert Smethergell was the cook assisted in the kitchen by a man and a woman. Substantial quantities of eggs and butter were consumed. Two pecks of flour, one strike of salt, and half pecks of oatmeal and cockles were regularly bought each week. Mary Drury's weekly bills for meat supplied by 'wait', chiefly beef, mutton and veal with the occasional neats tongues and calves heads, was rarely less than 23 stones per week, the heaviest being 29 stones 13 pounds for £4 15s. 11d. Other meat consumed included pullets, chickens, green plovers, teal, mallard, smee (widgeon), 'sosiges', bacon, rabbits and pigeons. Fish was eaten, particularly pike, cockles, shrimps and perch, and to a lesser extent gudgeon, grayling, smelts, red and white herring, lobster, salmon, crayfish, whiting, 'flownders' and salt codfish. Cream cheese and turkey eggs figure, and the gardener supplied herbs for Lent 'porag' as Ash Wednesday was on 9th February 1687. More luxurious items included sugar, raisins, currants, 'chayney' and 'sivill oringes' and 'lemonds' and, less frequently, pepper, 'sallet oyle', prunes,

---

31 NUMD, Pw1 642 (17th January 1686/7).

32 NAO, DD4P/58/74 (bundled).

anchovies, spice, cloves, ginger, cinnamon, 'nutts', 'care comfits', 'caraway cumfetts' and 'ryce'. John Newton supplied oil, honey, elixirs and cordials, as well as sand and writing paper.

Although the Ducal Palace's kitchens had facilities for brewing, beer and ale were bought in, including bottled ale. Of wines sack, rhenish and claret were regularly drunk with champagne seemingly a favourite, and three bottles 'of Shampane given to ye sarvants', and also Tent (a deep red Spanish wine). Less favoured were sherry and white wine, and only one bottle of brandy was bought. The usual strong and small ales and beers were bought and also 'Mumm', a wheatmeal beer.

Besides having insufficient accommodation for large parties, the Ducal Palace was deficient in two other commodities. The first was water. Robert Eyre regularly bought water at 4d. a 'loade' and weekly consumption was about ten loads (3s. 4d.) although in the first three weeks to 25th February 1686/7 thirty-three loads were bought. A lead cistern survives bearing the ducal coat-of-arms and dated 1681.[33]

The second was stables. Frances and Margaret brought their own staff and equipage. Mrs Mary Greathead billed Eyre for stable rooms, coach house and chamber, horse fodder (oats, beans, corn, straw, hay and horse ale) and bedding, plus accommodation for seven servants, their suppers, breakfasts, beer and candles. She also accommodated horses for guests and other staff from Welbeck such as John Putnam. The total number of horses is unclear but there were certainly six coach-horses, three hackneys and a number of saddle horses. There was one coachman, John Jackson, and postillions. The senior groom was Robert Radcliff whose responsibilities may have included some horse doctoring as he submitted bills for 'barme, for baking of it, fenicreek, doges Grease, heating balls' and 'for ye surup of Coltsfoot'. Margaret had her own groom who was billed separately for 'Peacocke', presumably her horse. Frances and Margaret each had a coach and calash and John Hawkings was responsible for their maintenance. He sent for coach wheels from Welbeck and fitted them; he greased, cleaned, 'blact & oyled' a coach and calash and fixed 'ye Coronett' and did the same for 'ye ladys [Margaret's] coach' and 'callash'; one calash was totally re-fitted, with a new seat for its coach box, and its

33 NCMG 1992-1658.

roof altered. Hawkings also supplied for Margaret 'a Crimson velvett Sidesaddle of the French Fashion' (£6 10s.).

Every week Frances ordered 10s. to be given to the poor and once £4. Twice Mrs Barker submitted bills (£1 9s. 11d. and 19s. 6d.) for cloth and thread 'for Shirting ye Poore', £1 was given at St Mary's church, Nottingham, and 5s. 'To ye Clark and Saxton att S^nt Peters [church]', Nottingham. Frances saw her tailor and had her slippers mended, and Joshua Wilkinson, joiner, perhaps related to Caleb Wilkinson, made two chests of drawers (8s. 5d.) for Margaret.

While at the Ducal Palace Frances was not a recluse. A number of visits and small entertainments appear to have been made. There were reciprocal visits to and from the Earl and Countess of Rutland. Mary Greathead presented a bill of 1s. 'for alle for ye Coche horses when the[y] came from Belvoire'. Visits were made to or from Frances's nephew William Pierrepont fourth Earl of Kingston. A small party may be indicated in the week 19th to 25th February 1687 by payments to the grooms of Mrs Bennett, old Lady Byron (Elizabeth Booth), Lord Byron, Lord Rutland, Mrs Mulliner, Sir William Stanhope (of Shelford, Nottinghamshire, MP for Nottingham in 1685) and Mrs Wright's 'made'. 'Mrs Mulliner' was probably Elizabeth wife of Darcy Molyneux, high sheriff of Nottinghamshire in 1687. A similar list of names with the addition of Mrs Warin's groom exists for the week 8th to 16th April. Perhaps a small party for the week 4th to 11th March is indicated by Mary Greathead's bill for fifteen extra horses. Arabella visited 22nd to 29th April when Dr Brigges administered 'Phisick'. Payments were made 'To see a Poppit [puppet] play' (10s.) and 'To see a band dance' (2s. 6d.). A payment of 5s. 'Given at the Glasshouse' would suggest a visit to the locally celebrated glass works on Barker Gate, Nottingham.

The accounts end on 4th June 1687. On 28th June Reresby went to Welbeck and 'found the Duchesse of Newcastle returned, who had been parted some months from the Duke, but yet not perfectly reconciled'. Feversham, through Reresby, renewed his suit but the atmosphere at Welbeck was hostile. Newcastle allowed Feversham and his retinue, which included Colonel Theophilus Oglethorpe, his second in command at Sedgemoor, and Sir Richard Graham, first Viscount Preston, the king's Master of the Robes, 'to make use of his castle at Nottingham in their return to London, where they went on Wednesday [13th July], and were greatly entertained at the Duke's charge'.

Newcastle 'being of an unsteady, fickle humour' lost his temper with the duchess and Margaret on 16th October over the Feversham proposal 'used them very roughly in discours' and 'behaved himselfe after soe brutal a manner' that the duchess left. By 26th October she was back at the Ducal Palace, for which no accounts survive, and intended to go to London the following week.[34] Ill, bewildered, but obdurate, Newcastle wrote to her:

> I intreat you to Consider y^{t} your parting with me and goeing to London will be a prejudice to you, and your two daughters unmarryed: and to me; Though you told me on munday was seven-night you would not keep me Company, yet you have Commanded my house, and may doe; ... I thinke it a strange proceeding you will goe from a place you Love so well as this, and Leave your Children out of ill will to me; It troubles me very much; If you will goe, I desire you will promise me under your hand, you will spend me not above a thousand pound a year, includeing Servants wages; and all Expences.[35]

The duchess did eventually return and both she and Newcastle may have stayed in the Ducal Palace in September 1690.[36]

Newcastle was loyal to James II despite his religion. Personally he had no qualms about Roman Catholics 'for they are my kinsmen and friends' and 'I am a frend to many of y^{m}, but I shall never be of their Religeon ...'. He encouraged his neighbours to celebrate the birth of James, Prince of Wales (10 June 1688).[37] However, his relations with the king were strained and he played no part in the Nottingham uprising in November 1688 organised by his kinsman the Earl of Devonshire. Princess Anne arrived in Nottingham on 2nd December, while fleeing from her father, James II, so that the uprising is often viewed as comparable to Charles I raising the Royal Standard at Nottingham (1642). In fact Anne's appearance was not premeditated. Yet many

---

34 *Reresby*, 458, 461, 472, 474-6.

35 NUMD, Pwl 548.

36 Implied in NAO, DD4P/58/75a/51.

37 HMC, 159; *CSPD 1687-1689*, 208; NUMD, Pwl 658.

were pleased to see her. The mayor and alderman gave her two noble banquets and she 'seemed wonderful pleasant and cheerful'. However, the Corporation was required to contribute financially to her guard of honour. Celia Fiennes claimed that Anne was housed in the Ducal Palace. Whether Newcastle was consulted is not known. Anne left Nottingham on 9th December.[38] Newcastle refused to swear loyalty to the new monarchs, William and Mary.

On Easter Monday (13th April) 1691 Newcastle declared he was ill and took to his chamber. Hectored to the end by his wife, daughters and their husbands Henry, second Duke of Newcastle, 'most Illustrious Prince' died on 26th July 1691.[39]

For a decade Newcastle and his family had resided periodically in the Ducal Palace, certainly twice a year seemingly in late spring and late autumn and for shorter periods in the year. Its heyday as a residence was short-lived. It passed to Margaret, Henry's favourite daughter, who married John Holles, fourth Earl of Clare in 1690. Clare appears never to have used it: perhaps it reeked too much of Cavendish. Significantly after his death Margaret stayed at the Ducal Palace in June 1712.[40] Clare divided the Cavendish-Holles inheritance between his daughter Henrietta and his nephew Thomas Pelham who was not a blood relation of the second duke. When Pelham acquired the Ducal Palace (1717) it was 'a Bare shell', the windows were all broken, some of the furniture and all the Cavendish portraits had gone. The State Apartments were 'very magnificent but out of Repair'. Nevertheless the Ducal Palace remained impressive 'wth a pretty Impudent countenance' wrote Sir John Vanbrugh as he admired it in 1718.[41]

---

38 E. Gregg, *Queen Anne* (1980), 66-7; D.H. Hosford, *Nottingham, Nobles and the North* (1976), 110-18; A.C. Wood, 'Revolution of 1688 in the North of England', *TTS* 44 (1940), 72-104; *RBN* (1900) v, 354-5.

39 NUMD, Pw1 623.

40 *RBN* vi (1914), 55.

41 G. Webb, ed., *The Complete Works of Sir John Vanbrugh: the Letters* iv (1928), no. 97.

7

An Officer and an Antiquary: Major Hayman Rooke and the beginnings of archaeology in eighteenth-century Nottinghamshire

Sarah Speight

Hayman Rooke (1723-1806) is remembered in Nottinghamshire for his association with the Major Oak, named in his honour, and in recognition of his publications on Sherwood Forest.[1] Yet he deserves commemoration for his contribution to antiquarian and archaeological research in Nottinghamshire and Derbyshire, a contribution spanning some thirty years and including numerous articles in the journal *Archaeologia* as well as a legacy of sketches and note books now residing in archive offices and museums in Derby, Sheffield, Oxford

---

1 H. Rooke, *Descriptions and sketches of some remarkable oaks in the park at Welbeck* (1790); H. Rooke, *A sketch of the ancient and present state of Sherwood Forest, in the County of Nottingham* (1799); D.J. Bradbury, *Secrets of Sherwood* (1987), 11. My thanks to the staff of the Gloucestershire Record Office and to Jonathan Wallis and Ruth Bellamy who kindly allowed me access to the sketches and watercolours held by Derby City Museum, Derby Local Studies Library, and Sheffield Museum.

and London.[2] In 1965 Andrew Sherratt explored Rooke's career via a chronological survey of his correspondence and published works.[3] This essay seeks to place Rooke in a wider context by a thematic approach that uses aspects of his work, and particularly that on Roman Nottinghamshire, to illustrate contemporary standards in antiquarian research.

When Rooke died, on 18th September 1806 at his home at Mansfield Place in Mansfield Woodhouse, he had enjoyed a moderately successful military career, a respectable retirement as a 'local authority' on things ancient, and had served his community as justice of the peace and deputy lord lieutenant of Nottinghamshire.[4] Despite the onset of rheumatism in his sixties, he remained active and well-connected into his old age.[5] In 1793 he was to be found acting as an intermediary for the third Duke of Portland in a disagreement over rents on the Welbeck estate, and he was still on the bench in 1803 when the *Nottingham Journal* records him committing a man to the county gaol for rape.[6]

Although Rooke has not made the first rank of celebrated antiquarians such as William Stukeley, his careful researches and collaborations, the swiftness and regularity of his publication, and the range of his illustrations, have preserved information in many cases now lost. His finished sketches and watercolours range beyond the East

---

2 Rooke was a regular contributor to *Archaeologia* between 1776 and 1796. Details of the Rooke archive are on the HMC website at www.hmc.gov.uk/NRA; Sketches collated and bound by John Joseph Briggs in the nineteenth century are held in the D(erby)L(ocal Studies) L(ibrary) (Ref. 10627) along with copies of letters to Rooke from Samuel Pegge and others (MS 844). D(erby) C(ity) M(useum) holds over one hundred and sixty individual sketches and watercolours. Sheffield Museum holds four of Rooke's field notebooks in the Bagshawe collection, purchased in 1870 from a London bookseller.

3 A.G. Sherratt, 'Hayman Rooke, F.S.A. – An Eighteenth Century Nottinghamshire Antiquary', *TTS* 69 (1965), 4.

4 *NJ*, 27th September 1806; G(loucestershire) R(ecord) O(ffice), D1833, Memoir by Sir Henry Willoughby Rooke (1853); 'Obituary', *The Gentleman's Magazine*, September 1806, 886-7. Rooke is buried in the chancel of Mansfield Woodhouse parish church.

5 H. Rooke, 'Observations on the Roman Road and Camps in the neighbourhood of Mansfield Woodhouse', *Archaeologia* 9 (1789), 205.

6 NUMD PWF 8 159, Rooke to the third Duke of Portland, 24th December 1793; *NJ*, 10th December 1803.

Midlands to Cumbria, the Isle of Wight, and even to Newfoundland (visited in 1773). His subject matter goes beyond prehistory and the Romans to medieval churches and the great estates of Derbyshire and Nottinghamshire: Welbeck, Bolsover, Haddon Hall, Hardwick, Papplewick, Thoresby. In an eclectic mix of sketches he records 'stone quarries in a romantic valley near Mansfield', Sir Richard Sutton's 'Turkish kiosk' near Farnsfield, the 'Druid's Temple' at Skegby, the 'sole of King Henry VI and his spoon' and the 'remarkable fungus' growing amongst the carrots and parsnips in his own kitchen garden (attributed to his 'gipsum or alabaster compost').[7]

In his published works in *Archaeologia*, Rooke demonstrated a working knowledge not just of the classical historians but of more recent European scholars. For example, his collaborations with Samuel Pegge on Arbor Low reveal his familiarity with Olaf Worm (1588-1654), the Danish father of topographical survey and pioneer of illustration.[8] Rooke illustrated that late-eighteenth century mix of reason and romanticism. He sees the sacred groves of the Druids on Stanton Moor but was able, at Mansfield Woodhouse, to recognise, excavate and accurately plan a Roman villa.[9] He was slowly cognisant of stratigraphy and relative dating, but at a loss to grasp the length of human prehistory. In other words he was typical of his generation.

Rooke was named for his grandfather, Major Hayman Rooke (1653-1725), first cousin to Admiral Sir George Rooke (1650-1709) the captor of Gibraltar in 1704 during the War of the Spanish Succession.[10] His father, Brudenell Rice Rooke, used his connections to secure army commissions for his four boys: Hayman (b.1723), Robert (b.1727), Henry (b.1742) and Charles (b.1746). Hayman's sister Selina married

---

7 DLL 10627.

8 S. Pegge, 'Arbor Low with illustrations by Hayman Rooke', *Archaeologia* 7 (1785), 131-48.

9 H. Rooke, 'An Account of the remains of two Roman villas discovered near Mansfield Woodhouse, in May and October 1786', *Archaeologia* 8 (1787), 363-76; A. Oswald, 'A Re-Excavation of the Roman Villa at Mansfield Woodhouse, Nottinghamshire, 1936-39', *TTS* 53 (1949), 1-14.

10 For a genealogy of the Rooke family see GRO catalogue for D1833. The fullest account of the family is Pamela McInally, 'Resurrection Major: A Biography of Major Hayman Rooke (1723-1806), Soldier and Antiquarian', Unpublished BA dissertation, University of Sheffield, 2000.

John Douglas, Bishop of Carlisle and subsequently of Salisbury, one of his antiquarian correspondents. Rooke himself never married but his nephews continued the family tradition of army service; Lieutenant-Colonel John Charles Rooke died of wounds at San Jean de Luz in 1813, and General Sir Henry Willoughby Rooke served at Waterloo in 1815. After his retirement Rooke kept in touch with his serving brothers, exchanging letters with Bob at Fort Louis in Senegal, and Henry at Fort Washington. In 1778 Henry wrote to Hayman, the 'Dear Major', telling him of his recent appointment as Deputy Inspector General of Provincial Forces at Philadelphia.[11]

The Rooke family archive was put together in the 1850s by Rooke's nephew General Sir Henry Willoughby Rooke (1782-1869). Married to his first cousin Selina, daughter of Rooke's brother Henry, General Sir Henry had clear reasons for wishing to preserve the family's history and wrote a memoir of each uncle.[12] Brudenell Rice Rooke had two principal patrons: the Duke of Beaufort and Lord Bath. Both were prevailed upon to support young Rooke in his military career although his route was not a smooth one. Rooke entered the army at sixteen and received his first commission as ensign on 25th August 1737. He was soon made up to second lieutenant in General Bisset's Regiment of Foote. By March 1740 he was a full lieutenant, becoming a Captain Lieutenant in October 1748. In October 1755 he was a Captain in Lord Loudoun's Regiment and in 1760 he commanded the Loudoun grenadiers.[13] Much of his early service was spent in Ireland with occasional recruitment drives bringing him back to England.

In France Rooke acted as a Brigade Major under General Sir John Mordaunt during the Seven Years War. After the capture of the island of Belle Isle in 1761 it was Rooke who was deputed to bring the news back to England, reporting to Prime Minister Pitt and to King George III.[14] Yet letters reveal the desperate efforts of Brudenell Rice Rooke and Lord Bath to secure Rooke promotion. Their frustration led eventually to accusations that the Secretary at War, Charles Townsend, was deliberately holding him back. On 23rd July 1762 Townsend wrote

---

11 GRO, D1833 F2 44.

12 GRO, D1833.

13 GRO, D1833 F2 4 1-3.

14 GRO, D1833 F2 9.

in his own defence to Lord Bath: 'It was at my request he [the king] made Captain Rooke a Major, after the reduction of Belle Isle when General Hodgson returned the vacancy a blank to be filled up by me, and His Majesty at my solicitation, in opposition to competition gave the majority to Captain Rooke'.[15] Rooke was old to be a major, and soon after Belle Isle he appears to have retired from the army, perhaps as part of the general demobilization that followed the end of the Seven Years War. His final regiment, Colonel Grey's 98th Regiment of Foote, was probably a scratch-built unit intended for a short life-span (as indicated by the high regimental number). He subsequently settled in Mansfield Woodhouse, close to his army friend Sir William Boothby.[16]

The eighteenth century saw a switch in antiquarian interest from the ancient world of Rome and the near and middle east, to Britain's own past. This new focus upon domestic antiquity led to a growing interest in the local landscape and, in the words of Alain Schnapp, to an emerging 'vision of the earth not just as a potential treasure-chest, but as a repository of interpretable traces'.[17] Rooke was one of those attempting to interpret the traces.

Developments in antiquarian study can be related to eighteenth-century politics and the search for a national identity.[18] When the British Isles were in conflict, searching the past could be seen as a threat to central authority and an occupation best carried out alone and discreetly. But with the Union of Scotland and England in 1707, and then the passing of the Jacobite threat after Culloden in 1745, the ground became fertile for public and communal antiquarian activity. This represented nostalgia for more certain times, and an unconscious but politically useful search for a common heritage. The French Revolution and the beginnings of the Napoleonic wars halted British participation in the Grand Tour and denied access to the European classical heritage. This, plus the patriotism of war time, encouraged a focus on British antiquity.

Communal intellectual activity was stimulated by the emergence of national societies, notably the founding in 1660 of the Royal Society.

---

15 GRO, D1833 F2 11.

16 GRO, D1833, Memoir by Sir Henry Willoughby Rooke (1853).

17 A. Schnapp, *The Discovery of the Past* (1996), 213.

18 D. Douglas, *English Scholars* (1939), 23.

Although antiquarianism was marginal to its interests, the methodology it promoted was a precursor of the development of archaeology.[19] It stood for rational and orderly data collection, for measurement and illustration, for systematic description and publication. Rooke's own great-grandfather, the astronomer and geometrist Lawrence Rooke (1622-62), professor at Gresham College, London, was one of the founder members.[20] In 1717 the Society of Antiquaries of London was re-founded and, in 1770, launched its journal, *Archaeologia,* with a clear remit to record and illustrate British antiquities.[21] Alongside the emergence of national societies was an associated growth in reference materials; for example, in 1709 Roger Gale published an edition of his father's commentary on the Antonine itinerary, a source that Rooke knew well three generations later.[22] With the right climate, and the availability of books, country gentlemen could become antiquaries, if not progressive thinkers.

Yet, by the time that Rooke was elected a fellow of the Society of Antiquaries of London in 1775,[23] antiquaries were providing a source for ridicule and satire in the literary and popular press. They were lambasted as men of leisure obsessed with petty detail and dead bodies; men who accumulated vast amounts of raw data and did not know what to do with it, amassing eclectic collections of dodo eggs and ancient weaponry.[24] Rooke himself was the target of a friendly hoax in 1796.[25] Called to investigate a barrow on the land of the Gell family of Derbyshire, he found an urn cover inscribed *Gellius* and proceeded to publish in *Archaeologia* this remarkable discovery of the Roman ancestors of his good friend Phillip Gell of Hopton.[26]

---

19 M. Hunter, 'The Royal Society and the Origins of British Archaeology', *Antiquity* 65 (1971), 113-21.

20 *Dictionary of National Biography*, 17, (1921-2), 209-10.

21 J. Evans, *A History of the Society of Antiquaries* (1956); B.M. Marsden, *Pioneers of Prehistory: leaders and landmarks in English archaeology (1500-1900)* (1983), 7.

22 Rooke (1787), 374.

23 Sherratt, 4.

24 M. Myrone and L. Peltz, *Producing the Past: Aspects of Antiquarian Culture and Practice 1700-1850* (1999).

25 Marsden, 13.

26 *Archaeologia* 12 (1796), 3-4. The original illustrations and Rooke's interpretation can be found in DCM, DBYMU 2002 98/106-107.

The scorn of some eighteenth-century commentators has been matched in recent times by the belittling of the period by modern historians of archaeological thought. Stuart Piggott, for instance, noted a general collapse in intellectual standards within historical and antiquarian research from the 1730s: 'The necessity of an empirical approach was forgotten, the British foundation-myths were rewritten, philological speculation took on even more fantastic forms, and antiquarian studies became, understandably enough, discredited by serious scholars in other fields'.[27] Yet Rooke was part of an increasingly popular hobby taken up by retired officers, clergymen, gentlemen and landowners. The format of his articles in *Archaeologia* reveals the significant networks that connected these people throughout the country (including for instance the Reverend Brian Fausset and his work on Anglo-Saxon barrows in Kent 1757-1773), and enabled them to keep abreast of the latest findings. The articles are all structured as letters designed to be read out at meetings of the Society of Antiquaries; letters to local friends, respected authors of papers on related themes, possible patrons. In Derbyshire, Rooke collaborated closely with the Reverend Samuel Pegge, illustrating many of Pegge's own offerings to the Society or addressing letters to him. In Nottinghamshire, his discoveries at Mansfield Woodhouse merited an introductory letter, appended to Rooke's own letter to the Society, by the then Secretary at War, Sir George Yonge. Sometimes it seems as if the connections reinforced or created by these dedicatory epistles are more significant than the information contained. A good example is found in Rooke's letter to his brother-in-law John Douglas, Bishop of Carlisle, written on 23rd February 1788, describing Roman remains at Buxton:

> I must beg leave to acknowledge my obligations to Mr. Heaton, not only for his information of these Roman works near the Crescent, but for his politeness in reserving them for my inspection; the ground being intended to be planted and laid out in walks to complete those elegant improvements of public utility, carrying on by his Grace the Duke of Devonshire.[28]

---

27 S. Piggott, *Ruins in a Landscape* (1976), 21.

28 H.Rooke, 'Account of a Roman Building and Camp lately discovered at Buxton, in the County of Derby', *Archaeologia* 9 (1789), 140.

To be an antiquary was to be a gentleman and to belong to a gentleman's club. In 1792 Rooke was impressed by a clergyman's tenant who refused payment for providing labour to examine some strange pits near Crich. As the Reverend Mr Mason wrote to Rooke, 'my tenant thanks you for your kind offer, but desires no other gratification than the pleasure he has already received in being somewhat instrumental to elucidate this curious remain'.[29] The gentleman antiquary did not undertake physical labour himself. At Mansfield Woodhouse in 1786 Rooke employed three men to excavate the villa. His job, as the learned authority, was to supervise.

This is not a criticism. Rooke and his contemporaries engaged in antiquarian research as a hobby, a pleasant pastime. They took their researches seriously but they did expect to enjoy them, otherwise they would have turned to alternative pursuits. There can be detected the emergence of some sense of social duty, an idea that to investigate the past was to provide useful and inspiring knowledge that could ennoble mankind. Rooke never explicitly states his antiquarian aims but it is clear that he sought knowledge for its own sake, and also, where possible, knowledge to enable evaluation of the early ancestors of the Britons. His deductions were compromised by the then absence of relative dating tools but he knew his limitations, or perhaps expressed himself with standard literary humility: 'Where no certain conclusion can be deduced from scattered remains of remote antiquity, the probability of these I shall now leave to the consideration of a more learned antiquary'.[30] The sense of a mixture of learning and aesthetic pleasure comes through in Thoroton reviser John Throsby's account of his private view of the Mansfield Woodhouse villa and mosaic: 'The view of them was gratifying to both (Throsby and friend); but his account of these discoveries, and the accurate manner of his describing the different apartments of the villa, contributed, in a great degree, to the entertainment of a day set apart, in some measure, as a visit to that friendly gentleman'.[31]

---

29 H. Rooke, 'Description of Certain Pits in Derbyshire', *Archaeologia* 10 (1792), 114-17; DLL MS 844, 161-2.

30 H. Rooke, 'Letter to the Rev.Samuel Pegge', *Archaeologia* 12 (1796), 9.

31 J. Throsby, *Thoroton's Antiquities of Nottinghamshire* (1790-6, reprinted 1972), 2, 319n.

Rooke's skills as an illustrator were limited and his method inconsistent but he did value objects and places on an equal footing with documentary sources, thus revealing an increasingly archaeological mentality. A letter of 1760 describes him as 'something of an engineer and a pretty good draughtsman' and his early drawing of the fortifications of the island of Gorce survive.[32] He was capable of careful, measured illustration (particularly of artefacts), noting the angle of view, date of composition and recognising form, fabric and function. Yet many of his architectural drawings are little more than cartoons with poor detailing and perspective. In his 1792 account of Roman remains in Sherwood Forest, he was careful to provide measurements of all earthworks and artefacts described, and produced a plate illustrating Holly Hill, Arnold, Oxton camp and barrow with a section through the latter (p. 125).[33] Yet he was inconsistent with compass points and omitted any context map to support his arguments for inter-site relationships. Samuel Pegge deployed Rooke as his roving illustrator, constantly sending him instructions for sites to visit and people to contact.[34] He did not hesitate to tell his friend when a detail required correction.[35] Rooke's illustrations of 'Druidical remains' on Stanton and Hartle moors reflect the fewer certainties of prehistory. His 1782 plates of Rowtor and Bradley Rocks carefully note the angle of view but intensify the 'spiritual' quality of the site by the addition of human figures in contemplation (p. 126).[36] The majesty of the rocks is more important than any routine data that could be collected.

Ironically this concern to illustrate can be seen as retardant to the growth of archaeology. Peltz and Myrone have argued that publication *became* the reason for much antiquarian work and that journals were themselves 'objects of desire', treated with as much reverence as the

---

32 GRO, D1833 F2 4; D1833 F2 50.

33 H. Rooke, 'Roman remains in Sherwood Forest', *Archaeologia* 10 (1792), 378-85, plate 34.

34 See for example see Pegge's letters to Rooke dated 23rd December 1783, 18th May, 12th July 1784: DLL MS 844, 7-8.

35 Pegge corrects Rooke's drawing of Arbor Low in a letter of 22nd November 1780: DLL MS 844, 5.

36 H. Rooke, 'An Account of Some Druidical Remains on Stanton Moor and Hartle Moor in the Peak, Derbyshire, *Archaeologia* 6 (1782), plates 12-13.

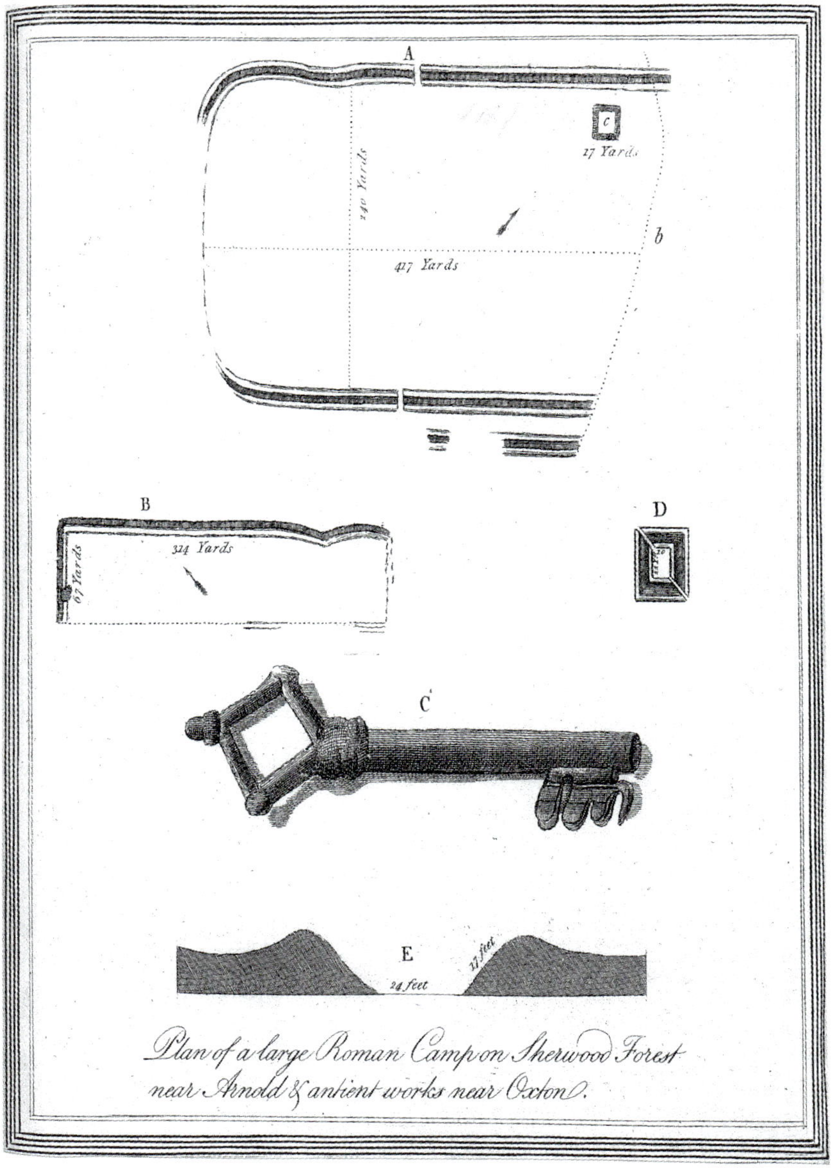

'Plan of a large Roman camp on Sherwood Forest near Arnold and ancient works near Oxton'. Scale of 100 Yards to an Inch. *Archaeologia* 10, Plate 34. Key: A Holly Hill, Arnold; Ab Continuation of earthworks beyond hedge; Ac Proposed site of *praetorium*; B Lovely Grange camp, Oxton; C Brass key found in Sherwood Forest; D Oxton barrow; E Section through Oxton barrow.

No. 1, South View of Rowtor Rocks. No. 2, S. W. View

No. 3 N. W. View of Rowtor Rocks. No. 4 Bradley Rocks.

A. South-west view of Rowtor Rocks, *Archaeologia* 6, Plate 12; B. Bradley Rocks, *Archaeologia* 6, Plate 13.

monuments and artefacts they illustrated.[37] The market demand for such expensive volumes suggests a wide public for antiquarian discoveries but, at the same time, perhaps a public that was satisfied by an 'armchair' participation. Once a monument or artefact had been engraved, was there less concern for its preservation? Perhaps but, at Mansfield Woodhouse, Rooke backfilled his site to protect it during harvest,[38] and secured viewing facilities to both safeguard the monument and allow for visitor access:

> The antiquary has to lament the frequent devastation made among the curious remains of antiquity (if I may be allowed to say) from a too eager desire for cultivation; but I have the satisfaction at this time to acquaint the Society, that the above mentioned *villa urbana* is upon the estate of John Knight, Esq. of Langold, who has obligingly expressed his intentions of erecting a building over the tesellated pavements for the inspection of the curious; the *villa rustica* and sepulchres, are on the estate of my worthy neighbour Mr. Mompesson, who is equally desirous of preserving the curious remains of Roman antiquity. It may be necessary to mention that the rooms with tessellated pavements are now filled up with earth, the only means of preserving them till the buildings can be erected.[39]

Rooke shared his contempories' preoccupation with the part rather than the whole where the part was most glamorous. Although he excavated and planned both the winged corridor house and the aisled hall at Mansfield Woodhouse, he saw the mosaic as the chief attraction of the site, sending up pieces of the painted plaster and tesserae to the Antiquaries by the 'Leeds Fly'.[40]

His generation were marked by their obsession with collecting. They wanted to own pieces of the past out of some aesthetic and ethereal thrill from connecting physically with the prehistoric and Roman

---

37 Myrone and Peltz (1999).

38 Sherratt, 5.

39 Rooke (1787), 376.

40 Rooke (1787), 363; GRO, D1833 F2 15, William Norris, Society of Antiquaries, to Rooke, 25th January 1787.

worlds. John Throsby described Rooke's house at Mansfield Place as 'enriched with a selection of things valuable to a mind like Mr. Rooke's'.[41] Rooke could recognise the portraits on Roman coins because he had a private museum or 'Cabinet of Curiosities' including coins of Vespasian, Marcus Aurelius, Antoninus Pius and Constantine.[42] In this he was conforming to current practice, although by doing so he may have been responsible for the loss of some important finds – for example the first-recorded Anglo-Saxon seax found in the county, excavated by Rooke at Oxton barrow in 1792.[43] He gave artefacts as gifts to friends and patrons, as recorded in the tantalising thanks of Lord George Cavendish in 1788: 'By the Duke of Devonshire's baggage I received your most obliging present, for which I am most exceedingly obliged....it will be a find of great amusement and information. The next time that I shall have a little time in Derbyshire, I shall indulge my curiosity in tracing these remains on the spot.'[44]

How many of Rooke's finds now sit unnoticed in private collections? However, the end of century does seem to mark a turning point in curating practice with a gradual shift towards the opening of public museums and a growing sense that the evidence of the past belonged to all. Susan Crane relates the process to a wider view of antiquity: 'The transition from one form of passionate historical collecting to another can be described as a shift from stories to histories, from fragments to totalities, from cabinets to museums'.[45] For those who followed Rooke, the key to changing attitudes and conceptions was the arrival of typology and stratigraphy (borrowed from the geologists); the adoption of the three-age system of stone, bronze and iron, and the application of this scheme to national collections, making antiquarian researches accessible to a wider public for the first time. Unfortunately, Rooke was not alive to read the work of Christian

41 Throsby, 2, 173-6, 319.

42 Rooke (1789), 205.

43 H. Jones and D. Knight., 'An Anglo-Saxon Seax from Rampton, Nottinghamshire', *TTS* 106 (2002), 47-51; H. Rooke, 'Roman Remains in Sherwood Forest, *Archaeologia* 10 (1792), 378-85.

44 GRO, D1833 F2 12, Lord George Cavendish to Rooke referring to antiquarian discoveries in Derbyshire, and to the king's illness, 1st December 1788.

45 S. Crane, 'Story, history and the passionate collector', in Myrone and Peltz, 187.

Jurgensen Thomsen (1788-1865) and hear of the opening of the Danish National Museum at Copenhagen in 1819.[46]

Rooke played a particularly important role in uncovering Roman Nottinghamshire. In 1786 he was directed to Northfields near Mansfield Woodhouse where stone and brick had been coming up in the ploughsoil.[47] He noted the local tradition of the 'country people' that there were 'fairy pavements' in the area. Setting his men to dig, Rooke soon identified Roman bricks about a foot beneath the surface, and had them followed until a range of rooms was discovered forming the *villa urbana*. As he recounted in his report to the Society of Antiquaries, he was then able to reason the function of many rooms by size, position, decoration and finds. The central reception room contained the fine mosaic, badly damaged in recent tree and shrub clearance. Rooke described this room as a summer *triclinium* (dining room) on the basis that it contained no obvious form of heating, and that the mosaic was not centrally positioned, thus allowing room for dining couches along one side. As more artefacts appeared, he recognised coins of Constantine and Claudius Gothicus and a number of radiate crowns; he identified roof *tegula* (tiles), an oil lamp and a ceramic strainer, the latter finds prompting him to identify a room set slightly apart from the main house as the kitchen. He made reasoned deductions and, crucially, he described his finds in measured and systematic detail, recording the dimensions of all rooms on his building plan. When his team returned for further investigation in October 1786 the discovery of a second building allowed him to apply the terminology of the Roman author Columella to his *villa urbana* (landowner's house) and *villa rustica* (servant's house). Although he continued to talk of two villas he related the buildings to each other in terms of status and function. He recognised later layers, seeing the signs of squatter occupation in his *villa rustica* and noting from the blocked flues: 'A proof that this part was inhabited, after the Romans left it, by persons of inferior rank who could not indulge themselves in all the luxeries of that people'.[48] He attempted reconstruction, (p. 130) restricting the *villa urbana* to ground floor only as he had found no evidence of a staircase.

---

46 G. Daniel, *The Origins and Growth of Archaeology* (1967), 90-2.

47 Rooke (1787), 363-76.

48 Ibid, 368.

Pen and ink drawing showing three reconstructed views of the Villas Urbana and Rustica, DLL 10627-26/2. Top: A sketch of the elevation of the east front of the Villa Urbana near Mansfield Woodhouse as it was supposed to have been originally, as no traces of a staircase could be found, the building probably consisted of one floor. The foundation walls of the front of the projecting buildings, at the ends were 5 feet thick, from whence there is reason to suppose they might have been designed for a little porch. (a) the Cryptoporticus. (b) the room over the Hypocaust. (c) the Kitchen. Middle: The west front of the Villa Urbana. (a) door in the Triclinium. (b) the Kitchen. Bottom: The south and west fronts of the Villa Rustica. (a) the entrance at the west front, which faces the Villa Urbana at 10 yards distance. (b) servants rooms. (c) the court for exercises. (d) the hot bath and sudatorium over the hypocaust. (e) the cold bath.

He tried to contextualise the site by linking it to a lost Roman road: 'Some old men in the village remember having seen some remains of it, but now there are no traces of it left'.[49] Rooke needed visible remains. If the traces were invisible and the location unknown he lacked the skills to search.

Via the 'fairy pavement' tradition, Rooke uncovered a villa estate in an area of west Nottinghamshire where villas were rare. He was unable to reconstruct the villa landscape but the subsequent re-excavation by Adrian Oswald in the 1930s, and the re-assessment of recent writers, has pointed to the significance of the site.[50] Oswald's excavation revealed late-first-century timber structures (identified as a Romano-British village) and traced the evolution of the site from a series of round huts to a fourth-century stone villa. Although Rooke had removed dating evidence from the uppermost occupation levels, Oswald was impressed by the accuracy of his plan and proceeded to work down to undisturbed layers.[51]

The discovery of the villa was promptly notified to the Society of Antiquaries and samples despatched to London. The Society was impressed and decided to hasten publication of Rooke's letter and his illustrations 'so as to gratify the publick curiosity with as little delay as possible'. Secretary Norris wrote to Rooke in January 1787:

> Your very curious account of the two Roman villas and other antiquities, illustrated with elegant drawings and specimens of the tessellated pavements and stuccoed walls....came safe to hand, and with as little damage, as the friableness of the stuccoed specimens, and mode of carriage could be supposed to admit, such excellent caution was offered in the arranging and packing them up.[52]

The excitement of the Mansfield villa pushed Rooke into a more systematic search for Roman occupation in Nottinghamshire and to further despatches to London. He was becoming the east midlands

49 Ibid, 374.

50 Oswald, 1-14; M. Todd, *The Coritani*, (1991), 90-1.

51 Oswald, 1.

52 GRO, D1833 F2 15, William Norris, the Society of Antiquaries, to Rooke, 25th January 1787.

correspondent for *Archaeologia*. His brother-in-law, the Bishop of Carlisle, told him in March 1788: 'I can assure you that any thing that comes from you is much attended to at Somerset Place, and you are considered as one of our most useful members'.[53]

Considering his military background, it seems surprising that Rooke did not assume a military role for the Mansfield Woodhouse villa until directed into such an enquiry by Sir George Yonge. Following the initial discovery Yonge initiated a correspondence with Rooke that continued for several years, and he became a vicarious antiquary via Rooke.[54] In 1789 Rooke published an article on the Roman roads and camps around Woodhouse, with an introductory letter by Yonge.[55] Yonge believed the Mansfield Woodhouse villa to be the residence of a Roman military commander and anticipated that his camp would be nearby with a connecting road. He encouraged Rooke to look for the Roman military presence in Nottinghamshire and pressed the Society of Antiquaries to endorse the work, concurring with Rooke that the Society needed to be far more pro-active and move beyond the mere publication of 'the labours of others'.[56]

Rooke subsequently explored a variety of other sites in the Mansfield area: Whinney Hill, Pleasley Park, Sookholme, Oxton, and Ramsdale Park.[57] The surviving sites have since been re-evaluated and Rooke's classification as Roman often altered to Iron-Age or Anglo-Saxon. However, in some cases, his record is all that survives. In 1792 he published his third article on Roman sites in Nottinghamshire and demonstrated the development of his methodology in a reasoned classification of Holly Hill:

> My informant, an old farmer at Arnold, assured me that he remembers the camp complete, extending a long way into the adjoining field, and that he is certain it was above twice the length

---

53 GRO, D1833 F2 17, John Douglas, Bishop of Carlisle, to Rooke, 8th March 1788.

54 Sherratt, 6-9, 12, 14.

55 Rooke (1789), 205.

56 Rooke (1789), 193-4; Copies of Yonge's letters to Rooke can be found in DLL MS 844.

57 D.J. Bradbury, *Mansfield Woodhouse Vol.1, The Villa and the Vale* (1990), 10-26.

> of what is now distinguishable. He likewise told me he heard his father say that, when he was a boy, this work was pointed out to him as a large Roman camp. This is the only traditional account I could procure; but it is sufficient to strengthen my conjecture, that it was the principal camp of the main body of the Roman army in these parts.[58]

His conjecture was strengthened by local folklore but was not formed solely by it. He noted the double ditch and *vallum* of the site, the likely position of a square *praetorium* (commanding officer's residence) at the highest part of the camp, and the almost linear relationship of Holly Hill to other 'exploratory' Roman camps at Oxton, Combs and Hexgrave (p. 125). Rooke used local contacts to inquire after Roman coin finds in the area, in this case unsuccessfully: 'But I could not find out in whose possession they now are, notwithstanding the obliging exertions of my learned friend Dr Oakes to procure every information relative to antiquities near Arnold that could be any ways serviceable to me in my researches'.[59]

He was trying to find supporting evidence for his Roman identification. Where possible he classified by analogy, as in the case of a key pronounced Roman by its green patina and resemblance to a key found at Montfauçon in France (C on p. 125).[60] His reconstruction of the Roman tomb found close to the villa at Mansfield Woodhouse rested both on the surviving fabric and upon a tomb found near York in 1768 and previously published in *Archaeologia*.[61] His identification of the Combs camp as Roman was disputed by a fellow antiquary but Samuel Pegge came to his support, publishing a Roman coin found near the camp in the *Gentleman's Magazine* and observing that 'it admirably confirms your conjecture'.[62]

The term 'archaeology' was not used in Rooke's day and did not become common in Britain until the second decade of the nineteenth century, when new ideas from Scandinavia and the adoption of relative

---

58 Rooke (1792), 378-85; DLL MS 844, 71.

59 Rooke (1792), 380.

60 Ibid, 380-1.

61 DLL 10627-22/1.

62 G. Daniel, *150 Years of Archaeology* (1975), 25.

dating techniques helped form a new branch of knowledge. Rooke was a true antiquarian with his wide-ranging interest in all things and all periods. He had only the most rudimentary understanding of stratigraphy, as when he recognised the squatter levels at the Mansfield Woodhouse villa. The startling contrasts between his observations on prehistory in Derbyshire, and upon the Roman period in Nottinghamshire, show that, like his peers, he went astray into Piggott's world of myth when the prop of historical record was pushed away.

Yet, like his peers, he was a polymath. Numismatics, epigraphy, philology, anthropology: aspects of all disciplines can be seen in his attempts to understand material culture and British prehistory. Excluding the Gell episode, he was liberated from the old search for family ancestors. He stumbled when without the historical record, but he made the attempt, unlike Dr Johnson who famously declaimed: 'All that is really known of the ancient state of Britain is contained in a few pages. We can know no more than what old writers have told us'.[63]

Rooke could not understand the remains of prehistory, but he knew they had a story to tell: 'By the number of Druidical remains on Stanton Moor, we may reasonably suppose this place to have been inhabited by the Druids. Here are temples, caves, rock bastions, rocking stones, rock idols and cairns. Their sacred groves have long since given way to cultivation, but their more durable monuments have stood the ravages of time, and remain as helps to illustrate their history.'[64]

With Roman Britain he was on safer ground. Rooke used the literary and historical sources to provide explanations for the sites and monuments he saw. The Roman author Columella explained Mansfield Woodhouse to him but he recognised that the archaeology had a primary value, hence the care taken over his plan and the illustrations of artefacts. At Mansfield he could pin his discoveries to a historical chronology and move from mere identification to interpretation. He could date the site via coin finds; he could classify sites, monuments and artefacts. He could draw the occasional inference, as in his comment upon post-Roman occupation at Mansfield. In prehistoric

---

63 DLL MS 844, 78, Samuel Pegge to Rooke, 8th July 1790.

64 H. Rooke, 'An Account of Some Druidical Remains on Stanton Moor and Hartle Moor in the Peak, Derbyshire, *Archaeologia* 6 (1782), 115.

Derbyshire he had un-dateable evidence and, as a result, his work tended towards the speculative and the derivative. This is shown by his illustrations.

Rooke was a scientist in the eighteenth century sense of being a master of systematised knowledge in several fields. His work included publications on the flora and fauna of Sherwood and Saucey Forests, as well as metereological treatises and historical pieces for the *Gentleman's Magazine*.[65] His observations of weather patterns brought him the friendship of Lord Middleton of Wollaton, and of Erasmus Darwin's friend Mrs Seward of Lichfield who wrote thanking him for a copy of his metereological register in 1805: 'It is pleasing to examine records of this ever varying climate, to compare its past influences, and to be enabled to calculate upon the immediately ensuing weather from the experience and observations of so accurate a mind'.[66]

In Nottinghamshire, Rooke was an early and important contributor to the growth of an archaeological record.[67] Thoroton's 1677 *Antiquities* was singularly lacking in archaeology,[68] and although William Stukeley sketched the Roman Fosse Way sites of *Ad Pontem* and *Crococalana* in 1722 little else appeared until Rooke's work late in the century.[69] He also acted as 'archaeological consultant' to John Throsby for his revised edition of Thoroton in the 1790s.[70]

Rooke was a collector and an aesthete with 'archaeological' thoughts. He discovered and he speculated. He disseminated his ideas via print at both the scholarly and more popular ends of the market –

---

65 H. Rooke, *A Metereological Register, kept at Mansfield Woodhouse, in Nottinghamshire* (1795), Continuations published annually until 1804/5; Rooke (1790); Rooke (1799); H. Rooke, *A Description of the Great Oak in Salcey Forest in the County of Northampton*, 1797; H. Rooke, 'Revolution House', *The Gentleman's Magazine* 59 (February 1789), 124-5.

66 GRO, D1833 F2 22, 23, Lord Middleton to Rooke, 6th February 1796, and Mrs. Seward to Rooke, 14th December 1805.

67 R.M. Butler, 'Archaeology in Nottinghamshire – Achievements and Prospects', *TTS* 58 (1954), 1-20.

68 A. Henstock, 'Nottinghamshire', in C.J. Currie and C.P. Lewis, eds., *A Guide to English County Histories* (1994), 315.

69 S. Piggott, *William Stukeley: An Eighteenth-Century Antiquary* (Revised edn. 1985), 162.

70 Throsby, 2, 319; Sherratt, 14-15.

Archaeologia to the *Gentleman's Magazine*, a monthly that covered every aspect of eighteenth-century life. His wide-ranging textual referencing, his collaborations with Samuel Pegge and the interconnections of his local contacts and correspondents show him at the early stages of the process that would produce the county societies of the nineteenth century. He represents the country-dwelling gentry that would move antiquarianism from a lone to a communal pursuit.

Major Hayman Rooke was a soldier, a gentleman, and an antiquary. If his military background prepared him for organised study, his membership of the Society of Antiquaries and his association with like-minded members of the gentry and aristocracy slowly propelled him from the study of the past for aesthetic reasons towards the search for knowledge. His surviving works represent perfectly the polarities of eighteenth-century thought; reason in the Romans and romanticism in the Druids. The accident of discovery and visible remains also meant that whereas in Derbyshire his investigations might produce little of continuing academic value,[71] his Roman studies in Nottinghamshire have left a corpus of information of continuing relevance to the history of the county.

---

71 In 2003 English Heritage used Rooke's illustrations to help them restore the landscape around the Nine Ladies stone circle: Jonathan Wallis, *pers. comm.*

8

Edward Trollope, the Archbishop's Palace, and the Founding of the Diocese of Southwell in 1884

John Beckett

In the Great Hall of Southwell Minster today in pride of place above the mantelpiece is a portrait of Dr Edward Trollope, Bishop of Nottingham. Since the Anglican diocese of Southwell covers the county of Nottingham, but there is no Bishop of Nottingham (although there is a Roman Catholic bishop of this title), Trollope seems to be an anomalous figure from a world which has now passed away. Consult the *Dictionary of National Biography* however, and you may be surprised to find that Trollope is attributed virtually sole responsibility for founding the diocese of Southwell in 1884: 'the new see of Southwell ... in great measure owed its formation to Trollope's exertions and munificence, he himself raising £10,000 towards the fund'.[1] In fact this is not entirely accurate. He was undoubtedly the principal fund raiser for the project, but his unique contribution was in the restoration of the Archbishop's Palace in Southwell. Who was Trollope, and how did he come to play such a key role at Southwell?

Edward Trollope was a Lincolnshire man. Born in 1817, he was the sixth son of Sir John Trollope, Baronet, of Casewick, Lincolnshire,

---

1 *Dictionary of National Biography*, 19 (1917), 1170.

by his wife Anne (Thorold) of Cuxworth. Trollope was a man of independent financial means. He became rector of Leasingham in 1843, and his household in 1851 included a footman, a groom, a gardener, a lady's maid, a nurse, a kitchen maid and a house maid. Grace, his first wife, was the daughter of a baronet, Sir John Palmer, and the eldest of Trollope's two daughters married a baronet. Trollope was in the classic Victorian tradition of the gentleman-scholar-parson.[2]

Trollope was a firm supporter of the Gothic Revival. He provided all but 10 per cent of the £1,000 needed to restore Leasingham church when he arrived there in 1843, and he insisted on adopting the moralistic and stylistic concerns of the Oxford Movement. At Leasingham he discovered 'almost every conceivable mischief has been wrought' when he became rector, but he prided himself on making changes such that 'now, even the parishioners of Leasingham can scarcely recognise their old degraded place of worship in its present greatly enlarged and beautiful condition'. He helped to found the Lincoln Diocesan Architectural Society of which he was the driving force from the mid-1850s.[3] An obituary in *The Times* following his death in 1893 described Trollope as 'an archaeologist of considerable repute devoting particular attention to the churches of Lincolnshire'. According to the *Stamford Mercury* 'he was for a long time the life and soul of the Lincolnshire and Nottinghamshire Archaeological and Architectural Society, and he was ever ready to give a helping hand to others in popularising and preserving the antiquities of his native county'. It added that he was 'an excellent organizer', but only 'a fairly effective preacher'.[4]

Trollope retained the rectory of Leasingham until his death in 1893, but in 1867 he was appointed Archdeacon of Stow within the diocese of Lincoln, and it was in this position that he first became involved in the creation of a new diocese of Southwell. Nottinghamshire was an archdeaconry within the archdiocese of York, until in 1837 it was

---

2 I am grateful to Sheila Stevens of Leasingham for providing this background information in respect of Trollope.

3 Terence R. Leach, 'Edward Trollope and the Lincoln Diocesan Architectural Society', in C. Sturman, ed., *Some Historians of Lincolnshire* (1992), 13-26.

4 *The Times*, 11th December 1893; *Stamford Mercury*, 6th November 1863, 15th December 1893.

transferred to the already large diocese of Lincoln. This was never likely to be either a satisfactory or a permanent arrangement. In 1852 Bishop Jackson of Lincoln told the Ecclesiastical Commissioners that his diocese was too large, and urged them to create a separate diocese for Nottinghamshire,[5] and three years later the Cathedrals Commission recommended in its third report that Lincolnshire and Nottinghamshire should be separate dioceses. Such pleas were largely wasted since government support for diocesan sub-division was not forthcoming in the mid-Victorian years.[6]

It was accepted at Westminster in 1869 that, in view of the pressure on some diocesan bishops, unrepealed legislation from Henry VIII's reign could be reactivated to permit the appointment of suffragan bishops. Within a few months of his enthronement at Lincoln in 1869 Bishop Christopher Wordsworth petitioned the Crown for the appointment of a suffragan bishop of Nottingham within his diocese. Nottingham was chosen because it was one of the towns named in unrepealed legislation from Henry VIII's reign as places from which suffragans might take their titles, but the implication was obvious - the suffragan was to have responsibility for the archdeaconry of Nottingham, effectively Nottinghamshire.[7] Henry Mackenzie, Archdeacon of Nottingham, was consecrated suffragan bishop of Nottingham in St Mary's on 2nd February 1870.[8] The consecration of a Bishop of Nottingham in the cathedral-like church of St Mary's, albeit a suffragan, was a portentous event. Bishop Wordsworth accepted that 'the appointment of a bishop suffragan, with a title derived from it, may be expected to lead to ... a bishop of its own'.[9]

---

5 Bishop Jackson was quoted in the *Guardian*, 6th June 1883.

6 A. Burns, *The Diocesan Revival in the Church of England* (1999), 192-205.

7 Bishop Wordsworth's argument for a suffragan at Nottingham is set out in BL, Additional MSS, 44,346, f. 384.

8 *NJ*, 4th February 1870; John Henry Overton and Elizabeth Wordsworth, *Christopher Wordsworth, Bishop of Lincoln, 1807-1885* (1888), 223-4; P.T. Marsh, *The Victorian Church in Decline: Archbishop Tait and the Church of England, 1868-1882* (1969), 101-2.

9 Overton, 302; Laura Ridding, *George Ridding: Schoolmaster and Bishop* (1908), 164.

In the years that followed, the idea of a separate diocese for Nottinghamshire continued to bubble below the ecclesiastical surface, and at the Lincolnshire Diocesan Conference on 13th October 1876 Archdeacon Trollope made his views plain. With Bishop Wordsworth in the chair, Trollope 'devoted a large portion of his paper to the advocating the erection of Nottinghamshire into a new see', and he went on to announce a fund raising scheme designed to make the case secure. The conference backed the plan unanimously.[10] In fact this scheme proved a non-starter, and when legislation was finally passed in 1878 paving the way for the creation of a new diocese in the Midlands it was proposed that Derbyshire should be taken from the existing diocese of Lichfield, and Nottinghamshire from Lincoln, to form the new ecclesiastical territory. Southwell Minster was to be the cathedral.

Trollope was by now Bishop of Nottingham. In the summer of 1877 Henry Mackenzie retired as suffragan Bishop of Nottingham as a result of ill health.[11] His successor might have been expected to be Canon Francis Morse, the vicar of St Mary's, whose candidature had been unsuccessful in 1870. In fact, Bishop Wordsworth recommended Trollope, who was consecrated suffragan bishop of Nottingham at Westminster Abbey on 21st December 1877. Somewhat surprisingly, hardly anyone from Nottingham attended. Even Wordsworth was absent, as the event coincided with a presentation in Nottingham to Mackenzie on his retirement.[12] According to the high church *Guardian* considerable regret was expressed in Nottingham that Trollope had not been consecrated in St Mary's, like his predecessor, but the coincidence of events suggests a rather lukewarm local response to his appointment.[13]

Trollope immediately grasped the nettle over the new diocese. Wordsworth could hardly have chosen a better lieutenant for the task in hand, and he told Archbishop Tait of Canterbury in June 1879 that his suffragan had 'taken the most active part in this work in this

---

10 *Guardian*, 1st November 1876.

11 *D[erby] M[ercury]*, 15th August 1877.

12 *NJ,* 22nd December 1877.

13 *Guardian*, 27th December 1877, 1779.

diocese'.[14] Trollope devised what we would today term a development plan. He set financial targets for each county within the existing dioceses of Lincoln and Lichfield (Lincolnshire, Nottinghamshire, Derbyshire, Staffordshire and Shropshire) to raise the £70,000 required to establish the new diocese with a minimum endowment of £3,500.

Trollope may have set the targets, but the various counties showed rather muted enthusiasm when it came to meeting them. By 1883 fund raising had virtually come to a halt, and it was revived only when the Lord Mayor of London convened a meeting at the Mansion House on 1st June. On that occasion Archbishop Benson told the assembled company that Trollope was 'one of the best and one of the most devoted Suffragans ... a man whose energy was only equalled by his liberality', and who on Wordsworth's behalf was 'now doing the whole work of a bishop'.[15] Suitably impressed, Trollope was sufficiently reinvigorated to see the rest of the funding for the new diocese gathered in by the end of 1883.

How much Trollope contributed directly is not known, but as early as 1879 he had taken an alternative and, in the event, costly initiative. In June 1879, when the funding process was slowing down, he commented to Wordsworth that if the Ecclesiastical Commissioners were 'able and willing to restore the old Palace at Southwell of which a portion remains, this would, I believe, be considered to be equivalent to £500 a year of the £3,500 required for the endowment of the proposed new Bishopric'. In other words, the capital fund would need to be only £60,000 rather than the £70,000 proposed – hence, perhaps the assumption in the *Dictionary of National Biography* that he contributed £10,000 towards the new diocese. Trollope and Wordsworth attended a meeting of the commissioners 'and offered it as a contribution towards the endowment of the See of Southwell'. It was agreed that Trollope would buy the house and grounds 'with the view of presenting the property as an additional endowment for the new See of Southwell', and that the completed palace could be conveyed back to the commissioners. The purchase was completed in December 1880 when the site was invested in four trustees:

14 L[ambeth] P[alace] L[ibrary], Tait Papers 253, f. 296.

15 *Guardian*, 6th June 1883.

Archdeacon Maltby, Rev. J.J. Trebeck, rector of Southwell, Rev. R.H. Sutton and Brant Broughton.[16]

The Archbishop's Palace at Southwell was an extensive range of buildings to the south of the Minster built on a courtyard plan during the fourteenth and fifteenth centuries for the Archbishops of York. The palace was started by Archbishop Thoresby c.1360 and completed by Cardinal John Kemp, who added the Great Hall c.1436. Cardinal Wolsey was among the archbishops who used the house. It was not systematically maintained after Archbishops of York ceased in the sixteenth century to use Southwell as one of several homes within their archdiocese. John Williams, who was translated from Lincoln to York in 1641, was the last occupant of the throne of York to be resident at Southwell. During the civil wars the palace was occupied in turn by combatants of both sides. Towards the end of the conflict the Scottish Commissioners used it as their quarters, and it was to them that Charles I formally surrendered in 1647. The palace was then given over to Parliamentary troops and it was soon uninhabitable. The lead was removed from the roofs and anything that could be made use of quickly disappeared. It was left open to the elements and soon became a ruin. Only the outer walls survived (now as the walled garden to the present Bishop's Manor).

The original west range, which included the Great Hall, was owned by the Chapter and kept in some sort of repair, although by the 1870s this was also dilapidated. During the eighteenth century a house was built within the walls of the old palace. This seems to have been used partly as a court house for Southwell magistrates, and partly as a girls' school. The Ecclesiastical Commissioners owned all the buildings on the site from 1840, but as far as they were concerned the accommodation (notably the eighteenth-century house) was not adequate to be the seat of a bishop.[17]

---

16 C[hurch of] E[ngland] R[ecord] C[entre], file 47749 part 1/8

17 H.F. Summers, 'Southwell Old Palace', *S[outhwell] D[iocesan] M[agazine]*, n.s. 8 (1935), 26, 50, 139, 158, 183. Another brief account, with pictures and a plan of the Old Palace, can be found in H. Gill, 'The Palace – Southwell', *TTS* 10 (1907), 73-6. CERO, file 47749 part 1/6; NAO, DD 223/1; *SDM*, 19 (1906), 39; n.s. 2 (1929), 157; 8 (1935).

The Archbishop's Palace, Southwell, showing the Great Hall, restored by Bishop Edward Trollope.

Trollope commissioned G.F. Bodley, the architectural high priest of the Oxford Movement, to undertake a partial restoration of the Great Hall. Bodley restored and furnished the banqueting hall, renewed the roof and windows and built the stone staircase at the east end. The work was undertaken with great care. The windows, for example, were restored using as much as possible of their original tracery, and then filled with rich glass bearing the arms of former occupants of the manor, and of ancient county families. Trollope's expectation was that these public rooms, added to the existing house on the site, would collectively provide accommodation fit for the bishop's residence.[18] Apart from the £1,600 he paid for the palace and the five acres of adjoining grounds, Trollope 'spent £3,655 9s 9d upon its partial restoration so that it has cost me altogether £5,255'.[19] Most of this seems to have been his own money, although he received help from others, including the Dowager Duchess of Cleveland. Archbishop Benson of Canterbury noted in June 1883 that the Palace had been 'restored by the liberality of the Bishop Suffragan, and handed over free of expense'.[20] Trollope certainly put a good deal of effort into the restoration work, and few observers doubted that it had been expertly undertaken.

Unfortunately the Ecclesiastical Commissioners proved difficult to please. In July 1883, shortly after the Mansion House meeting had reinvigorated fund raising, they began to express doubts as to whether they would accept the restored buildings as suitable accommodation for the bishop. When in October 1883 Trollope urged them to fulfil the agreement the commissioners responded that it was 'very doubtful' as to whether or not they would. The commissioners' objections were particularly frustrating because they came so late in the day. Sir George Pringle, on behalf of the commissioners, explained that if they were to accept the restored buildings as part of the endowment they needed to be 'in a present fitting condition', and already reconveyed to them for the purpose. The key phrase was 'fitting condition'. No one doubted

18 N. Summers, *A Prospect of Southwell* (1988 ed.), 56

19 *SDM*, 7 (1894), 6; *The Times*, 3rd January 1881; LPL, Benson Papers, vol. 100, f. 359.

20 *The Times*, 30th June 1880; 9th January 1884; *Guardian*, 6th June 1883.

that Trollope had spent a great deal of time and money, but his alterations were not considered sufficient as an upgrading of the existing property to 'make a sufficient dwelling place for the bishop'. Trollope had acted in good faith, and could reasonably claim to have been let down by the Ecclesiastical Commissioners at this late stage in the proceedings. Bishop Wordsworth, anxious to see his diocese divided, was distraught by this intransigence. He argued that the see should be founded immediately, and the commissioners should allow five years for a residence to be completed. Pringle rejected this view.[21]

Ewan Christian, the Ecclesiastical Commissioners' architect who had for years been overseeing the refurbishment of the Minster, was asked to survey the house. However, the Commissioners made it clear in advance that a further £3,000 to £5,000 would be needed for restoration work 'before it is accepted as "a fitting residence" for the Bishop'. Unless the trustees of the Additional Home Bishoprics' Fund were willing to guarantee the availability of this sum for any work Christian might recommend, the bishopric could not be founded.[22]

It was clear to the Southwell promoters that there was no way round the Ecclesiastical Commissioners' objections, particularly when Christian pronounced the restored buildings to be inadequate for their intended purpose. He estimated that a further £9,000 was needed to pull down the existing eighteenth-century house and build an entirely new home 'in keeping with the architectural character of the ancient remains of the palace and the restored portion'.[23] Frustrated in their hopes, but anxious to have the diocese founded as quickly as possible, the Southwell promoters proposed to give a bond undertaking to raise sufficient capital within five years to yield an additional £500 a year on the endowment.[24] George Strutt of Belper helpfully gave £500 as an indication that funds would be forthcoming.[25] They then drew up plans for a new house.

---

21 BL, Additional MSS, 44, 484, fos. 287-96; CERO, file 47749, part 1/9-14.

22 *Official Year-Book of the Church of England* (1884), 277.

23 BL, Additional MSS, 44,485, f. 36.

24 *DM*, 16th January 1884.

25 *NJ*, 10th January 1884.

On 17th January 1884 a deputation from the Midlands arrived at the offices of the Ecclesiastical Commissioners for a meeting chaired by the Archbishop of Canterbury. Trollope, Archdeacon Maltby, the Secretary of the Additional Home Bishoprics Fund (Rev. Arthur Ingram), the Sub-Dean of Lincoln, and several 'trustees', came to report that the funding was complete and Southwell diocese could be founded. Knowing as they did that the episcopal residence would be a problem, they arrived armed with plans for a new house, which was to be built on the site of the old archiepiscopal palace within five years. They were willing, they claimed,

> to enlarge the existing remains of the old palace at Southwell in such a manner as to make the same, in the opinion of the Commissioners, a fitting residence for the Bishop, and the building is thereupon legally vested in the Commissioners to their satisfaction, the same will be accepted by the Commissioners as an equivalent for the additional £500 per annum of episcopal income.

The Commissioners accepted the plans, subject to the approval of Ewan Christian, but wanted greater security than a vague promise. After some argument it was agreed that a surety of £15,000 would need to be put up in terms of stocks and bonds redeemable as soon as the house was completed. Bishop Wordsworth, evidently foreseeing this eventuality, immediately pledged the required sum.[26] On 5th February 1884 the diocese was officially founded.

Trollope had been Suffragan Bishop of Nottingham since 1878, and was widely recognised both at the time and subsequently as the man who had made sure the new diocese came into being. Why then did he not become the first bishop? Trollope's position in 1884 was an unusual one. He was the only English suffragan whose responsibilities lay largely in an area (Nottinghamshire) which was about to be placed in a new diocese. This presumably gave him some hopes of the preferment, and his claims were certainly discussed in both London and Nottinghamshire,[27] but he did not have Wordsworth's backing.

---

26 *Official Year-Book of the Church of England* (1885), 256-7; CERO, 47749 part 2/ 1-2; *The Times*, 18th January 1884.

27 LPL, Benson Papers, vol. 17, f. 110.

Bishop Wordsworth wrote to the prime minister, W.E. Gladstone, in December 1883 with a long and rather platitudinous list of the qualities he thought would be needed in the first bishop of the new diocese. He thought it inappropriate to suggest names,[28] but others were less diffident. Lord Monson proposed his friend Dr Stirling, Bishop of the Falkland Islands, a training which the Lincolnshire landowner clearly considered ideal for an English diocese with a number of large industrial towns.[29] Wordsworth's son John, fearful that his father's reticence might be misinterpreted in Whitehall, told Gladstone that he knew 'there is one person that he would really like to see [at Southwell] the Warden of Keble College'. This was the Rev. Edward Talbot.[30] Canon Edmund Venables, Precentor of Lincoln, also favoured Talbot.

Some correspondents of the prime minister were simply fearful of candidates they had heard mentioned in the press. The *Nottingham Journal* carried an article on 5 January 1884 suggesting that 'the two names which will be sent to the Queen by the Prime Minister for the see of Southwell will be those of Canon Hole and the Hon. and Rev. E.C. Glyn. Either would be a good appointment, but the selection of Canon Hole would be immensely popular in the new diocese and would be universally approved'.[31] Two Nottingham evangelical clergymen, the vicars of Holy Trinity and St Andrews, wrote to Gladstone early in January 1884 to contradict the assertion about Hole.[32] Hole was also

---

28 BL, Additional MSS, 44,346 f. 433; LPL MS 2148, Wordsworth Papers, General Correspondence, Wordsworth to Gladstone, 23rd December 1883.

29 BL, Additional MSS, 44,484, f. 152.

30 BL, Additional MSS, 44,484, f. 283. Rev Edward Talbot (1844-1934) was the first warden of Keble (1869-88), and subsequently bishop of Rochester, Southwark and Winchester.

31 *NJ*, 5th January 1884. Rev. Samuel Reynolds Hole (1819-1904) was Vicar of Caunton, 1850-87, and prebendary of Lincoln from 1875. In 1887 he became Dean of Rochester. An enthusiastic huntsman, he was well known as a successful rose grower, as well as being a popular preacher and platform orator. He had referred to the possibility of his being raised to a bishopric in 1881, although apparently in jest: G.A.B. Dewar, ed., *The Letters of Samuel Reynolds Hole* (2nd edn., 1907), 85. There is no mention of such hopes in his various volumes of recollections, although *The Memoirs of Dean Hole* (1903) contained pen portraits of Wordsworth and Bishop King (his successor at Lincoln). The Hon. Rev. Edward Carr Glyn was Vicar of Kensington, and Honorary Chaplain to the Queen.

32 BL, Additional MSS, 44,485, f. 9.

the subject of a vitriolic denunciation by Canon Venables, but Venables was also vehemently opposed to Bishop Trollope's appointment. Neither Canon Hole, nor Bishop Trollope was, in Venables' view 'such as one looks for in a bishop of a new see'. Trollope he particularly singled out for criticism: 'with all his excellencies, unsparing of his time, his labour, his money, the kindest and most liberal of men, is a second rate man who will carry no moral weight. He should be liked, not looked up to, very far from being what a bishop should be, a head and shoulder fuller, morally and intellectually, than the diocese.'[33]

Whether this character assassination had any impact on Gladstone we do not know. Possibly Trollope was too old for the position. It had been dioceses in which illness or incapacity had prevented the bishop from carrying out his duty that had been loudest in supporting moves for a reform of the episcopate.[34] Trollope, born in 1817, was approaching his 67th birthday when the diocese was finally confirmed, and he would inevitably have been a stop-gap appointment. In the event, George Ridding, the first Bishop of Southwell was 56 (as was Edward King when he was appointed to Lincoln in 1885). In any case, the Church of England was reluctant to appoint senior local clerics to the position of first bishop.[35] Possibly Trollope had no designs on the position. He had, after all, lived all his life in Lincolnshire where he still held the rectory of Leasingham, and where he died in 1893.

In any case the Church of England preferred schoolmasters as bishops of new dioceses. Archbishop Benson has been head master of Wellington School before subsequently moving via Lincoln to be the first bishop of the diocese of Truro. Perhaps on his advice, in February 1884, Gladstone offered the bishopric to Dr George Ridding, headmaster of Winchester School. Gladstone told Wordsworth: 'I have both inquired and consulted a good deal about Dr Ridding, and I believe him to be one of those large minded men who will work on the one hand with great devotion and energy, on the other hand with a liberal and just regard to the various shades of sentiment and practice united in this commission of the Church'.[36] Ridding was consecrated

33 BL, Additional MSS, 44,485, f. 97.

34 O. Chadwick, *The Victorian Church* (1970), 343.

35 P. Morrish, 'Parish-Church Cathedrals, 1836-1931: Some Problems and their Solution', *Journal of Ecclesiastical History*, 49 (1998), 443-4.

36 LPL, MS 2148, Wordsworth Papers, General Correspondence, fos. 95-9.

bishop in St Paul's Cathedral on 1st May. The array of attendant bishops including Lincoln, Lichfield, and the suffragan bishop of Nottingham.[37]

Trollope's position now became anomalous for two reasons. First, he remained suffragan bishop of Nottingham, but *not*, as might have seemed logical, within the diocese of Southwell - in which position he would have been subject to Ridding - but within the diocese of Lincoln. In effect, he and Wordsworth together retired from Nottinghamshire once Ridding was appointed. Trollope remained active in Lincolnshire. In October 1884 he chaired the Lincoln Diocesan Conference in the absence of Wordsworth through illness, and when in December Wordsworth announced his resignation as of 25th March 1885 he passed all his episcopal duties immediately to Trollope. However, any hopes Trollope may have entertained of succeeding to Lincoln disappeared when Bishop King was appointed in 1885 following Wordsworth's death. Perhaps significantly, until 1884 Trollope was billed in the Lincoln Diocesan Conference proceedings as the Suffragan Bishop of Nottingham. From 1885 he was referred to as the Right Reverend the Lord Bishop of Nottingham, taking a title usually reserved for a diocesan bishop. He helped out in Southwell diocese for a while when Ridding was seriously ill in 1888, and consecrated St George's Church in the Meadows, Nottingham, on 12th June.[38] One of his obituaries in 1893 noted that 'of late years his Lordship had visited Nottingham occasionally but as will be understood in an altogether unofficial capacity'.[39]

The second reason Trollope's position was anomalous was that he owned Ridding's theoretical home. The agreement reached between the Ecclesiastical Commissioners and the Southwell delegation in January 1883 meant that approximately £9,000 had to be raised to complete the house in a manner which would satisfy Ewan Christian. A 'Building Committee' was set up, consisting of the Archdeacons of Derby and Nottingham, the Secretary of the Derbyshire committee, the Sub-Dean of Lincoln, and Canon Ingram. Their task was to raise funds

37 *Guardian*, May 1884, 688.

38 Ridding, *George Ridding*, 252; *SDM*, 1 (1888), 132; 7 (1894), 6.

39 Nottingham Local Studies Library, St Mary's 19th Annual Report, 5.

and at the same time to oversee the planning and building of the new episcopal residence. By the end of 1884 about £2,500 had been raised, leaving £6,500 outstanding.[40]

Meantime Bishop Ridding and his wife had to find temporary accommodation. They were obviously choosy since they 'found no possible house in Southwell, Nottingham, Derby, or elsewhere'. As a 'last hope' they visited Thurgarton Priory which 'to Dr Ridding's relief, proved to be remarkably well adapted to a Bishop's special wants'. This was a house of 1777 built on the ruins of Thurgarton Priory.[41] Ridding regarded this as a temporary move, but he soon came into conflict with the Building Committee over the plans being drawn up for Southwell. Put simply, he saw the Southwell residency project as an unfortunate diversion from his work of setting up the diocese. Southwell was virtually inaccessible by railway, and the fund raising required for the residence left him short of money for diocesan affairs. As one of his chaplains recalled many years later 'He always loved the Old Palace very dearly, and always delighted to have any gatherings there, but he lived at Thurgarton because he felt it much better generally for the diocese that he should do so'.[42]

Ridding's hostile attitude towards Trollope's project soon became abundantly clear to the Building Committee. In December 1884 Ridding told Arthur Ingram that

> I think the true thing is to raise the additional £500 and leave me to find my own house. When politics are more settled the diocese would probably find a Palace for a future Bishop but I really dont think the diocese will help the least now towards a Palace at Southwell where a Bishop would have nothing to do and would be inaccessible. I dont think the people whose imagination is taken by the idea of restoring the Palace at Southwell will be gratified by such a bald house as the one planned.[43]

---

40 *Southwell Diocesan Church Calendar* (1885), xiii.

41 Mr Hutchinson of Epperstone offered to rent out Thurgarton Priory as a temporary home for the bishop: CERO, file 47749, part 2/4.

42 H.F. Summers, 'Southwell Old Palace', *SDM*, n.s. 8 (1935), 26, 50, 139, 158, 183.

43 LPL, Benson Papers vol. 17, f. 125.

Nor did he leave it at this, writing in the first edition of the *Southwell Diocesan Church Calendar* that 'the natural place for the Bishop's residence is the chief town', and requesting freedom to live where he considered most appropriate.[44]

Not surprisingly Trollope was offended. Ingram pointed out to Ridding that 'I need hardly say that the throwing over of the house plan would deeply pain the Bishop of Nottingham'. He then forwarded the tetchy correspondence to the Archbishop of Canterbury, and was gratified to find Benson 'adheres to the view taken by the promoters of the Southwell Bishopric from the first, viz that the Bishop's house ought to be built at Southwell'.[45] Ridding was not to be put off easily, and he told the Southwell Bishopric Endowment Fund in January 1885 that 'I think the Ecclesiastical Commissioners have been misguided in introducing any special clause about the Southwell Palace. Southwell has been the idea of a special and limited though leading set of contributors; its appeal to historic imagination is a delusion; its situation for present use absurd.'[46] It was certainly not a point of principle that the new bishop should live in Southwell. The bishops of Durham lived at Bishop Auckland, of Carlisle at Rose Castle, and of Winchester at Farnham. In theory, there was no reason why the Bishop of Southwell should not have lived in Nottingham or Derby, or at another location within the diocese - even Ilkeston, a border town proposed by Ridding[47] - but Southwell was where the traditionalists wanted him to be.

Conflict over the residence came to a head at the first diocesan conference for the new diocese, held in Nottingham in October 1885. Ridding gave a long speech in which he reiterated his objections to Southwell. His principal concerns were that it was not on a main railway line, and that a bishop should live among his people and be able to travel to all parts of his diocese with ease. A few of the subsequent speakers sympathised with the bishop's position. Canon Andrews suggested that he might compromise and have residences in Derby and Nottingham; Canon Morse thought he should live 'at or near the largest centre of population in his diocese'; and Canon Trebeck

44 *Southwell Diocesan Church Calendar* (1885), xiv.

45 LPL, Benson Papers vol. 17, fos. 125-7; vol. 28, fos. 78, 80.

46 LPL, Benson Papers vol. 17, f. 127.

47 *DM*, 21st October 1885.

proposed that he should be allowed to live where he wanted. But the mood of the meeting was against Ridding. The Derbyshire contingent thought he was angling to live in Nottingham, which they were unwilling to accept, and a motion put by Canon Hole to the effect that the bishop was required to live in Southwell was 'carried amidst considerable applause'.[48] Ridding had lost, but no house was built and he stayed in Thurgarton. After all, as Laura Ridding later recalled 'a railway station was within ten minutes' walk, on a good line, with an adequate supply of trains by which the Priory could be reached by noon from all parts of the diocese'.[49]

The impasse which ensued was clearly awkward for all parties. First, came the financial problem. In January 1884 Wordsworth had pledged a bond of £15,000 to cover the five year term during which the proposed house was to be built. Wordsworth died in 1885 with no progress having been made, and the Ecclesiastical Commissioners demanded that the £15,000 should be raised. This was not achieved until 1889-90, just prior to the point at which the bond would otherwise have been forfeited in the absence of a house.[50] Laura Ridding claimed that the need to raise this money cut across her husband's plans for setting up the machinery of the new diocese, and in some frustration he paid off the final £3,600 himself.[51] Meanwhile Trollope was left with his white-elephant, a restored Great Hall which was neither home for the bishop nor required by the Ecclesiastical Commissioners. Towards the end of 1890 he offered it to Ridding as property for the bishopric.

Not surprisingly, the offer caused Ridding 'much embarrassment', although 'I have never doubted that it would come some day'. Through Archbishop Benson, Ridding referred the matter on to the Ecclesiastical Commissioners who, rather disingenuously, offered to accept it as 'an addition to the endowments of the See without regard to any possible future use'.[52] It was an offer with which Trollope was not impressed.

---

48 Ibid. Ironically, the Conference was meeting in Nottingham because it was far more accessible than Southwell.

49 Ridding, 167-8.

50 It did at least mean that eventually the Ecclesiastical Commissioners had to take responsibility for funding the new house: CERO, file 47749 part 3/1-3, parts 4-5.

51 Ridding, 160, 163-7.

52 LPL, Benson Papers, vol.100, f. 356.

He asked for the return of the £1,600 he had spent purchasing the old Palace, offering to allow his outlay on restoration to represent 'my gift towards the see of Southwell'. The Commissioners refused his request despite the fact, as Trollope pointed out, that 'it is not purchasing of the Southwell Palace I am seeking for on the part of the Commissioners, but a repayment of my purchase money on the return of that property very greatly increased in value, for which increase I do not require one farthing'. When this failed to move them, he made the only retort he could: 'I think I shall retain the property for the future, as it will be sure to be wanted either for an Episcopal residence or a Diocesan College in due course of time, and indeed was fixed upon as a suitable site for the first Diocesan College before it was finally decided to establish it at St Augustine's Canterbury'.[53] It was an unsatisfactory end to a generous offer by Trollope. He died in 1893, and the trustees then formally made over the Palace to the see. Ridding subsequently spent £1,500 on its drainage, heating and water supply, and on making it 'convenient for dispensing hospitality on the occasions of his Chapter meetings, ordinations, committees, visitations, and great diocesan festivals'.[54]

Bishop's Manor, the home today of the Bishop of Southwell, was commissioned in 1905 for Bishop Edwyn Hoskyns, second bishop of the new diocese. The foundation stone was laid in March 1906, and the architect was Christian's partner W.D. Caröe:

> After careful consideration and consultation with the clergy and laity, the Bishop has decided that Southwell shall be the Bishop's home. There are, without doubt, disadvantages attending this decision, but there would be others, equally great, wherever the Bishop lived.... The new house is planned to incorporate the ancient hall, the only complete part of the ruin, which was restored by Bishop Trollope in 1884, as well as other parts of the ruined palace. The Architect ... has planned the new residence in such a manner that almost every stone of historic significance will be reverently incorporated in the new edifice.[55]

---

53 LPL, Benson Papers, vol. 100, f. 359.

54 *SDM*, 19 (1906), 39; NAO, DD 223/1, Notes on Bishop's Manor.

55 Summers, 'Southwell Old Palace'; NAO, DD 223/1

The cost was estimated at £7,000. Caröe turned the surviving north, south and east outer walls of the old palace into a walled garden. The building was dedicated on 18th June 1905. It is not regarded as a particular success: Norman Summers has written of Bishop's Manor that 'The new house is an undistinguished building with the cottagey character popular in the early years of the present century'. He accepted however that Caröe had made a skilful job of incorporating the house within the west side of the old ruins which occupied the site of the original great hall, and of restoring the porch and the arches which once led to the service rooms and the detached kitchen.[56]

Yet symbolically this was an important moment: a bishop was once again living on the site of the old archiepiscopal palace built in the fifteenth century. 'This ancient house', ran the (Latin) inscription in the porch of what was the new Manor, 'once a retreat of the Archbishops of York, was restored from the ruin and desolation of more than two hundred and fifty years, to the glory of God and the benefit of his brethren, by Edwyn, Second Bishop of Southwell'.[57] Bishop Trollope, meantime, was commemorated through his portrait in the Great Hall, and the Archbishop's Palace of which he was so proud lives on as a place for gatherings of church people in Southwell.

---

56 Jennifer M. Freeman, *W.D. Caröe: his architectural achievement* (1990), 172-3.

57 Summers, *Prospect*, 56.

58 Summers, 'Southwell Old Palace'.

9

Unhealthy Areas in Victorian Nottingham: the Rookeries

Ken Brand

On 3rd February 1873 Edward Seaton, MD was appointed Nottingham's first Medical Officer of Health.[1] He was selected from thirty-four candidates and as agreed in Council earlier he was to receive a commencing salary of £400 per annum. Such an appointment was obligatory under the terms of the Public Health Act of 1872. The town might well have had a medical officer as early as 1858 but the Local Government Act of that year made the post optional. In fact after an initially favourable response the Council later 'Resolved to defer for consideration the appointment of an Officer of Health'.[2] On 11th December 1871 subsequent to an outbreak of smallpox the Sanitary Committee appointed Dr E.B. Truman, Public Vaccinator, as Medical Officer of Health (temporary).[3] Once Dr Seaton took up his full-time position Dr Truman continued as the town's Analyst.

There was much to occupy Seaton, starting with an inspection of the town's schools.[4] Soon he was working in unison with M.O. Tarbotton the Borough Engineer. Their first joint report, on the insanitary conditions of certain houses in the Meadows, was presented

---

1 RBN, IX, 224, Reports to Council, 3rd February 1873.

2 Ibid, 139.

3 Ibid, 218, Report of Sanitary Committee.

4 E. Seaton, *A Report on the Sanitary Condition of the Borough of Nottingham* (1873). This 56-page report was prepared within months after his appointment.

to the council on 8th October 1874.[5] At that time Seaton could act only within the limited powers of the Artisans and Labourers Buildings Act 1868 - the Torrens Act - which gave local authorities the power to demolish individual houses lacking drainage or water closets. He was well aware that the clearance of Nottingham's slum housing could never be completed in this fragmentary way. Thus when the Artisans and Labourers Dwellings Improvement Act 1875 gave local authorities the provision to compulsorily purchase areas 'unfit for human habitation', Seaton was quick to spot the opportunities thrown up by the new legislation.

Seaton was well aware that Nottingham had several problem areas, none more so than the Rookeries.[6] In his 1873 report he had referred to the 'buildings lying between the Long Row and Parliament Street' as forming 'a specimen of some of its worst localities'.[7] Two years later the Public Buildings Committee presented to the Council a graphic account of this area, prepared by Tarbotton:

> Those [houses,] on the west of Greyhound Street, and a few others here and there, as in Trinity Passage and Ram Yard, may be considered tenantable, and have an aspect of respectability, but the majority of the small houses are filthy, back-to-back and offensive in the extreme. Some of the occupants are as repulsive as the slums in which they have their being, and those of the female gender are so well known by the police that I need not trouble you with their description. A clearance of an acre or two of land to the South of Parliament Street would relieve the district from much impurity and unwholesomeness, and at the same time, open out a most valuable space for commercial purposes. As in many other instances, this site displays to the passing crowds the lives where 'wealth accumulates' but shields from view the dens where 'men decay'. The shop fronts and premises adjoining and

---

5 RBN, IX, 240-1 Report to Council.

6 Rookeries, used of a specific area of Nottingham, was often employed generically in Victorian England for 'a cluster of mean tenements densely populated by people of the lowest class' (*Oxford English Dictionary*).

7 Seaton, 53.

> immediately behind the Long Row, are in good condition; but all the rest of the property, as estate, would be classed in the lowest scale.[8]

Robert Mellors's description can hardly be bettered:

> Grocers, drapers, boot stores - every variety; eating houses and pie making establishments, some of which were not remarkable for their cleanliness; sweetmeat manufactories carried on in attics; fried fish emporiums, where a colouring material had to supply the lack of freshness and given an attractive look to please the eye; bacon curing establishments in dingy basements; rag and bone assorting rooms, a visit to which caused lively feelings afterwards; laundries, in which clothes and children, and steam and soap suds were strangely mixed up; bird fanciers and showmen.[9]

Although the problems with this area were well understood in the 1870s nothing was immediately done, but in March 1881 Seaton drew up a document for the General Purposes Committee ... 'with regard to an unhealthy area situate to the north of the Long Row, in the Market Place, and comprises that portion of Parliament Street which lies between the top of Rigley's Yard and Redgate's offices, and the several yards communicating between that street and the Market Place, viz:- Rigley's Yard, Hulse's Yard, Ram Yard, Bellfounder's Yard, Pennell's Yard, Crown Yard, Wheatsheaf Yard, Greyhound Street, and Crackle's Yard.'[10] Seaton's report was considered by the committee on 29th March. His research suggested that drastic action was required:

> During the past three months I have carefully inspected every part of every house, and all the premises situate within the above defined area, with regard to their sanitary conditions. I have also made such enquiries and researches as enable me to form a correct

---

8 RBN, IX, 245.

9 R. Mellors, *In and About Nottinghamshire* (1890), 474.

10 Minutes of the General Purposes Committee 29th March 1881.

> estimate of the average state of health of the population residing therein during a long series of years. I find that diseases indicating a generally low condition of health amongst the population have been from time to time prevalent in this area, and that such prevalence may reasonably be attributed to the closeness, narrowness, and bad arrangement of the streets and houses within the area, and to the want of light, air, ventilation, and proper conveniences, or to other sanitary defects, one or more of these causes combining to render the houses unhealthy. And further, it appears to me that the evils connected with the houses situate in the above defined area, and the sanitary defects in this area, cannot be effectually remedied otherwise than by an improvement scheme for the rearrangement and reconstruction of the streets and houses within such area.

The area was given as 12,813 square yards, with a working-class population of about 400.

Seaton's proposals were referred to the Health Committee for detailed consideration, which proposed that the council should take all the necessary steps under the 1875 legislation 'with the view of having such area cleared and the land sold for building purposes'. The General Purposes Committee, in effect the full council, followed this lead, and the proposals became 'The Nottingham Improvement Scheme 1881'.[11]

What was to be done with the area? The corporation had three issues to face: clearance of the area, reuse of the land, and rehousing of those displaced. Seaton was aware that this was prime development land: he was subsequently to argue that 'the value of the land is against it being used for the re-erection of property of this kind', i.e. working-class housing.[12] Tarbotton had even suggested as early as 1875 that the land might be used for a new town hall.[13] The corporation was uncertain, and 'resolved to invite architects and others to send in competitive plans for the utilisation of the area'. They offered two prizes of 50 and 25 guineas respectively to the authors of the plans judged first and second in merit. Following advertisements, plans and

---

11 Reports Presented to Council 1880-1 Appendix, 738-40.

12 RBN, IX, 305.

13 Ibid, 245.

full details were sent to local architects in May 1881.[14] The intention was for proposals to be submitted by the 1st August 1881, although the time was extended. Eventually nine sets of plans were received.[15]

Those wishing to take part were instructed that they had to produce

> Plans and Designs [which] must show not only the laying out and disposition generally of the land, but the nature of the buildings in the opinion of the Architect or Surveyor most appropriate and profitable and architecturally effective to be erected on the said land and a Report must accompany each set of designs or plans, stating the principles of dealing with the 'Unhealthy Area' and of establishing an Improvement Scheme, the character of the buildings proposed to be built, the mode of proceeding with the works and disposing of the land and giving as nearly as possible the financial result of the scheme.

There followed some general indications of what was expected. In particular it was desired 'to form, pave and complete one or more streets with a gradient of not more than one in 14, the principal street to be not less than 45 feet in width'.

The results of the competition were given to the General Purposes Committee in a note of 21st October 1881 written by William Ford, Chairman of the Health Committee. The identification of the architects submitting schemes was concealed by rather fanciful noms de plume. Their real names were submitted in separate envelopes. Fortunately the envelopes have survived. The first prize was awarded to the plan labelled 'Sweetness and Light' which was entered by Evans and Jolley,[16] while the second prize went to the plan marked 'Albany' from Truman and Pratt. Several other well-known local architects submitted unsuccessful schemes.[17] No drawings survive of their proposals but

14 NAO, CA/PE/III/9 Proposed improvement scheme: instructions to architects competing (with plan) May 1881.

15 NAO, CA/PE/III/10 Printed notice to candidates of extension of time 22nd July 1881.

16 NAO, CA/PE/III/13 and CA/PE/III/16 Scheme entitled 'Sweetness and Light' and letter giving real names.

17 NAO, CA/PE/III/11-22 Covers all entries and envelopes with real names.

descriptions of the entries appeared in the *Nottingham Daily Express* on 4th and 5th October 1881, where they were still identified only by the noms de plume. T.C. Hine entered under the name 'Just What's Wanted' and Fothergill Watson chose 'I Take Aim for the Mark'. Hine, who seldom entered competitions, no doubt had some reflected satisfaction on discovering the winning practice was that formed by two of his former pupils.

Estimates of likely costs involved in re-developing the area were given by the two prizewinners[18] and, independently, by the Borough Surveyor.[19] He estimated the cost of acquiring the land and buildings at £84,500 and the value of the surplus land for resale £49,000. Thus he arrived at a figure of £35,500 as the net cost of the improvement scheme.

The award-winning scheme proposed direct access from the Market Place to Parliament Street by means of one street 45 feet wide and two parallel side streets 36 feet wide. The sites on this main street and on Parliament Street were intended for first class shop premises while the greater proportion of the sites on the side streets were to be for residential use. The entrance to the main street on Long Row was through an archway with buildings above. The existing piazza would be reinstated.

Although the corporation had passed the buck by holding an architectural competition, it did not regard itself as bound to implement any of the schemes, winning or not. Indeed, on 3rd October 1881, by which time the results of the Health Committee's Competition had been decided, Samuel Johnson, the town clerk, circulated a proposal by the Improvement Committee on the 'Siting of an intended Central Railway Station' to members of the General Purposes Committee. After ending his introduction '... the Improvement Committee think that the plan now proposed is one that is feasible, and would be for the good of the town', Johnson set out the broad outlines of this plan:

---

18 NAO, CA/PE/III/29 Architects' estimate of costs.

19 NAO, CA/PE/III/31 Borough Engineer's estimate of costs revised 23rd January 1882. The Borough Engineer was now Arthur Brown, formerly Tarbotton's assistant. He was promoted in October 1881when Tarbotton resigned to become Engineer to the Town's Gas and Water undertakings.

> It is requisite that such an important factor in determining Town Improvements as a Central Railway Station should be definitely fixed. For some time past it has been felt that the present Railway Stations are not sufficiently central, and that their sites could not be regarded as final. The Town Council having declared that a considerable portion of the property bounded by Parliament Street is an unhealthy area, the time seems opportune for the suggestion of a Central Railway Station. The site would include, not only the unhealthy area, but a very considerable portion of ground extending as far as the Gaol. The scheme, however, would not involve any level crossing. The principal streets, such as Clumber Street, George Street, Broad Street, would pass over the Railway at their present levels; of the remaining streets, only Beck Street would be interfered with, and then but to a slight extent, namely, by deviating the traffic going towards the south-west, whilst the south-east traffic would pass along New Parliament Street... The Station would be in a cutting, but would be approached from the Great Market Place on the level... Market Street will not be interfered with, and opposite the Theatre the line would pass into a tunnel.[20]

Johnson ended by pointing out 'The Railway Companies will not attempt any works of the kind unless on the invitation of the Town Council. The scheme would be costly under any circumstances but without the moral support of the Town Council the costliness would be increased to such an extent as to render the scheme impracticable.' To help the members visualize the proposals, lithographs of the site as it might be developed and how it could fit into the existing railway network were attached to these outline proposals. The preparatory work on the intended station was carried out by the engineers Edward Parry M.I.C.E., County Surveyor for Nottinghamshire and T. Greenhalgh Walker.

It must have seemed inconsistent, to say the least, to some councillors for the corporation first to organise a competition, and then to propose an entirely different scheme, although it was entitled to do

---

20 RBN, IX, 289 General Purposes Committee meeting; Reports Presented to Council 1880-1, 717-24 including plans (damaged).

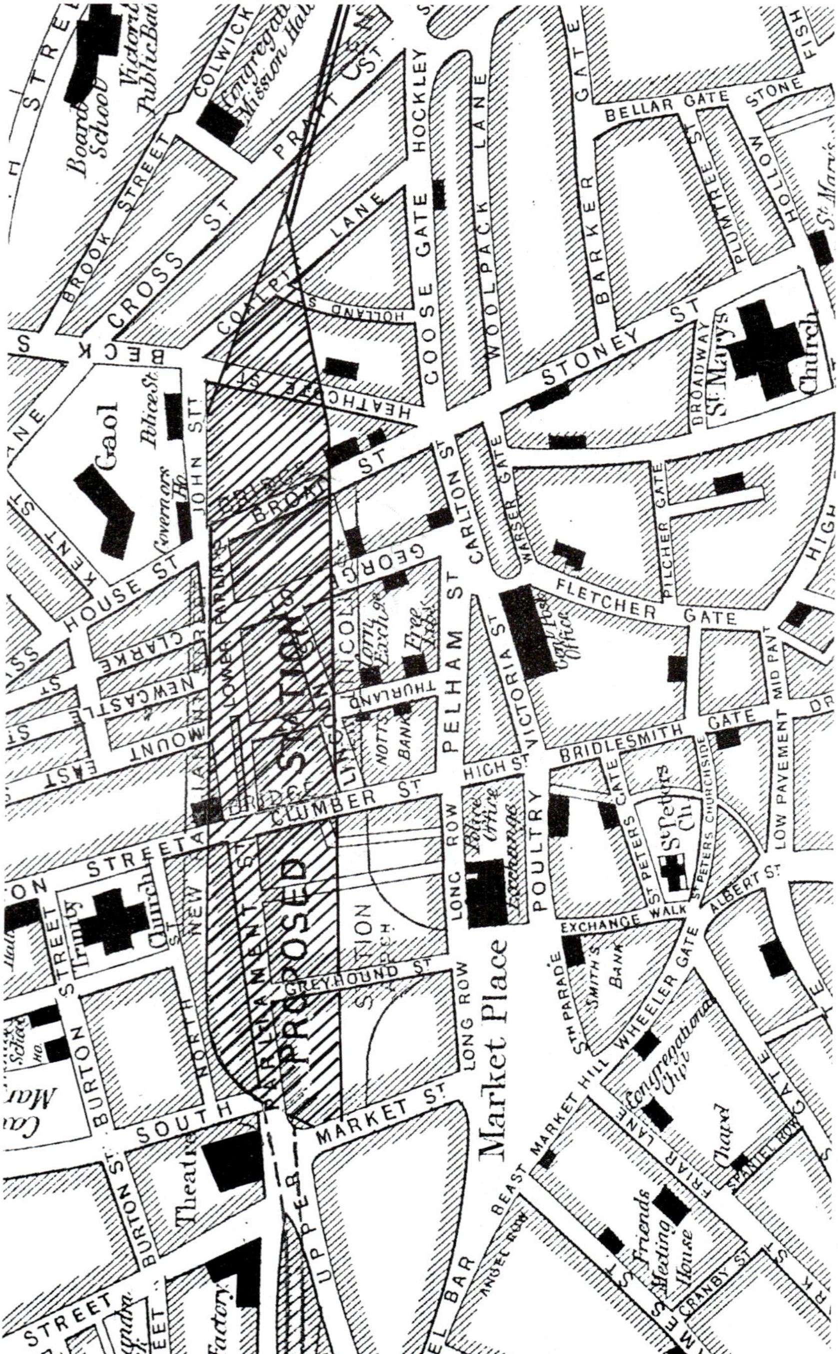

The Proposed Nottingham Central Station and its approaches as presented to the corporation, 3rd October 1881.

so.[21] Clause eight of the 1881 Improvement Scheme specifically made provision for disposing of the land 'for the construction thereon of railways and auxiliary works, and the erection thereon of a railway station, with other necessary offices and buildings'. Who decided that this clause should be activated is not known, but it was wholeheartedly endorsed by the General Purposes Committee on 3rd October 1881 (p. 162). The railway would have occupied ten acres of potentially valuable centrally placed land about 300 feet wide stretching from Market Street to beyond Heathcote Street. The approach from the east would have been over a long viaduct, while extensive tunnelling would have been needed both to the east and immediately to the west as well as to provide links to the existing lines. Despite the potential expense, the General Purposes Committee could clearly see the financial advantage of persuading private companies, in this case railway companies, to meet the cost of clearance, and it resolved that ' a Memorial be sent ... to each of the following Railway Companies, namely, the Midland, the Great Northern, and the London and North Western, requesting them to take into consideration the desirability of cooperating for the purpose of establishing a Central Railway Station according to the plan produced'.

It must have been galling for those architects who had entered the competition to redevelop the Rookeries area to read in adjoining columns of the *Nottingham Daily Express* for 5th October 1881 not only detailed descriptions of their entries, but the General Purposes Committee's consideration of 'The Proposed Joint Central Railway Station' optimistically intended to include within its ten acres site the same area of the Rookeries they had been invited to redevelop. As far as we know, the railway companies made no response. The only further mention of the railway idea was in an internal memo. On 5th December 1881 the General Works Committee recommended that any extension of the tramways should be deferred until the site of a central railway station was settled. Perhaps the council was too dictatorial in its approach, telling the railway companies where and how to build a railway station and setting out the approaches.

While the memorial of 3rd October 1881 was sent to and no doubt perused by the railway companies, the Health Committee passed on the results of their competition to the General Purposes Committee on

21 Reports Presented to Council 1880-1 Appendix, 739.

21st October and recommended the adoption of the plan awarded first prize - with certain modifications. As this modified scheme was later referred to as 'trident like' it would appear that the alterations did not take the intended three streets through to Parliament Street, but left them as three prongs. However, in their subsequent dealings with the Local Government Board, the Council deliberately withheld the details of their true intentions, to which the Board not surprisingly objected. The Council's excuse was they wanted to clear the area first and then see 'to what uses it could be applied with the greatest economy'. In the end, to appease the Board the Council sent the award-winning plan without having any immediate intention of proceeding. The Local Government Board originally approved the Council's scheme by a Provisional Order of 3rd May 1882; this was later confirmed by the Board's Provisional Order Confirmation (Artisans and Labourers Dwellings) Act 1882. The Board expected the work to be carried out as soon as possible.[22]

Where were those about to be displaced to go? The 1875 legislation which underpinned the whole Rookeries scheme obliged local authorities to provide alternative accommodation for those displaced. This created difficulties. If the Rookeries was to be redeveloped for commercial premises the council had to provide housing elsewhere. It needed to be nearby: in Seaton's words, 'if no substitute be found near at hand nothing will prevent the former occupants of the poorest class of dwellings, which are demolished, from crowding into others close by – rendering them still worse'. At the same time 'building healthy houses of this class so as to make them fairly remunerative', was virtually impossible.[23] Faced with these difficulties, on 25th October 1881 the General Purposes Committee adopted a scheme for re-housing those 'persons of the working classes displaced' from this unhealthy area, on the Hunger Hill gardens.[24] The corporation maintained the option to dispose of the allocated land by public auction on building leases, with the Estates Committee initially offering 7,900

---

22 NAO, CA/PE/III/296 and CA/PE/III/297 Local Government Board order permitting modification 23rd April 1890; and further modification 30th August 1892. Gives a resumé of original permission.

23 RBN, IX, 305.

24 Ibid, 289.

square yards for the erection of seventy houses. In fact the Estates Committee actually leased 6,331 square yards of the Bridge Estate[25] to three developers on ninety-nine year leases from 25th March 1883. The Council gave clear indications of the standard of dwelling houses they expected to be erected and further that 'All the streets to be made shall be efficiently drained, paved, and lighted'. There was, of course, the matter of compensation for those allotment holders whose gardens would be taken for building purposes. The terms of a satisfactory agreement were not presented to the Council for approval until 2nd March 1885, although they were backdated to 25th March 1884.

The annual report of the Estates Committee presented on 2nd July 1883 noted that 'building is proceeding on the Hunger Hill'. In total eighty-four houses were erected on Westminster Street; they probably formed the Darby, Franchise, National, Reform and Simons Terraces on that street.[26] Twenty years later the houses of two of the developers were said to be in fairly good condition whilst those of the third developer needed repairs to brickwork. Seaton noted in his 1882 annual report that there were 'within a mile walk of any of the slums hundreds of cheap and healthy houses being erected'. Possibly by offering the Hunger Hill solution the Council hoped to shift the undesirables to an out of centre location, but as Seaton was well aware the value of the Rookeries land was such that commercial rather than domestic buildings were the most suitable for the area.[27]

---

25 The Bridge Estate was one of the money raising estates managed by the pre-1835 Nottingham Corporation. The other two were the Chamber Estate and the School Estate. The latter disappeared after the 1835 Municipal Reform Act. The Bridge Estate was set up to repair the two Trent Bridges on the London Road, one the major bridge, the other over an old loop of the Trent. The estate was made up of houses and land granted or received as bequests. The principal grant was that of 21st February 1551 from Edward VI, being the properties of the former chantry of St. Mary's and the Hospital of St. John. In 1838 the Bridge Estate had a rental of £1,400 and owned 265 acres: RBN, IX, 11-19.

26 The Terrier of the Chamber, Bridge and Freemen's Estates 31st December 1903, 150-1. One of the original developers was W.H. Simons.

27 Medical Officer of Health, *Annual Report* (1882).

Seaton left Nottingham in 1884 and was succeeded as MoH by Dr Arthur Whitlegge. A report submitted by the Health Committee on 1st June 1885 noted that all except three of the seventy owners of property in the 'Unhealthy Area' had agreed to accept the price arbitration fixed by Robert Evans, in total £141,341. This is the architect Evans in another role as a highly respected arbitration assessor. After six months' deliberation Evans announced his decisions in March 1885. He split the arbitration award into £13,460 as trade compensation and £127,881 as property valuation. This was somewhat less than the owners' original total demand for £178,030. Three unresolved claims were referred to a Q.C. appointed by the Local Government Board, who subsequently fixed a figure c.£5,000. The report was approved.[28]

As noted no plan showing the details of Evans and Jolley's proposals has so far been traced, however the rather wide, almost parallel, Ford Street shown on Goad's Insurance Plan of the area, dated 1886, indicates what actually happened. In the second half of 1885 the property abutting on each side of Crown Yard was pulled down and an experimental street, Ford Street, which bore no resemblance to the winning entry, was constructed (p. 167). Gradually the whole of the properties acquired were demolished and cleared away, the work being completed by June 1886. The ground was levelled and remained unaltered until 1890.

Ford Street was never formally set out and it was not reported to the Local Government Board. The Goad organisation was then currently preparing their insurance plan of central Nottingham and drew in what they saw. They may not have been fully aware of its temporary nature but entered it as a piece of commercial opportunism. In trying to be up to date the company 'covered' the area with a faulty document, which was not rectified for over thirty years when a second edition appeared. The name Ford Street was provisional, no doubt being chosen as an acknowledgement of William Ford, chairman of the committee that set up the competition. In Wright's *Directory* for 1889 Ford Street is actually listed on Long Row East, between No.22 and 'The Bell' public house. In the same directory, as the result of demolition, only

---

28 318 documents relating to the 'Unhealthy Area', including many claims for compensation survive, and give a good idea of the protracted nature of the intended clearance. These documents can be consulted at the Nottinghamshire County Archive Office (CA/PE/111).

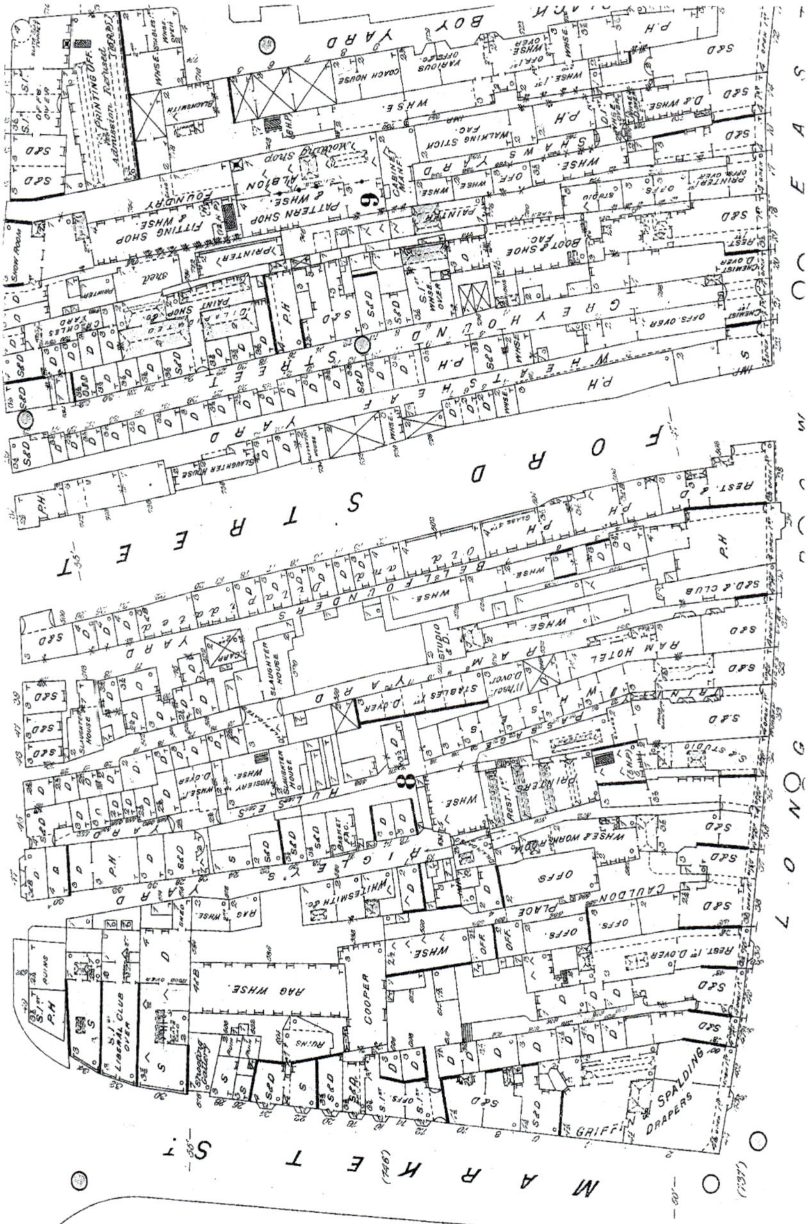

Goad's Insurance Map 1886 (Long Row Central) showing Ford Street, projected but never built.

Nos.1 and 3 Greyhound Street, at the Long Row end, survive compared with Nos. 1-41 and 4/6-34 in 1885.

Arthur Brown, the Borough Engineer and Surveyor, prepared the scheme for unhealthy area site, the familiar Y layout of King and Queen Street that was finally accepted. King and Queen Streets were each to be 50 feet wide, increasing to 60 feet where they joined. The Estates Committee had been requested by the Health Committee 'to undertake the laying out and disposal of the land lying between Land Parliament Street acquired under the provisions of the Artisans and Labourers Dwelling Act', for the Council had by now considered that the plan originally adapted and adopted for laying out the streets, in the form of a trident, would not develop the land to its full potential as too much back land would be created. The Estates Committee reported on Brown's proposal to the Council on 17th June 1889, but the plan was withdrawn for the time being.

It was resubmitted and approved on 7th October 1889.[29] Local architects and others interested had been sent a copy of the plan and invited to submit suggestions and criticisms. This modified plan was approved by the Local Government Board order of 23rd April 1890; subsequent alterations were approved in April 1892 and confirmed in August. There were certain provisos that had to satisfy the Board. The improvements would not: 'require larger public expenditure than that agreed, would not require the taking of any property otherwise than by agreement, nor affect injuriously other property in a manner different to that by the said scheme'. The contractor for the laying out of Queen and King Streets was Mr F Messom. The usual dates quoted for their opening are 1891 for Queen Street and 1892 for King Street, although there is no mention of either in Wright's *Directory* for 1892-3. Once the work was finished the final cost of clearing the Rookeries and reinstating a street pattern was taken up by the local press. On 19th October 1892 the *Nottingham Daily Express* concluded: 'The actual capital outlay, reverting to the time of the clearing of the area, was, in

29 NAO, CA/PE/III/295 Arthur Brown: Plan Showing Proposed Method of Laying Out the Unhealthy Area 7th October 1889. Five areas A – E marked out with a total area of 8068 square yards. (Printed)

round figures, £160,000'.[30] The overall deficit on the scheme must have been in the order of £75,000, although benefits to city were largely uneconomic and unquantifiable.[31]

The problem remained of what to build in the new area? On 10th October 1890 a deputation from Nottingham Corporation visited the office of the Postmaster General in London with a proposal to sell land on one of the proposed new streets (Queen Street) to H.M. Government in order to erect a new building to house under one roof, several government offices scattered around the town. A letter from the General Post Office, London put before the council on 5th January 1891 stated that the Treasury had turned down the offer of land, even at a lower figure of £42,000. On 6th July 1891 the Council reduced their original asking price of £10 per yard to £4 per yard of 'the land on the western side of the Unhealthy Area redevelopment to be sold only for the purposes of a new Post Office and other Government Buildings' (later the Inland Revenue Office). These eventually opened on 1st August 1898.

Government buildings were never going to fill the whole area, and the Council prepared a comprehensive 'Plan of Building Land: Long Row and Parliament Street' comprising twenty-seven freehold and leasehold plots, which were offered for Sale by Auction at the Guildhall on 19th October 1892. Although this auction attracted a large and influential gathering, including the mayor, aldermen, councillors and businessmen, only one plot was sold. This was the second largest, of 384 square yards near the bottom east side of King Street, which went for 8s. 7d. a yard leasehold. Offers were made for other plots but none reached the asking price. Mr. Kidd, the auctioneer, having opened the proceedings with great gusto, concluded the day by saying he had little fear that a very satisfactory disposition of the estate would eventually be made by private contract. He was right, the "plum" plot at the junction of King and Queen Streets, the centre of the **Y**, and some land

---

30 *Nottingham Daily Express*, 19th October 1892 has a concise resumé of events relating to the clearance of the Unhealthy Area. This was in fact the figure given by the town clerk, Samuel Johnson, in evidence to the Select Committee on Town Holdings, 1888 (Parliamentary Papers (313) XXII).

31 NAO, CA/PE/III. The figure of £75,000 was calculated by N.A. Ferguson, 'Working Class Housing in Bristol and Nottingham, 1868-1919' (University of Oregon Ph.D thesis, 1971), 130.

on the eastern side of Queen Street was acquired soon after the auction by the Prudential Assurance Company and the plans for their new offices, designed by Alfred Waterhouse, were ready by 1894. Government offices, including the new head post office, took up most of the western side of Queen Street.[32]

On King Street early arrivals were the Borough Club (Gilbert Smith Doughty 1893-4) and Watson Fothergill's grand new department store for Jessop and Son (1895-6).[33] In 1898 plans were approved for Albion Chambers, shops and offices, where the eastern side of King Street turned into Parliament Street. Several smaller shops were erected before the end of the decade, but a few plots, which much later formed the site of the Elite Cinema on Upper Parliament Street, were still not taken up at an auction conducted on 15th July 1903.

On Long Row, new buildings framed King Street for businessmen displaced by the changes. They appear to have been favoured by the council for neither site was offered for auction on the 19th October 1892. On the eastern side Arthur Marshall designed Russell Chambers, shops and offices, for Herbert Butler (1895-6), whilst on the western side Watson Fothergill was the architect of Queen's Chambers, four shops with workrooms over, for Ernest Skipwith (1896-8).

Other building work changed the appearance of the centre of Long Row. The Ram Hotel, which had been tucked into Ram Yard, was rebuilt with a prominent Long Row frontage adjoining the Fothergill building. Existing shops were altered for new clients, one being converted into banking premises for the London and Midland. The Mikado Café was redesigned. Once Jessop and Son had moved from Long Row East, by the side of the Black Boy Hotel, Fothergill prepared

---

32 RBN, IX, 390 Annual Report of the Estates Committee.

33 NAO, CA/PL Building Plans Register, etc. Individual folders classify planning applications c. 1870 – 1902 (to 1920 for some) by streets alphabetically. Refer to King Street, Queen Street and Long Row (Central). For a description of the earlier history of the redeveloped site see J. Holland Walker, 'An Itinerary of Nottingham', *TTS*, 36 (1932), 2-11. Holland Walker pointed out, among other things, that the General Post Office, which opened on 1st August 1898 stood on the site of the Mellers bell foundry – 'where the fortune was made which was so nobly expended in funding the High School'. One of the eminent Sandby brothers, painters, lived for a time in Mannings Yard, and Pennel(l)s Passage was named after Alderman Pennell, Mayor of Nottingham and architect of the original Exchange (1724-6).

plans for two shops and additions to the hotel to replace the vacated premises.

On the 5th October 1896 the Improvement Committee proposed, and the Council agreed, to set out a new street from Parliament Street, immediately opposite King Street, to North Street, now Forman Street. This street had it been constructed would have linked the Market Place directly but obliquely, via King Street, to the new Central (later Victoria) Station. What actually happened, as reported to the Council on 10th September 1900, was the widening and improvement of the streets abutting on Holy Trinity Church Yard (Trinity Square). This resulted in the cutting of King's Walk, and to the east, widening New Yard, thus providing some limited improved access to the new station via Trinity Square. Parliamentary approval was sought and granted to round off the eastern corner of King Street, where it turned into Parliament Street, by taking land from Redgate's Albion Foundry. This was where Albion Chambers were subsequently erected. Since 1931 New Yard has been known as Trinity Walk.

Although the corporation failed either to implement the winning competition entry of 1881, or to persuade the railway companies to come together to set up a central station, by the time the Rookeries had been redeveloped a further opportunity had arisen that would provide Nottingham with a central station and this was successful. The council, sitting in committee resolved on 12th November 1888 'that it is desirable in the interests of this Town that there should be a Central Railway Station, and that it is the duty of the Town Council to assist in the erection of such a Station by all legitimate means [etc]'. This was not a revival of the 1881 scheme but a new initiative by the Manchester, Sheffield and Lincolnshire Railway (from 1897 the Great Central Railway), which led in the course of the 1890s to the redevelopment of another notorious area, centred on Charlotte Street to the north of Parliament Street, as the Victoria Station.

10

The Royal Visit to Nottinghamshire, 1903

Philip E. Jones

King Edward VII's visit to Nottinghamshire in September 1903, although the first visit of his short reign, was not his first visit to the county, nor would it be his last. As Prince of Wales he had visited Clumber in 1861, Welbeck in 1881, 1891 and 1897, and Rufford in 1886, 1899 and 1900. As King Edward VII he stayed at Rufford every year from 1903 to 1909 during Doncaster race week in September. He was following in the footsteps of a long line of other royal visitors to Rufford, including James I, Charles II, William III and George IV, but he was the only regular royal visitor. It was one of his favourite locations and he was often heard to remark that coming to Rufford was 'like coming home'.[1]

Rufford Abbey was founded in 1146 as a Cistercian monastery by monks from Rievaulx Abbey in Yorkshire. Its transformation into a country house was begun under the ownership of the sixth Earl of Shrewsbury, and completed by the Savile family of Thornhill in Yorkshire who acquired the estate in 1626. When Edward VII visited Rufford as Prince of Wales in 1886 the estate was owned by Augustus William Savile, who had succeeded his brother Henry in 1881. Augustus was a popular socialite and Master of Ceremonies to Queen Victoria. He was also a very successful artist. He had painted a full-length portrait of Edward as Prince of Wales wearing the robes and

1 A.E.T. Watson, *King Edward VII as a Sportsman* (1911), 333.

order of the Garter. The portrait hung over the mantelpiece in the library at Rufford during the king's later visits. When Augustus died in April 1887 he was succeeded by his elder brother John Savile, created 1st Baron Savile in 1888.

All Edward VII's visits to Rufford as king were made during the ownership of John Savile Lumley-Savile, 2nd Baron Savile. He was the son of Reverend Frederick Savile-Lumley, rector of Bilsthorpe, and nephew of the 1st Baron, whom he succeeded in 1896. John Savile Lumley-Savile was born in 1854 and educated at Eton, afterwards entering the diplomatic service. From 1881 to 1889 he was employed in the Foreign Office before retiring from official life and returning to live with his uncle at Rufford. Here he looked after the estate and managed the stud farm, the shooting and the hunting with the Rufford hounds until he succeeded to the estate in 1896 on the death of his uncle. Two years earlier, in 1894, he married Gertrude Violet, the only daughter of Charles Francis Webster-Wedderburn, and widow of Horace Augustus Helyar of Coker Court in Somerset. In her younger days Lady Savile had been considered one of the beauties of Brighton society, with her wealth of golden hair, delicate features and charming manners. After her husband's succession to the barony in 1896, both Lord and Lady Savile acquired the reputation of being the foremost of the smart entertainers of the day. It is perhaps therefore not surprising that they were honoured by the intimate friendship of Edward VII, who came to Rufford Abbey seven years in succession.

The 1903 royal visit to Nottinghamshire was just one of a succession of engagements that was almost immutably fixed. The king's life followed a regular pattern that was mapped out with extraordinary exactitude. He usually spent a week each January with the Duke and Duchess of Devonshire at Chatsworth. He visited Paris and Biarritz in spring, then went on a Mediterranean cruise. In April he was usually in Copenhagen for his father-in-law's birthday, in June at Epsom, then at Ascot. In July and August there were invitations to country houses, plus Cowes for the yachting and Bolton Abbey for the start of the grouse shooting season. A three weeks' cure at Marienbad in August usually immediately preceded his visit to Lord and Lady Savile at Rufford Abbey in September. He was at Balmoral for the shooting season in October, and at Windsor, Sandringham or Buckingham Palace in November and December. Christmas Day and New Year's Day were always spent at Sandringham.

In August 1903 Edward made his regular annual visit to the mineral springs of Marienbad, the celebrated spa town of West Bohemia, for the 'cure'. When he succeeded to the throne on 22nd January 1901, on the death of his mother Queen Victoria, 'Bertie' as Edward VII was affectionately known, was fifty-nine years old and not in the best of health. Even the coronation ceremony, arranged for 26th June 1902 had to be postponed until 9th August because he had appendicitis. It was undoubtedly his increasing corpulence which led him to spend three weeks each year at Marienbad,[2] although as his reign progressed he suffered increasing bouts of bronchitis and respiratory difficulties, possibly in part due to his addiction to tobacco.

The king returned to Buckingham Palace on 4th September 1903 from Marienbad. His physician at Marienbad, Dr. Ott, was pleased that the treatment had gone well and that the king had lost some weight. After a brief rest in London Edward prepared to leave for Rufford. On Monday 7th September he accompanied Queen Alexandra and Princess Victoria to Charing Cross Station en route for Copenhagen on a visit to the queen's father, King Christian IX of Denmark. King Edward then travelled to King's Cross Station where a special royal train was due to leave at 3.40 p.m. and to arrive at Ollerton Station (just under two miles from Rufford Abbey) at 6.27 p.m. A trial trip of the train had already been run on the Friday afternoon under the supervision of Mr. W.H. Hills, superintendent of the Running Department.

The departure platform (No.1) was closed to the general public and only the railway officials and a few privileged persons were present. These included Mr. Proud, General Superintendent, Mr. T. Smith, stationmaster at King's Cross, and Mr. Carr, who was in charge of the railway police. As was customary, a strip of red carpet had been laid on the platform. The king wore a black frock coat and was reported as looking in the best of health.[3] He drove up in an open carriage and immediately proceeded to his saloon on the train. He was accompanied by Victor Albert Spencer, Viscount Churchill (Lord in waiting), Captain George Lindsay Holford and Colonel Arthur Davidson

2 In 1902 he measured 122 cm round both his chest and his waist, causing him to leave the bottom button of his waistcoat undone. The public followed suit and this eventually became the height of fashion.

3 *Nottinghamshire Weekly Express*, 11th September 1903.

(equerries in waiting). Among Lord Savile's house guests who were travelling on the royal train were Countess Howe, Viscountess Churchill, General Lyttleton-Annesley, Mr. and Mrs. Arthur James, the Honourable Mrs. George Keppel, the Honourable Ronald and Mrs. Greville, Consuelo, Dowager Duchess of Manchester and the Marquis de Soveral, the Portuguese Ambassador. Some of them had been invited by the king to travel in his saloon. Railway officials travelling on the train included Mr. O. Bury, General Manager of the Great Northern Railway Company, Mr. W.H. Hills, Mr. W.J. Grinling, Chief Traffic Manager, and Mr. T.R. Johnson, Assistant Engineer. Mr. H.A. Ivatt, locomotive engineer, was on the engine.[4]

The train used was the Great North of Scotland royal train which consisted of engine, two brake vans, two composite carriages and two saloons, painted in cream and gold. The drawing room portion of the royal saloon was furnished in Louis XV style and the smoking room portion in Queen Anne style. The train was pulled by a Great Northern Railway Atlantic engine as far as Tuxford, on that Company's main line, and was preceded by the 3.25 p.m. express from King's Cross to the North which acted as pilot. Once under way all gates along the route were locked, points clamped and platelayers posted to guard all level crossings for thirty minutes before the arrival of the train. From King's Cross to Tuxford there was no stop and the scheduled time was strictly maintained.

When King Edward paid his first visit to Rufford in 1886 the Dukeries route had not been constructed and he had to make the journey by road from Tuxford Station to Rufford Abbey. In September 1903 he travelled to Ollerton from Tuxford on the Lancashire, Derbyshire and East Coast Railway, which had opened in November 1896. The engine selected for the last eight miles to Ollerton was a 0-6-2T, No.26. At Tuxford the locomotive had been thoroughly examined and the brass polished under the watchful eye of Robert A. Thom. Born at Aberdeen in 1873 and apprenticed as a boilermaker, he had become Locomotive Superintendent of the Lancashire, Derbyshire and East Coast Railway in 1902, a post he was to hold for four years. He was a true Scotsman with a sharp manner and quick temper. He was even known to suspend his crew half a day's pay for the most trivial

---

4 *Nottingham Evening News*, 8th September 1903.

offences. The train set off on the short distance to Ollerton, allegedly reaching a maximum speed of sixty-four miles per hour, and pulling a load of 200 tons.[5]

For many weeks previously the king's visit to Rufford had been a topic of conversation locally. A large crowd gathered at Ollerton station to greet the royal train. Sightseers began to arrive soon after 5 p.m., many of them by train from Nottingham, Sheffield, Chesterfield, Mansfield and Lincoln.[6] None of them was allowed on the platform. In deference to the king's wishes there were no decorations around the station, although the premises had been smartened up by a recent coat of paint and a white ensign had been hoisted on the station-master's house. Crimson carpet had been laid on the platform and in the booking hall through which the king had to pass to get to the waiting carriage to take him to Rufford.

The preparations at Ollerton station had been carried out under the expert guidance of the stationmaster, Francis Glanville Kemp, a Yorkshire man. His father Charles had been stationmaster at North Ferriby and Kemp junior had commenced his working life as a railway porter.[7] The police arrangements at Ollerton were in the hands of Captain William Hugh Tomasson, Chief Constable of Nottinghamshire, assisted by Superintendent Samuel Herod of the Worksop Division and Superintendent John Thomas of the Retford Division. All traffic on the road between the station and Rufford Abbey was temporarily stopped and a policeman posted at each crossroad.

Lord Savile, accompanied by his estate agent Joseph Bell, arrived at the station to meet the train. The royal special arrived on time and running through the station on the down side was backed to the up platform so that the royal saloon was drawn up immediately opposite the carpeted portion. On alighting from the train the king exchanged greetings with Lord Savile and then proceeded through the booking hall and out of the station. Here he was greeted with enthusiastic cheers from the crowd along the station approach. The king's carriage, drawn by four bay horses, with postillions in the Rufford black and white

---

5 J.Cupit and W. Taylor, *The Lancashire, Derbyshire and East Coast Railway* (1984), 37.

6 *N(ottingham) D(aily) G(uardian)*, 8th September 1903.

7 PRO RG11/4749, 1881, f. 26.

livery, set off down the incline from the station and turned in the direction of Rufford Abbey, preceded by two mounted police constables. Inside the carriage were the king, his equerry Colonel Arthur Davidson and the Marquis de Soveral. The other house guests who had travelled from London on the royal train were conveyed in carriages to Rufford after the king's departure. The Earl and Countess Cadogan were due to arrive on Tuesday evening and Captain and Mrs. Heneage later in the week. The king's luggage and servants from Buckingham Palace had arrived at Ollerton by the 2.33 p.m. train, while one of the royal motor cars had arrived from Balmoral the preceding Saturday.

The king was given a suite of rooms in the north-west corner of the abbey overlooking The Wilderness. The suite included bedroom, bathroom, dressing-room and parlour. Even when the contents of Rufford Abbey were sold at auction in 1938 the rooms were still known as King Edward VII's Suite.[8] For the duration of his stay at Rufford Edward had asked that the house should be connected with the telegraph so that he could receive important communications from London. A gang of men was therefore employed on Monday morning erecting a temporary wire from a point on the east side of Ollerton across country to Rufford Abbey. A room at the Abbey was set aside as an instrument room in charge of the court telegraphist. Extra instruments had to be installed at Ollerton and a staff of telegraphists and messengers sent out from Nottingham.[9]

Tuesday 8th September was the first full day of the king's visit and also the opening day of the races at Doncaster. The royal train had been stationed at Doncaster overnight. It returned to Ollerton just before noon to take Edward, his hosts and the Rufford house party to Doncaster. The driver in charge of the train from Ollerton to Doncaster and back for the week was Mr. Andrews, who had been driving all the royal trains on the Great Northern system for several years. He was a reliable, cool-headed, clear-visioned man who always felt a great sense of pride when driving the royal train.[10] The train was due to

8 Christie, Manson and Woods, *Catalogue of the Rufford Collection to be sold by auction on 11th October 1938 and nine subsequent days* (1938), 3.

9 *NDG*, 8th September 1903.

10 *Doncaster Gazette*, 11th September 1903.

depart from Ollerton at 12.25 p.m. by which time the crimson carpet had been laid out on the platform and all arrangements made for a prompt departure. Three mounted policemen were employed to keep the roads clear of traffic.

Two minutes before the train was scheduled to depart, the king arrived at the station in his glass-topped motor car, a 22 h.p. Daimler emblazoned on the back and sides with the royal coat of arms. Like all of his cars, it was distinguished by its claret colour and absence of number plates. In addition to the chauffeur and his mechanic Stamper, the king was accompanied in the car by Lady Savile and two of the Abbey guests. Few members of the public had turned out for the occasion, perhaps forty or fifty people all told. However they cheered loudly and a group of children waved their handkerchiefs. In return the king raised his tall silk hat. Lord Savile and the other house guests arrived at the station in carriages and the train left on time for Doncaster. The Great Northern had printed a special timetable on a white card surmounted by the royal coat of arms for the royal trains travelling between Ollerton and Doncaster during the king's visit.[11] On Tuesday the train was timed to arrive at Doncaster at 1.10 p.m. The northern half of the platform had been barricaded off, but no red carpet had been laid.

Among those who had assembled to receive the king were the Earl of Scarbrough, lord lieutenant of the West Riding, whose seat was Sandbeck Park, near Rotherham; Mr. F.W. Fison, M.P., member for the Doncaster Division; Right Reverend John Nathaniel Quirk, Bishop of Sheffield; Councillor Robert Robinson, J.P., the Mayor of Doncaster; and Mr.W.H. Lindsey, the stationmaster.[12] After the introductions by Scarbrough, the king travelled by closed carriage to the racecourse, accompanied by Lord Savile, Scarbrough, and Lord Churchill, with a mounted police escort. The king's visit was a private one, and consequently little had been done to decorate the town. One or two businesses had made an effort, notably Messrs. Parkinson and Son, butterscotch makers and confectioners in the High Street, who displayed welcoming mottoes draped with flags.[13] As he arrived at his

11 *NDG*, 9th September 1903.

12 *The Times*, 9th September 1903.

13 *Doncaster Gazette*, 11th September 1903.

private stand the royal standard was run up. The royal box had recently been constructed by knocking two old private boxes into one and an electric lift had been installed. Apart from lunch, the king stayed in his box until he returned to Rufford. There were seven races on the card, beginning with the Fitzwilliam Stakes. The next race was the Clumber Plate, for which only three horses ran, one of them the king's three-year-old colt *Persistence*, which came in last. The king and his guests left for the station at 4.55 p.m., and were back at Ollerton before six o'clock. They returned to Rufford by car.

Wednesday, the most important race day of the week, was fair with some sunshine, although quite blustery.[14] Shortly before noon the royal train arrived at Ollerton Station from Doncaster. During the half hour before its departure at 12.25 p.m. a small crowd of onlookers gathered to admire the train. As on Tuesday, Edward motored from Rufford Abbey, accompanied by Lady Savile and two other guests in the rear of the car. The other members of the house party travelled to the station in omnibuses. Joining them were the Earl and Countess Cadogan, who had proceeded to Doncaster from York on Tuesday morning and travelled to Ollerton on the royal train on Tuesday evening. Also joining the train were the railway officials who had travelled to Doncaster on the previous day. The crimson carpet had been laid throughout the booking hall but not on the platform because of the wind. Police arrangements on this occasion were in the hands of Superintendent Herod of the Worksop Division.

Although the weather was bright and sunny at Doncaster on Wednesday morning, the wind was cold and rain fell intermittently throughout the morning. This did not stop crowds of people arriving for the St. Leger. Every train was packed and Doncaster station was busy between 10 a.m. and 2 p.m. Over 350 trains were expected during the day. The main streets of Doncaster were congested long before the first race at 2 p.m. and vendors of butterscotch did a tremendous trade, as did the proprietors of eating-houses and hostelries.

The royal train reached Doncaster at 1.10 p.m. and the king was received by Mr. Fison, representing the Great Northern Railway, in the absence of the Company's chairman, Lord Allerton. The king was driven in an open carriage and pair to the racecourse in time for the

---

14 *NDG*, 10th September 1903.

first race, appropriately called the Rufford Abbey Plate. The main race of the day was the St. Leger Stakes at 3.15 p.m. There were only five runners, including the king's pair *Mead* and *Persistence*. The race was won by four lengths by Sir James Miller's *Rock Sand*. *Mead* came second, but *Persistence* came in last. This was a disappointment for the king, whose had won the St. Leger with *Persimmon* in 1896 and *Diamond Jubilee* in 1900. The royal train returned from Doncaster at 4.50 p.m., fifty minutes earlier than had originally been intended.[15] There were reported to be about a hundred spectators to welcome the king when the train arrived back at Ollerton Station at about 5.35 p.m.

No special festivities had been planned at Rufford for the evenings of the king's visit. Monsieur F. Casano's string quintet, which had been invited to play at Rufford on Edward VII's previous visits, had arrived from London during the day and played a selection of music on Wednesday night during and after dinner. Frederick Casano was well-known in musical circles in London. He was born in Croydon in 1871, the son of an Italian father and Belgian mother.[16] His father Edward, professor of singing in Kensington, had distinguished himself by composing the music for a number of popular songs of the day, including *You Love Me Not* and *A Flower Pledge*.[17] In 1901 Frederick was still living in fashionable Kensington with his parents and styled himself a musician.[18]

The king did not attend the races on Thursday, which was a disappointment to the many people who had travelled to Ollerton station to see him depart for Doncaster. The royal train did run, but it was used to convey a number of the Rufford house party who attended the races, including Earl Cadogan, the Honourable Ronald Greville and Mr. Arthur James. Meanwhile the king spent much of Thursday morning walking his long-haired, rough-coated fox terrier Caesar in the grounds and gardens of Rufford Abbey.[19] The gardens close to the house were laid out in beautiful geometric patterns like an intricate

---

15 Ibid.

16 PRO RG11/36, 1881, f. 122.

17 *Catalogue of printed Music in the British Library to 1980. Volume 10: Cae-Caste* (1982), 349.

18 PRO RG13/28, 1901, f. 32.

19 Sidney Lee, *King Edward VII : A biography* (1927), 65.

tapestry, each flower bed outlined by neatly trimmed box hedging. The king took a special interest in the gardens. Not so Caesar, who on more than one occasion was seen lifting his leg against one of the rose bushes. The king was so impressed with the gardens that before he left Rufford he presented John Doe, the head gardener, with a scarf pin composed of the monogram 'E.R.' set in diamonds.

Soon after 2 p.m. the king set off in the royal car in the pouring rain for a drive through the Dukeries and on to Bolsover Castle and Hardwick Hall. Lord and Lady Savile and some of the house guests followed in two other cars. Word had reached the castle long before the royal party and Bolsover town had been liberally decorated with flags and bunting. Crowds of people stood in the pouring rain awaiting the king. The party arrived at 3 p.m. and stayed for forty minutes. They left by way of the High Street where children from the National School had assembled to cheer them. After a brief visit to Hardwick Hall, the party returned to Rufford via Mansfield. Passing through the town about 6 p.m., the route was along West Gate, Church Street and Ratcliffe Gate. A few residents recognised them, although no official stop was made in the town.[20] Back at Rufford, the evening entertainment was again provided by Monsieur F. Casano's band.

The arrangements for the king's journey from Rufford to Doncaster on the Friday morning were the same as those on Wednesday. The sun shone at Doncaster for the sale of yearlings which always took place on the last day of the race meeting. The king had sent half a dozen brood mares up for the sale. He remained at the racecourse until the end of the meeting, anxious not to miss the last race. Before leaving for the station, he complimented the chairman of the race committee, Alderman F. Brightmore, on the general arrangements, especially those connected with his own reception and comfort during the week, and presented him with a scarf pin as a memento of his visit.[21] The king left Doncaster station soon after 4.30 p.m., arriving at Ollerton about 5.10 p.m.

After the visits to Doncaster, the king relaxed through a quiet weekend at Rufford. Much of Saturday morning he spent with his dog in the grounds of the Abbey. To commemorate his visit he planted a

---

20 *Mansfield and North Notts. Advertiser*, 11th September 1903.

21 *N(ottingham) E(vening) P(ost)*, 11th September 1903.

King Edward VII at Rufford Abbey.

mulberry tree in the newly laid-out Italian garden, close to the park. Unfortunately these formal gardens have not survived. After lunch, together with several members of the house party, he motored over to Newstead Abbey, then in the ownership of Lady Geraldine Chermside. As Prince of Wales he had visited the Abbey in June 1878 while staying with the Duke of St. Albans at Bestwood Lodge, on the occasion of the opening of the Midland Counties Art Museum at Nottingham castle. Even earlier than this, there had been some talk after the death of Thomas Wildman in 1859 of purchasing Newstead Abbey, but the difficulties of adapting it to a royal residence were considered insuperable.[22] In the end the Abbey was bought in 1861 by William Frederick Webb and the following year Queen Victoria purchased Sandringham for her son as a retreat from public life similar to her own houses at Osborne and Balmoral.

The king's visit to Newstead Abbey seems to have been unexpected. Until shortly before of his arrival nobody but the county police officials had been informed of his visit. Early in the morning a telegram had been sent to the Abbey, to the effect that Lady Savile and some of the house party would be visiting from Rufford, but no mention was made of the king. Newstead Abbey had been unoccupied since 1901, Lady Chermside being in Australia with her husband Sir Herbert, who was then Governor of Queensland. She had left her sister Ethel Webb in charge of the house,[23] and fortunately she happened to be passing through Newstead on her way to the north of the county and was informed of the anticipated visit.

The king's equerry, Colonel Arthur Davidson, and Mrs. Heneage left Rufford for Newstead Abbey in a carriage and pair soon after lunch. The king, accompanied by Lady Savile, Countess Howe, Lord and Lady Churchill, the Duchess of Manchester, Mrs. W. James, the Honourable Mrs. G. Keppel, the Marquis de Soveral and Captain George Holford, left later in motor cars. The twelve-mile journey to Newstead Abbey was made via Blidworth and Annesley. The king is reputed to have made a stop en route at The Badger Box public house in Annesley and to have bought a 4d cigar and 'lushed' the company

22 A.J. Lloyd, *A Guide to Newstead Abbey* (1916), 40.

23 R. Coope, 'The Webb family and its ownership of Newstead Abbey, Nottinghamshire, 1860-1925', *TTS*, 105 (2001), 147.

with him.[24] The Deputy Chief Constable, Superintendent Harrop, and a number of policemen were present at Newstead, but their presence was unnecessary since there was hardly anyone about. Miss Webb spent over an hour showing the party the Byron relics and the rooms of the house. Afterwards they walked through the gardens and the king stopped to read the wording on Boatswain's tomb. The party was served tea in the grand saloon before returning to Rufford just before 7 p.m.[25]

On Sunday morning the king again walked in the gardens at Rufford before attending a service in the private chapel. Many people, chiefly cyclists, attempted to get into the grounds of Rufford during the morning, but the main gates were closed except to those who had valid tickets of admission to the chapel. At this time the chapel was on the basement floor, originally part of the ancient abbey. The pews were of black oak and tapestries hung on the walls. The family pew, in which the king and house party sat, was reached by a small oak staircase from the grand hall. The service itself followed the ordinary form of morning prayer. The prayers and vesicles were recited by Reverend G.A. Grace, curate of West Retford, and the sermon was preached by Reverend J.P. Jones, chaplain at Rufford. The small Rufford Abbey choir had been augmented by principals from other churches, including Harry Tomlinson and Wilfred Brown, leading trebles at West Retford, James Thomson and Ernest Fenton from East Retford, and Harry Pemberton, alto at Clumber Church. The choir was conducted by Herbert C. Andrews from East Retford and the organist was A. Mettam. At the end of the service the whole congregation stood for the National Anthem.[26] A quiet Sunday afternoon and evening were spent at Rufford as the king was leaving early the next morning. He conferred the bronze medal of the Victorian Order on Horace Holman, Lord Savile's butler.[27] Horace, who was originally from Wickham in Kent, had been with the Savile family for many years and had come to Rufford with excellent references from the Earl of Sandwich at Hinchingbrooke House, just

---

24 *Notts. Free Press*, 18th September 1903.

25 *NEP*, 14th September 1903.

26 Ibid.

27 *Mansfield and North Notts. Advertiser*, 18th September 1903.

outside Huntingdon.[28] The bronze medal was presented in appreciation of the trouble he had taken in connection with the arrangements for the king's visit.

On Monday 14th September, the royal train left Ollerton at 8.10 a.m. for Ballater, via the East Coast route. The king travelled to the station by car, accompanied by Lord Savile. Crowds of cheering people, including many school children, lined the goods yard fence immediately opposite the station doors. Only officials and staff of the railway company were allowed on the platform and so the steps of the footbridge were packed with onlookers. Even the arrival of the royal servants and their luggage was watched with interest. Crimson carpet had been laid in the booking hall and across the platform to the door of the royal saloon, but there were no decorations around the station. The king bade farewell to Lord Savile and boarded the train accompanied by his equerries, Colonel Davidson and Captain Holford. Brief stops were made at Retford (for the purpose of taking on board official papers), at York (where the train was taken over by the North Eastern Company), at Newcastle-upon-Tyne, and at Edinburgh. The king reached Balmoral at 7 p.m.[29]

The king repeated his Doncaster race week visit to Rufford each September between 1904 and 1909, and had made preliminary arrangements to return in September 1910. Sadly September 1909 was to be the last visit because on 6th May 1910 he suffered a series of heart attacks and died that evening. His memory lived on at Rufford. Lord Savile erected a bronze sundial on a stone pedestal in the rose garden. It bore the inscription: 'In memory of Edward VII. Though the voice is hushed, his wondrous spell is on our hearts'.[30]

---

28 PRO RG11/1603, 1881, f. 139.

29 *The Times*, 14th September 1903.

30 *Catalogue of the Rufford Collection*, 202.

Adrian Henstock – An Appreciation

Barbara Sharp

Adrian Henstock started and ended his career as an archivist in the same county. He spent thirty-eight years in Nottinghamshire, during which time he became an authority on every aspect of the history of the county. His knowledge, however, is not restricted to Nottinghamshire; having been brought up in Derbyshire he retains a great interest in his native county and in Ashbourne in particular; indeed when an East Midlands regional project was mooted shortly after his retirement the first name on everyone's lips as qualified to help was Adrian's because of his knowledge of a large part of the area. This vast store of knowledge is not however the only attribute which characterises Adrian's professional career. He has made a significant contribution to the acquisition and care of Nottinghamshire's archives and dealt with the many challenges presented to him with professionalism, efficiency and good humour.

After taking his first degree at University College London in Medieval and Modern History in 1963, Adrian went on to gain his Diploma in Archive Administration from the University of Liverpool. He began his professional career in 1964 as Assistant Archivist to Nottingham Corporation being promoted to City Archivist in 1966. Two years later Adrian metaphorically 'crossed the river' and joined the staff of the Nottinghamshire Record Office as Senior Assistant Archivist on a salary of £1,485 per annum. On 1 January 1971 he began his 32-year tenure of the post of County Archivist, later re-designated Principal Archivist, from which he retired on 31st January 2003.

The last thirty years have seen great changes in the demands made on local archive offices both in terms of their greater usage by researchers and in the diversity of work undertaken. An early opportunity to branch out into something new came soon after Adrian became City Archivist. The Annual Report of the Archives Department for 1967-8 refers to a 'new medium for publicising the Department ... with the opening of the local radio station, Radio Nottingham.'[1] The report mentions the provision of material for two series of broadcasts and Adrian having been invited to take part in a further series. From this grew a close association with the media which continues to the present time. Two notable events were his being asked to provide the questions for a contestant on the BBC television programme *Mastermind* whose specialist subject was the history of Nottingham and his involvement in the *History Hunters* programme on Channel 4 dedicated to identifying the oldest public house in the city.

Nottinghamshire Archives is well known in professional circles for its outreach work which, with its popular annual series of lunchtime talks and occasional workshops, has again been fostered and encouraged by Adrian. The staff have produced a succession of education archive packs and it was the one published in 1993, entitled *Rufford: From Abbey to Country House,* devised and written by Adrian himself, which won the prestigious Phillimore prize for the best educational publication produced by a local record office in the year. Perhaps his most recent memorable moment came in 1999 when he donned full wig and frilly shirt to take on the role of the county's seventeenth century historian, Dr Robert Thoroton, for the Archives Open Day, a role which will no doubt continue to haunt him even in retirement. The increase in the usage of archives was country wide during these years as the interest in local history and more particularly family history grew. Adrian's first annual report as County Archivist for 1970/71 records the number of visitors to the archives as 2,256;[2] in 2003 the figure was nearer 16,000.

The holdings of archive repositories grew (as indeed they fortunately continue to do) and one of the developments which contributed to this growth was the passing of the *Parochial Registers and Records Measure* in 1978. As in other county record offices this resulted in the deposit of thousands of parish records. Adrian quickly foresaw the potential problems these might pose with regard to meeting the twin demands of access and conservation. The result was the

1 NAO, CA/LB 4/3.

2 NAO, CC/CL1/QC 02.

microfilming project he instigated on behalf of the County Council in conjunction with the Diocese of Southwell. Although similar projects have subsequently been carried out in other offices, Nottinghamshire was the first archive service to undertake a project whereby every parish register for the county was filmed up to and including 1900, whether or not the records were deposited in the Archives. Where they were not deposited, Adrian travelled the county collecting them and, in cases where they were still current, taking them back again! To this day the existence of these microfiche enables access to be given to these vital records in libraries throughout the county as well as in the Archives and has greatly saved 'wear and tear' on the originals. The project was `advertised' by Adrian in the *Journal of the Society of Archivists* in 1985,[3] and he received an enquiry about it as recently as 2002.

The early 1970s saw Adrian involved in the negotiations for a further huge transfer of records - those of his former employer, the City Council. The 'Battle of the Charters', as the local press described it, came to a satisfactory conclusion when the city and county record offices were amalgamated as a result of the implementation of Local Government Reorganisation in 1974. Thus, after relinquishing responsibility for the city charters and other city archives when he joined the County Council in 1968, he regained custody of them six years later.

By the late 1980s the storage problem had become acute and Adrian looked at building after building throughout the City in an attempt to find a suitable new 'home' for the ever-growing archives. No existing premises were found but fortunately a plot of land was and Adrian spent the early 1990s designing the new repository and then, once constructed, overseeing the move of the archives to their present location on Castle Meadow Road. After many months of planning and hard work, the Archives were officially opened by the Princess Royal in February 1993. For the first time all the city and county archives were together under one roof whereas before the move they had been scattered over four different locations around the city. This was no straightforward move, and it was no mean achievement that it was carried out so successfully.

---

3 A. Henstock, 'The Nottinghamshire parish registers microfilming project', *Journal of the Society of Archivists*, 7 (1985), 443-9.

The 1990s, of course, has witnessed the greater use of IT, a development which Adrian adopted with enthusiasm with the result that all collection management is now undertaken on a data base. It was the introduction of computers which facilitated the introduction of the Records Management Service. Records Management was largely unheard of in the 1960s; today the principle of the systematic destruction of routine administrative and financial records rather than storing them in odd corners and forgetting about them is now accepted as good professional practice by the many institutions faced with ever growing mountains of paper. Under Adrian's guidance Nottinghamshire Archives implemented a Records Management Service for the County Council and continues to provide a service which is the envy of many of our colleagues in other counties.

Thus during his four decades as a professional archivist Adrian has had to deal with many changes; the world of archives today is a very different one to that which he entered nearly forty years ago. Each decade has produced its own challenges. Adrian being Adrian has taken each in his stride with his usual pragmatic approach. He is too self-effacing to mention his achievements but they are clearly visible to anyone using Nottinghamshire Archives today. As a person, he is renowned for this kindness and patience; in the nine years I worked with him I never had any fears of asking him anything however ludicrous it might have appeared. His ability to see straight to the root of a problem and come up with the (often) simple and straight forward solution would leave me full of admiration. Working with Adrian was always a pleasure, very often a good laugh and I am pleased that I had the opportunity to do so. I tried my best to dissuade him from retiring (he even agreed with one of my reasons!) but to no avail. I conclude by thanking him, on behalf of his former colleagues and all users, past, present and future, for everything he has done for Nottinghamshire's written heritage. May he have the happy and fulfilling retirement he so justly deserves.

Adrian Henstock: a Bibliography

Compiled by Corinne Phillips

Books

Ashbourne: the historical setting (Ashbourne, Ashbourne Urban District Council, 1971).

Ashbourne: local history trail (Arkwright Society, 1977).

Bingham Parish Church: a history and guide (Bingham, Friends of Bingham Parish Church, 1994).

County House High Pavement, Nottingham: a Georgian and Regency town house (Nottingham, Thoroton Society, 1975).

Muniments evidences and writings: the history of archives in Nottinghamshire (Nottingham, Nottinghamshire County Council, 1999).

Tracing the history of your house: documentary sources for the history of Nottinghamshire buildings 1500-1950 (Nottingham, Nottinghamshire Local History Association, 1988).

Edited books

The diary of Abigail Gawthern of Nottingham, 1751-1810 (Nottingham, TSRS, 32, 1980).

Early Victorian country town: a portrait of Ashbourne in the mid 19th century by the Ashbourne Local History Group, Cyril Calderbank ... [et al.] (Ashbourne, Ashbourne Local History Group, 1978).

A Georgian country town, Ashbourne 1725-1825, Vol.1, Fashionable society (Ashbourne, Ashbourne Local History Group, 1989).

A Georgian country town, Ashbourne 1725-1825, Vol.2, Architecture. (Ashbourne, Ashbourne Local History Group, 1991).

Articles

Bulletin of Local History: East Midland Region

'The Archives and Local History Departments of Nottingham Public Libraries', 3 (1968), 9-19.

'Group projects in local history: house repopulation in the mid

nineteenth century', 6 (1971), 11-20.
'Nottinghamshire Record Office', 9 (1974), 3-13.
'Group projects in local history: buildings and society in a Georgian market town' [Ashbourne], 13 (1978), 1-7.

Derbyshire Archaeological Journal
'Cheese manufacture and marketing in Derbyshire and North Staffordshire, 1670-1870', 89 (1969), 32-46.
'The course of Hereward Street: a reappraisal', 100 (1980), 35-42.

Derbyshire Life and Countryside
'"A faire school house...": Ashbourne's Grammar School founded 400 years ago this month', 50, 7 (July 1985), 45-6.

Derbyshire Miscellany
'Longford cheese factory', 6, 1 (1971), 4.
'Four Ashover accidents in the 17th and 18th centuries' 7, 2 (October 1974), 71-3.
'The early Derbyshire Quakers and their emigration to America', 8, 1 (Spring 1977), 7-9.
'Ashover Fabrick: a lost 17th century folly', 14, 4 (Autumn 1996), 99-103.

Journal of the Society of Archivists
'The Nottinghamshire parish registers microfilming project', 7, 7 (April 1985), 443-9.

Local Historian
'Town houses and society in Georgian country towns: part 1, Architecture', 14, 2 (May 1980), 68-75.
'Town houses and society in Georgian country towns: part 2, Houses and society', 14, 3 (August 1980), 149-55.
'Politics and personalities in local communities', 15, 7 (August 1983), 388-401.

Local Population Studies
'House repopulation from the census returns of 1841 and 1851', 10 (Spring 1973), 37-52.

'An unusual lying-in asylum', 15 (Autumn 1975), 50.
Correspondence, 'Access to records', 6 (Spring 1971), 53.
Correspondence, 'An unusual 19th century census', 5 (Autumn 1970), 70.
Correspondence, 'Genealogical register entries in Nottingham parishes', 25 (Autumn 1980), 57-8.
'Miscellany' compiled by Adrian Henstock & Valerie Henstock, 5 (Autumn 1970), 61.
'Miscellany from the East Midlands' compiled by Adrian Henstock & D. Hool, 2 (Spring 1969), 56.

Mining History: bulletin of the Peak District Mines Historical Society
'The Ashbourne [Lead Mining] Inquisition of 1288: a Reply', 7, 2 (1978), 96-8.
'"T'owd mon wor frum Bonser": the origins of the medieval miner's effigy in Wirksworth Church', 14, 2 (Winter 1999), 68-9.

Nottingham Topic
'Bingham's butter cross', (December 1977), 15.

Nottinghamshire Building Preservation Trust Newsletter
'Tracing the history of your house, 1: The Old House, Bleasby', (September 1980), 5-9.
'Tracing the history of your house, 2: The Flying Horse Hotel, Poultry, Nottingham', (December 1980), 6-10.
'Tracing the history of your house, 3: Hoveringham Mill', (March 1981), 6-9.
'Tracing the history of your house, 4: County House, High Pavement, Nottingham', (June 1981), 5-8.
'Tracing the history of your house, 5: The Cooper's Cottage, Bingham', (September 1981), 10-13.

Nottinghamshire Historian
'"...A great Receptacle for Fanaticks..."' [Brewhouse Yard] 13 (Spring 1974), 7-9.
'Bingham's market revived', 16 (Autumn 1975), 2-4.
'Lodge-on-the-Wolds: an asylum for "Virgins chaste and fair"', 17 (Summer 1976), 5-7.

'Hitting the trail', [Town & village trails]18 (Winter 1976), 16-18.
'Brief lives: two 17th century orphans from Mansfield' (How they lived series no.5), 20 (Winter 1977), 2-6.
'A prospect of Nottingham', 21 (Summer 1978), 16.
'From Plum Pudding to Paradise: the study of Nottinghamshire field names', 22 (Winter 1979), 5-8.
'Murder and suicide: the Hockerton murder case of 1821-2', 25 (Summer 1980), 11-13.
'Justice at work: the notebooks of Sir Gervase Clifton J.P.', 29 (Summer 1982), 11-12.
'"Overwhelmed by calamities": the turbulent life of William Dickinson, historian of Newark and Southwell', 67 (Autumn/Winter 2001), 10-12.

Notts Local History Council Newsletter
'Two of the quorum and three of the peace' by Adrian Henstock and Reg Brocklesby, [Notts Court of Quarter Sessions] 9 (March 1972), 3-4.
'John Cockshutt, the miller of Bolham, near Retford', 'How they lived' series, 10 (November 1972) 4-5.

Post Medieval Archaeology
'The Monopoly in Rhenish Stoneware Imports in Late Elizabethan England', 9 (1975), 219-24.

Thoroton Society Transactions
'A parish divided: Bingham and the Rev. John Walter, 1764-1810', 85 (1981), 90-101.
'A road traffic census of Nottingham in 1819', 90 (1986), 94-100.
'"A very old and crasey howse": the Old White Hart Inn, Newark, Nottinghamshire', 100 (1996), 19-53.
'County House, High Pavement, Nottingham: a Georgian and Regency town house', 78 (1974), 54-67.
'Early Stuart Nottingham: new evidence from the St. Peter's Easter Book of 1624', 97 (1993), 99-116.
'Late medieval building contracts for the Nottingham area', 88 (1984), 103-5.
'The Halls of Whatton: the faltering rise of a Victorian landed family', 86 (1982), 97-105.

'The records of the Thoroton Society: a summary list', 77 (1973), 104-9.
(with Keith Train), 'Robert Thoroton: Nottinghamshire antiquary, 1623-1678', 81 (1977), 13-32.
(with Maurice Barley), 'Keith Sydney Sayer Train, M.A., F.S.A., 1905-1985', 89 (1985), 11-13.
(with Kenryo Ashikaga), 'A Nottinghamshire village in the Jacobean period: the East Bridgford estate maps of 1612-1614', 100 (1996), 77-93.
(with John Samuels), 'Post medieval glass-making and industrial activity at Awsworth, Nottinghamshire', 102 (1998), 99-101.

Chapters and introductions
'The changing fabric of the town, 1550-1750' in John Beckett, ed., *A centenary history of Nottingham* (Manchester University Press, 1997), 107-31.
(with Sandra Dunster and Stephen Wallwork), 'Decline and regeneration: social and economic life', in ibid, 132-64.
'Dr Robert Thoroton and the Antiquities of Nottinghamshire (1677)', 3-6, and 'Nottinghamshire historical writing, 1677-1997', 6-12, in John Beckett, ed., *The Thoroton Society of Nottinghamshire* (Nottingham, Thoroton Society, 1997).
'House repopulation from the Land Tax assessment in a Derbyshire market town 1780-1825', in M. Turner and D.R. Mills, eds., *Land and property: the English Land Tax 1692-1832* (Alan Sutton Publishing, 1986), 118-35.
'House Repopulation from the Census Enumerators Books of 1841 and 1851' in Dennis Mills and Kevin Schurer, eds., *Local Communities in the Victorian Census Enumerators' Books* (Oxford, Leopard's Head Press/Local Populations Studies Supplement, 1996), 363-82.
'John Chapman's Map of Nottinghamshire, 1774', in Nottinghamshire County Council, *Chapman's Map of Nottinghamshire 1774* (2003).
'Nottinghamshire', in C.R.J. Currie and C.P. Lewis, eds., *English county histories: a guide. A tribute to C.R. Elrington* (Alan Sutton Publishing, 1994), 312-22.

Index

Airmyn, William de, 14
Andrews, Canon, 151
Annesley, 183
Antrobus, George, 61
Arnold, 84, 124
Arnoll, Joan, 54
Ashby, John de, 14
Askewe, William, 48

Bankes, Richard, 84, 85, 86, 88, 90, 92
Barker, Elizabeth, 111
Barnard (nee Charlton), Emma, 61
Barnard, Elizabeth (wife of Sir James Brydges), 61, 63, 69
Barnard, Elizabeth, 71
Barnard, Emma, 3, 5, 59-76
Barnard, Henry, 59, 61, 68
Barnes, Thomas, 103
Barrow, Agnes, 47, 48
Basford, 55
Benson, Archbishop Edward, 141, 144, 146, 148, 151, 152
Bernewell, William de, 11
Bestwood, 79, 83, 84, 86, 95, 96, 183
Bigges, Ralph, 102
Bilhaugh, 79, 86, 87
Billyng, Sir Thomas, 33, 37
Bingham, Sir Richard, 30-7
Bingham, Thomas, 31
Birklands, 79, 87, 88
Bleasby, 49
Blidworth, 90, 92, 94, 97
Blyth Hospital, 5
Bodley, G.F., 144
Bolsover, 101, 106, 118, 181
Booth, William, 101
Boothby, Sir William, 120
Boun, Gilbert, 85
Bradshaw, Alice, 49
Bradshaw, John, 49
Bradshawe, Christopher, 35
Bradshawe, Roger, 35
Braunston, 9
Bristol, Robert de, 14
Brito, William, 27
Broughton, Brant, 142
Brown, Arthur, 168
Browne, Jeremiah, 102
Brydges, James Duke of Chandos, 60, 70, 75
Brydges, Sir James (Lord Chandos), 62, 63, 70
Buckingham, 2nd Duke of, 109
Bugge, Ralph, 12
Bulwell, 9
Bunting, John, 93-4
Burdin, James, 102
Burton Joyce, 54
Busli, Roger de, 26
Buxton, 122
Byron, Lord, 113
Byron, Sir John, 88, 92

Calverton, 84, 94
Canons, 71
Carburton, 90, 94
Caröe, W.D., 153, 154
Casano, Frederick, 180, 181
Caton, John, 49
Caunton, 52
Cavendish, Arabella, 100, 110, 111, 113
Cavendish, Elizabeth Duchess of Albemarle, 100, 105, 106, 107, 108
Cavendish, Frances, 100, 106, 112
Cavendish, Henry, 100
Cavendish, Katherine Countess of Thanet, 100, 109
Cavendish, Lord George, 128
Cavendish, Margaret Countess of Clare, 100, 109, 110, 111, 112-13, 115
Cavendish, Sir Charles, 88, 90, 94
Cavendish, William, 92-3
Charlton, Sir Job, 62, 65
Chatsworth, 173
Chermside, Lady Geraldine, 183
Child, Barnard, 71-2
Child, Lady Emma, 59-76
Child, Richard Earl Tylney, 59-60
Child, Richard, 71-2, 74
Child, Sir Josiah, 5, 59, 60, 67, 69-72
Chounan, David, 22
Christian, Ewan, 145, 146, 149, 153
Church courts, 3, 38-57
Cleadthorpe, 90
Clifton, 26, 27
Clifton of Clifton family, 22-35
Clifton, Sir Gervase, 28, 29, 34, 35
Clifton, Sir Robert, 36-7
Clipstone, 79, 83, 88, 95, 96
Clumber, 79, 95, 96, 172
Cossall, 9, 13
Cossall, Adam de, 11
Coup, John, 54
Cowper, Joan, 50
Crich, 123
Cromwell, Ralph, 28, 82
Crophill, Sir Ralph de, 14, 15
Cumbria, 118,

Danke, Elizabeth, 48
Dawson, Richard, 54
Derbyshire, 116, 135, 140, 141
Dobbes, Isabel, 48
Domesday, 10, 26, 27
Doncaster races, 172-85
Douglas, Bishop John of Carlisle, 122, 132
Doverbeck, River, 78
Dovey, Edward, 70
Drury, Mary, 111
Dunham, 49, 50
Dunsby, 9, 12, 14, 15

East Markham, 54
Ecclesiastical Commissioners, 139, 141, 142, 144, 145, 146, 149, 152, 153
Edwinstowe, 79, 85
Elite Cinema, 170
Enclosure, 92, 96-8
Evans & Jolley, Architects, 159, 166
Evans, Robert, 166
Eyam, 9, 12
Eyre, Robert, 112

Fairforth, Thomas, 55
Farfrae, Lucetta, 38, 42, 58
Farnsfield, 90, 92, 118
Farr, Thomas, 100-15
Fiennes, Celia, 103, 104, 115
Fitz James, James Duke of Berwick, 110
Fletcher, Francis, 87
France, John, 101

Gale, Joseph, 102
Garland, William, 45, 49
Gawthern, Abigail, 75
Gedling, 54
Gell, Philip, of Hopton, 121, 134
Gladstone, W.E., 147, 148
Glorious Revolution, 1688, 114-15
Glyn, Rev. E.C., 147
Gothic Revival, 138
Gower, Adam, 55
Graham, Richard Viscount Preston, 113
Granby, 49
Greasley, 50
Greathead, Mary, 111-13
Gresley, Richard de, 16
Gretton, 55

Haddon Hall, 118
Hall, Richard, 101
Hardwick Hall, 118, 181
Harwood, Joan, 45
Hawkings, John, 112-13
Hearth Tax returns, 22
Henchard, Michael, 38
Henchman, Rev Charles, 23
Henstock, Adrian 2, 4, 5, 186-94
Herring, Archbishop, 23
Hine, T.C., 160
Hole, Canon Samuel, 147-8, 152
Hole, Hugh, 52
Holly Hill, 132
Holt, Thomas, 74
Hoskins, W.G., 21
Hoskyns, Bishop Edwyn, 153-4
Hunger Hill, 164, 165

Ilkeston, 151
Illingworth, Sir Richard, 28-37
Ingram, Rev Arthur, 146, 149, 150, 151
Isle of Wight, 118

Jackson, Bishop John, of Lincoln, 139
Jackson, John, 112
Jackson, Joseph, 101
Jessop and Son, 170
Jessop, Francis, 68
Johnson, Sir Samuel, 160-1

Kemp, Cardinal, 142
Kerchivall, Anthony, 56-7
Keyworth, 21, 23
Kighill, 88
Kilby, John, 102
King Edward VII, 5, 172-85
King, Bishop Edward, of Lincoln, 148, 149
Kingston, 4th Earl of, 113
Kirkby in Ashfield, 90
Knight, John, 127

Lane, Margaret, 54
Langdon, Thomas, 88, 92
Langold, 127
Latimer, Lord, 42
Laxton, 54
Leasingham, 138, 148
Leen, River, 78
Lenton, 83, 93
Lincoln Diocesan Architectural Society, 138
Lincolnshire, 139, 141
Liverpool, 47
Lloyd, David, 55
Local Government Board, 164, 166
London, Lord Mayor of, 141
Louth, Archdeacon, 45
Lucas, Jonathan, 102
Luxton, Stephen, 44

Mackenzie, Bishop Henry, of Nottingham, 139, 140
Major Oak, 116
Maltby, Archdeacon, 142, 146
Mansfield, 51, 78, 118, 181
Mansfield Woodhouse, 5, 103, 117-34
Maps, 77-98
Marienbad, 173, 174
Marple, Richard, 102

Massey, Elizabeth, 44
Meden, River, 78
Mellors, Robert, 156
Metcalfe, Elizabeth, 56
Morse, Canon Francis, 140, 151
Mortain, Count of, 26
Morteyn family, 3, 7-20
Mountjoy, Lord, 88
Murrey, Thomas, 105, 106

Newark, 45
Newcastle, 1st Duke of, 90, 99-115
Newcastle, 2nd Duchess of, 99-115
Newcastle, 2nd Duke of, 3, 4, 99-115
Newcastle, 3rd Duke, 95
Newfoundland, 118
Newsome, Joseph, 111
Newstead, 88, 92, 183-4
Newton, John, 111, 112
Normanton, William de, 11
Nottingham Castle (Ducal Palace), 3, 4, 10, 100-15, 183
Nottingham, 27-8, 43, 45, 47-49,51, 55-56, 78, 83, 101, 103
corporation, 108
Estates Committee, 164-5, 168
General Purposes Committee, 158, 159, 160, 163, 164
Health Committee, 158, 160, 163, 166, 168
Rookeries, 155-71
Nottinghamshire, 44, 51, 57, 85, 116, 139, 140, 141, 146, 186, 187, 188
maps of, 79-80
Nuthall, 9

Oglethorpe, Colonel Theophilus, 113
Ollerton, 174-85
Ordnance Survey, 78
Oswald, Adrian, 131
Ousthorpe, John de, 14
Oxford Movement, 138
Oxton, 128, 132

Papplewick, 88, 118
Parr, Henry, 56-7
Pate, Henry, 22
Pearson, John, 101
Pecche, Gilbert, 11
Pegge, Samuel, 118, 122, 133, 136
Penance, 38-58
Perlethorpe, 85, 86
Peverel, William, 26
Pierrepont, William Earl of Kingston, 86-7
Piggott, Stuart, 122
Pleasley Park, 132
Porter, Matthew, 101
Portland, 3rd Duke of, 117
Princess Anne, 188
Pringle, Sir George, 144, 145
Prudential Assurance Company, 170
Public Health Act, 1872, 155
Putnam, John, 103, 106, 112

Radcliff, Robert, 112
Radford, 55, 93
Ramsdale Park, 132
Ravenshead, 9, 88
Ray, John, 64, 68, 69
Reresby, Sir John, 107-15
Retford, 52, 56, 185
Ridding, Bishop George, of Southwell, 4, 148-53
Ridding, Lady Laura, 150, 152
Risley, 9
Robin Hood, 3
Robinson family, 23
Robinson, Emot, 47
Roman Nottinghamshire, 129-36
Rooke family, 118-19
Rooke, General Sir Henry, 119
Rooke, Henry, 119
Rooke, Lawrence, 121
Rooke, Major Hayman, 3, 5, 116-36
Rookeries, 4, 155-71
Roos, Peter, 54
Rose, Robert, 102
Royal Society, 120-1
Rufford, 5, 93, 95, 110, 187, 172-85
Russell Chambers, 170

St George's Church, Meadows, 149
Salcey, Robert de, 27
Savile, Augustus William, 172
Savile, Baron John Lumley-Savile, 173-85
Savile, Baron John, 173
Savile, George Marquess of Halifax, 110
Savile, Henry, 172
Savile, Lady Gertrude, 173, 178,183
Saxton, Christopher, 81
Scarbrough, Earl of, 178
Seaton, Dr Edward, 3, 4, 155-8, 164-6
Selston, 53, 62, 68
Senior, William, 92-3
Seyliard, Bridget, 111
Shadwell, Thomas, 110
Shelford, 87
Shepherd, Stephen, 47
Sherwood Forest, 3, 9, 77-98, 116, 135
Shrewsbury, Earl of, 88, 172
Shropshire, 141
Skegby, 118
Skippon, Philip, 68
Smethergell, Robert, 111
Smith, Robert, 49
Smythe, Richard, 93
Smythson, John, 94

Sookholme, 132
South Carlton, 62
South Muskham, 62, 70
Southcote, Robert de, 15
Southwell, 43, 44, 45, 48, 49
    Archbishop's Palace, 3, 4, 137-54
    Bishop's Manor, 153, 154
    Diocese of, 137-54
    Minster, 137, 140, 145
Spanby, William de, 12
Speed, John, 81
Spicer, Hugh le, 15, 16
Stafford, Humphrey, 49
Staffordshire, 141
Stamford, Thomas de, 11
Stanhope, Sir Thomas, 87
Stannhope, Sir William, 113
Stanton Moor, 118, 124, 134
Stanton-in-the-Wolds, 3, 21-37
Stephenson, Edward, 55
Stoke Bardolph, 87
Strelley, Robert de, 10
Strutt, George of Belper, 145
Sturton, 51
Sturton, Thomas, 51
Sutton in Ashfield, 92
Sutton Passeys, 7
Sutton, Rev R.H., 142
Sutton, Sir Richard, 118
Swillington, Joan, 28
Sybthorpe, Simon, 27

Tait, Archbishop, 140
Talbot, Rev Edward, 147
Tarbotton, M.O., 155-6, 158
Tattershall Castle, 28
Thoresby, 79, 85, 86, 87, 95, 100, 118
Thoresby, Archbishop, 142
Thornhaugh, Peter de, 11
Thornholme, 12
Thoroton Society, 1, 2, 5
Thoroton, Dr Robert, 1, 2, 3, 6, 15, 21, 27, 35, 77, 135, 187
Thorpe-in-the-Glebe, 22
Throsby, John, 1, 2, 23, 123, 128, 135
Thurgarton Priory, 150, 152
Trebeck, Canon J.J., 142, 151
Trent, River, 78
Trollope, Bishop Edward, of Nottingham, 3, 4, 137-54
Truman & Pratt, Architects, 159
Truman, Dr E.B., 155
Tuxford, 175

Vanbrugh, Sir John, 115
Venables, Canon Edmund, 147-8
Vescy, William de, 9
Victoria County History, 1, 2
Victoria Station, 171

Walker, Myles, 102
Walker, Robert, 51
Walker, Trotha, 53
Walsall, 9, 12
Wanstead, 71-2, 74
Warde, William le, 16
Warren, Joan, 49
Warsop, 88
Waterhouse, Alfred, 170
Watson, Fothergill, 160, 170
Webb, Ethel, 183-4
Webb, William Frederick, 183
Welbeck Atlas, 93, 94
Welbeck, 79, 95, 99, 102, 103, 106-9, 112, 117, 118, 172
Wellum, Adam de, 17
Wendy, Lettice, 65-8
Wendy, Sir Thomas, 62, 68
Whinney Hill, 132
White, William, 1
Whitlegge, Dr Arthur, 166
Widmerpool. 27
Wigston Magna, 21
Wildman, Thomas, 183
Wilkins, John, Bishop of Chester, 63
Wilkinson, Caleb, 103
Wilkinson, John, 70
Wilkinson, Joshua, 113
Williams, Archbishop John, 142
Willoughby family, 3, 7
    Cassandra, 60-75
    Francis, 59, 65, 70-1
    Sir Henry, 7
    Richard de, junior, 12, 13
    Sir Richard de, 12-20
    Thomas Lord Middleton, 59, 68, 69, 70, 72, 74, 75
    Sir William, 62, 66, 68
Willoughby on the Wolds, 12
Willughby, Francis, 5, 59-68, 71
Wingfield, Robert de, 11
Winstanley, Catherine, 65, 66, 69
Wollaton, 2, 7-20, 68, 70, 71, 75
Wolsey, Cardinal Thomas, 4, 142
Wood, Professor A.C., 1, 22, 57
Wordsworth, Bishop Christopher, of Lincoln, 139-41, 145-7, 149, 152
Wordsworth, John, 147
Work, Olaf, 118
Worksop, 99, 102
Wright, Mary, 111
Wright, Richard, 101
Wymeswold, 24, 26

Yonge, Sir George, 122, 132